SEVEN SUMMERS FROM THE SHORE

Father Brawn Sullivan

Catholic California Press / Sullivan Media Group,
Los Angeles, CA

Sullivan Media Group

Back Cover Photo of Father Brawn Sullivan by: William Rolf
Front Cover Photo: Harbor at Dubrovnik, Croatia by: Matthew Nieschalk

Published by: Catholic California Press / Sullivan Media Group - Los Angeles, California
Sullivan Media Website, http://www.greenearthprintanddesign.com
http://www.catholiccaliforniapress.com

To the Kids.

Rejoice, O young man, while you are young,
and let your heart be glad in the days of your youth.

-- Ecclesiastes 11:9

AUTHOR'S NOTE

Medjugorje, the Bosnian site of alleged apparitions of the Blessed Virgin Mary, figures prominently in this story. Many Catholics, let alone general readers, know little or nothing about the events at Medjugorje, so I offer this thumbnail sketch to familiarize folks with them.

The apparitions began June 24, 1981. Six teen agers in the village of Medjugorje, in Bosnia-Hercegovina, (then Yugoslavia) claimed to have seen the Blessed Mother, and the apparitions continue to this day. If authentic, this is the longest-running Marian apparition in history; an unprecedented event in the mystical experience of the Church.

As was the case at Fatima, La Salette and other approved apparitions, the visionaries at Medjugorje have been given secrets pertaining to future events. The secrets are for the future. They are not for this time, and speculation about them is, in my view, a waste of time. More important are the messages coming from Medjugorje, or perhaps I should say, the single message which all these many messages add up to: know that God exists; know that Jesus is your Savior; convert your heart to peace.

Our Lady calls herself the Queen of Peace, the visionaries tell us, and she has asked for prayer, fasting and conversion, at Medjugorje, as she did at Fatima. The grace of Medjugorje in fact seems to be that of conversion. If your faith is weak, you will find it strengethened; if strong, it will be deepened; if you have no faith, you may find yourself beginning to doubt your disbelief, as a result

i

of a visit to Medjugorje. Our Lady has said, according to the visionaries, "I have come to remind the world that God exists." The visionaries also claim that Our Lady has told them that Medjugorje is her last apparition. There will be no more visions of Mary, after this one ends.

Medjugorje has not been approved by the Church. Neither has it been condemned. An initial investigation, called by the then-Bishop of Mostar (in whose Diocese Medjugorje is situated) claimed the visionaries were lying and condemned the apparitions, in 1984. This initial judgment was subsequently vacated by the pan-Yugoslav Episcopal Conference, which claimed that the Bishop had run a deliberately biased investigation toward a foregone conclusion. It was well-known at the time that the Bishop was an opponent of the apparitions.

The Yugoslav bishops subsequently conducted their own investigation, and reported in 1991 that it was not possible, at the time, to claim that there was anything supernatural happening at Medjugorje. This assessment may be understood as "wait and see." The bishops noted that the messages and the practice of the faith at Medjugorje were consistent with Catholic doctrine and belief, and they permitted priest-led pilgrimages, but asked bishops not to go. The presence of bishops as pilgrims in Medjugorje could be interpreted as official approval.

Despite the recommendation that bishops not travel to Medjugorje, many, many bishops have gone there as pilgrims, as have some 30,000 priests. This is almost eight per cent of all the priests on earth. The total number of pilgrims to Medjugorje runs to over a million a year.

A striking aspect of the history of Medjugorje is that, in view of the bias against the apparitions, from Mostar, the Church has removed the right to rule on Medjugorje from the local bishop (the Bishop of Mostar). When the time comes to decide on the authenticity of Medjugorje, the decision will be made by the pan-Bosnian Episcopal Conference, not the local bishop. This situation is without precedent in the history of the Church. It does not prove the authenticity of the apparitions. It proves that the bishops of Mostar (there have been two, since 1981) have shown themselves to be unreliable, with regard to assessing the authenticity of Medjugorje. To paraphrase one Vatican official, the Bishop of Mostar is entitled to his opinion, on Medjugorje. And his opinion is just that.

A couple of personal notes. This is a heavily-populated story. Its central cast consists of the teens (now twenty-somethings) from the Marysville youth group, with whom I worked, during the years in which SEVEN SUMMERS takes place. For brevity's sake, I have not attempted to introduce the young people individually: they simply show up as the story unfolds, most of them quite early on.

Second, and I am only going to say this here and now, with this first edition of my first book. My name is Richard Brawn James Sullivan. Many (most) know me as Jim. I am writing under my middle name for several reasons. First, I always did write as Brawn, not Jim, when I was a struggling young novelist, back in the eighties and nineties. Second, there already is a Father Jim Sullivan who publishes books. Google him and he comes right up. Third, to the extent that anything resembling literary renown may ever come my way, I want to do all I can to shield my parish ministry from it. Publishing as Father Brawn builds a layer of protection between my parish life, the everyday ordinariness of which I much cherish, and the vicissitudes of even so low-level a degree of fame as that which can come to a writer. I would, in fact, publish anonymously, if I could do so. Marketing realities preclude that possibility. Hence, Father Brawn Sullivan herewith makes his debut.

UPDATE ON THE STATUS OF MEDJUGORJE

The Vatican has recently announced the formation of a special commission to investigate Medjugorje. This commission will render the Church's final decision on the apparitions.

PROLOGUE

Seventy or eighty feet above the Adriatic Sea one golden afternoon in the summer of 2003, I was sipping peach iced teas in such succession that the friendly girl at the café counter came to know what I wanted before I asked. She remarked, in Croatian-accented but perfect English, that I really liked peach-flavored iced tea. In fact, I'd have preferred unsweetened, but they didn't carry it, and it was too early in the day for a real drink.

The girl asked me if this were my first time in Dubrovnik; I told her no, I had been here several times before. It was, however, my first visit to this terrace cafe, literally built into the cliff above the sea, and accessible only via the city wall. The medieval wall which surrounds Dubrovnik is the greatest intact city wall on earth. You can walk it just as people walk the Great Wall of China; it is so solid and so spacious that, at various points, it has cafes of its own. This particular café is not on the wall. It is on the cliff, outside and slightly below the wall. Its location gives it an advantage over almost any other café in Dubrovnik: it commands sweeping and unimpeded views of the harbor, the islands and the blue-green sea itself, sparkling that particular afternoon in the bright, hot sunlight.

I had seen this café on previous visits; seen it from the wall, with its palm-thatched roof and subtropical greenery spilling out along the railing, the railing which protected those seated at the tables from the almost sheer drop to the rocks below. I had wanted, on previous visits to the city, to take the time to visit this cafe, to spend a leisured couple or three hours watching the yachts come and go, watching the young men dive from the rocks.

I had not had the time for such leisure on previous trips: I was always here leading a pilgrimage and pilgrimages rarely afford entire afternoons free. There was the Old Town to see, with its Renaissance and baroque monasteries and churches, with its dazzling white pavements, its statues and fountains; there was lunch to get; there were pilgrims to assist: "Where can I go shopping after lunch?" "Which way to the beach?" Always, on previous visits to Dubrovnik, I had had to come down off the wall with my group, to attend to my work as a tour leader.

This trip was different. This trip, I had the luxury of time and, at this point in the trip, of reduced responsibility. I had indeed come to this part of the world once again on pilgrimage to Medjugorje. I will be saying a great deal more about Medjugorje later in this narrative, so if you have not heard of it, not to worry. When the pilgrimage ended, instead of flying home to California, I – and eight young and adventurous members of the group – stayed behind. An extra night in Medjugorje, and then, a week down the Dalmatian Coast, starting at Split, with its jazz clubs set in Roman ruins, through Makarska ("the Croatian Riviera") and ending here in Dubrovnik. This was the last full day of our Adriatic vacation, and I was doing exactly what I had dreamed of doing, those several previous trips to Dubrovnik: I was doing nothing, and loving it, the whole long and sundrenched August afternoon.

I suppose I was not doing absolutely nothing. I was keeping a relaxed eye on the young men diving from the rocks. They were off to the side, about halfway down to the water. From the bits and snippets of laughing conversation that drifted up to the terrace, I guessed them all to be Croatian, local youth who knew the rocks and knew the sea, knew where the depths were. I was saying lazy prayers for them, an occasional Hail Mary, maybe two or three Hail

2

Marys together, that none of them would break his neck. And I was watching to make sure that none of my young men, all eight of them Californians, joined them. I am certain I'd have been willing to wreck the serenity of the afternoon for everyone there -- café patrons, sunbathers on the rocks below, swimmers in the translucent sea, not to mention the young men themselves -- had any of my California boys climbed up from the sea rocks to join the daring Croatians. I am certain I'd have leaned out over the railing and barked an order in angry English to not even think about it, get back down to the sea rocks and no arguments, and do it NOW. I'd have climbed down the steep stone steps to the level of the divers, and repeated the order. I very much doubt, at my age, already that summer past the middle of my forties, and fully dressed, and in western boots yet, beneath my khaki slacks, that I'd have been able to negotiate the rock-climbing necessary to physically reach the divers. But I would have threatened it, had one of my boys decided to give a forty-foot plunge into the Adriatic a go.

I am not a dad, and never have been. What I am today is a Catholic priest. What I was that afternoon above the Adriatic was a seminarian and youth minister, one day before returning home with the eight young men from my California youth group who had opted for the Dalmatian tour. I was not about to come home with one of them injured -- or worse -- from a diving accident. I am usually described as relaxed and easy going, but when it comes to the well-being and safety of my kids, I can go from zero to dad-from-hell in less than two nano-seconds. My boys, of course, all knew this, and the desire to avoid a scene may have been what kept them from joining the divers. Or, perhaps, simple maturity did. They were all that summer in their early twenties: five years earlier, when we had first come to Europe together, they had all been teens. I lost ten pounds, on that first trip, and I think all of it from sheer worry.

Europe had been a lot less stressful with them, this second time around.

Most likely, though, what kept my kids safe at the level of the sea were the girls – Italian and Swedish, I was later told – whom they met there on the rocks. Dubrovnik – indeed, the entire Croatian coast from Istria south – is a magnet for the European young in the summers, and my boys, with their Mexican-American looks, their love of adventure and their easy California attitude, were rather magnetic themselves. This had been true already on the first trip, in 1998; it was doubly so the summer of 2003. If I hadn't seen five international romances develop among them on this trip, it is probably because I saw ten.

A familiar voice called my name, and I turned from the young divers to the sea, where I saw Jorge out in the water, maybe thirty feet from shore. Only his head and shoulders were above the water. There is no wading area off the rocks at Dubrovnik. If you get into the water there, you are almost always immediately in over your head.

"Why don't you come down?" Jorge called up.

A couple of the other guys, on the rocks with the girls, looked up. "Yeah, come down! Catch some rays, dude!"

I smiled and waved the invitation off. I have always loved the sun, and I love to swim, and in fact I had my swimsuit on under my slacks. But I was deeply content there at my little table, sipping peach iced tea, and…just being: being with my kids, in Dubrovnik, at the end of a grace-filled pilgrimage. I did not want to exert myself. We'd been swimming in the Adriatic all week, in any event. It is a calm sea, with little in the way of surf, and with a refreshing mix of warm-cool currents. It is also the third clearest sea in the world: you can see a dime at thirty feet in the Adriatic. It is, in fact, a great sea for swimmers.

But there are times when I prefer to observe, rather than participate; or maybe as the sociological method suggests, there are times when what most suits me is participant observation. I was not watching the scene before me on television, after all. I was part of it. But I was watching it. And I was more than watching it. I was soaking in it, quietly reveling in it, as surely immersed in it as was Jorge, a moment later, when he made a dolphin dive and disappeared beneath the sunlit water.

We had waited five years for this moment, my California boys and I. We had worked and prayed and hoped and…waited. The 1998 pilgrimage, the first time any of the kids from my youth group had been to Europe, had galvanized them, had opened a world of opportunity to them, a world of bright possibility. I had had seventeen teenagers with me, on that trip. Mercifully, I had also had two dozen adults from our hometown parish, St. Joseph in Marysville, including my mom and sister, and our pastor. We'd gone to London and Italy on that trip, as well as to Medjugorje. We had crossed the Adriatic Sea on a ferry. When the kids got their first look at the Croatian coast, from the windows of the bus that took us to Medjugorje, several of them said, "We have to come back," because we were not visiting beaches on that first pilgrimage.

I will not forget the joy I felt, that first trip, watching as my kids soaked in the experience of Europe, and more, so much more to me, being after all, a future priest, as they got their first taste of religious pilgrimage: as they visited the Vatican, Assisi and Marian shrines, as they saw for the first time the universality and deep history of the Catholic faith. That was August of 1998, and my kids and I had been together three years. I was to leave for seminary just ten days after we got home. I would no longer be youth minister in Marysville, and by any normal expectation, that 1998 pilgrimage should have been the grand finale for me and the kids. By any normal expectation, the 1998 trip should have been the end of our time together.

My kids and I have never been into normal expectations.

It wasn't just the kids who wanted to return. I wanted it, too. For the next several years, in fact, I would want it more than I wanted anything else. The goal became a passion, in me: a singular drive, a drive that I pursued with an intensity that I never thought about, at the time, but which, in retrospect, almost amazes me. In the midst of this drive to see my kids back in Europe, and back on pilgrimage, I would be asked by the Lord for a surrender so complete that I would not, until it happened, have thought myself capable of it. In every other realm of my life but this one, the realm of me and my kids, my will would be vanquished, my hopes and dreams dispersed in the void, and my spirit very nearly broken. Yet at the lowest point in all of that, I would hold to this one hope, this one dream: that my kids and I would return to Medjugorje. My passion for this one goal largely defined the middle years of my forties, and it re-shaped my seminary experience. I am, to some extent, the man I am today, the priest I am today, because of that passion.

And now here we were, eight of my boys and I, on the last full day of the trip we had spent five years dreaming of and working toward. It had been a phenomenal trip, rich with the kind of experiences that shape us, that get us thinking about experience, about life in new ways. This was the end of it: this last long and lazy afternoon on the coast. I wanted only to drink it in. The serenity and quiet joy I felt that afternoon seemed touched by eternity, as if the light bathing Dubrovnik and the harbor were streaming from heaven itself. I felt as if I could stay there forever.

It was August 12. The next morning we would board our flight for Frankfurt, and after a short layover, be on our way to San Francisco. This was in fact the last day of an entire chunk of my life, but I did not know it, at the time. Even if I had known it, it would not have mattered. All that mattered that afternoon was the sight of Jorge, dolphin-diving into the sunlit sea, was the sight of the rest of the guys spread out with their beach towels, their cameras, their sodas and bottled water, my boys from Marysville there on the sunny rocks with the girls from Italy and Sweden. All that mattered that serene afternoon was everything that had led up to it: seven years, with my kids; seven years that changed all of our lives. This is the story of those years.

ONE

It was a bright June morning in 1997, a weekday, and I was having coffee on the patio at my mom's house in Marysville. For those of you unfamiliar with California geography, Marysville is located on the confluence of the Yuba and Feather rivers, in the Central Valley. The city is about forty minutes north of Sacramento and two hours from San Francisco. On clear days, we can see both Mount Shasta, near the Oregon border, and Mount Diablo, one of the highest peaks in the Bay Area. We are eighty minutes from the ski slopes of the Sierra but Marysville's climate is Mediterranean, with long, hot, desert-dry summers and short, rainy winters – very like the climate of Croatia. Summer mornings in Marysville tend to make me happy in and of themselves. The sun may already be hot, but it is dry heat, and in the shade, it can feel cool and fresh 'til early afternoon. I have spent many summer mornings at my mom's, just taking my time with my coffee, watching the mockingbirds flit about in the overhead branches, and maybe playing with one of our cats.

This particular morning I had more than the usual domestic bliss going for me: I had just finished a heavy semester at the Dominican School at the Graduate Theological Union in Berkeley, and had come up from the house I shared in Oakland with my sister Anne, to spend a few days at Mom's. With the semester behind me, I was free to really start concentrating on "my kids," that is, the fifty or so teenagers who made up the youth group at St. Joseph Parish in Marysville. I was youth minister for the parish. I had taken the job against all my own best judgment in the autumn of 1995. In the twenty or so months since that reluctant acceptance, and to no one's surprise more than mine, the ministry had become a true passion in me, and my kids, one of the deepest joys of my life.

My studies at the Dominican School were nearing an end: the coming year would see two light semesters, compared to the semester I had just come through. The year ahead was doubly auspicious because I had also recently left my job at Cal. I had worked at UC-Berkeley's Career Planning and Placement Center since 1980. In the spring of 1997, in recognition of the number of hours I was putting in as youth minister, Father Leon, my pastor and boss at St. Joseph's, had doubled my salary. That raise freed me from the need to keep working my job, at the university. I felt as if God Himself were clearing the tracks for me and the kids, for the coming year. And I wanted, more than anything else, that summer of 1997, to make tracks with the youth ministry in Marysville. I wanted to do this above all because it would be my last year with the kids: after finishing up at the Dominican School, I would transfer to St. Patrick's Seminary, on the San Francisco Peninsula, to complete my studies for priestly ordination. Once a seminarian, I would no longer be able to hold my position as youth minister in Marysville.

And because I realized that the coming year, summer, 1997 to summer, 1998, would be my last year with the kids, I let myself dream that morning. I asked myself what I would do for the kids, if I could do anything. The answer came back like a boomerang: I would take them to Europe, next summer. I would take them on pilgrimage. And I knew where we would go, too: we would go to Rome and to Medjugorje.

Rome I don't need to explain. It has been a pilgrimage destination for millions, and for centuries. Medjugorje is another matter. To this day, more than a decade after that sunny morning on the patio, many Catholics have never heard of the Bosnian village where, if authentic, the longest-running Marian apparition in history is still taking place. Already in June of 1997 the apparitions were marking their sixteenth anniversary. Already by 1997, a million pilgrims a year were visiting Medjugorje. I had first heard of Medjugorje in the mid-eighties, three or four years after the start of the apparitions. I had wanted to go for years, but one way and another, it had never panned out. Now here I was on the patio at Mom's, a tough spring semester successfully behind me, my job at Cal forever behind me, and all of the coming year to look forward to, with my kids. What would I do for them, if I could do anything?

The air was fresh and cool, and scented with Confederate jasmine. The mockingbirds had a nest full of babies in the pyracantha which was a constant fascination and frustration for our several cats. It was maybe a Tuesday morning – I know anyway it was early in the week – and I was enjoying my coffee. And I was enjoying my contemplation of the year ahead, with the kids. And I let myself dream, for and about my kids.

And to better help you, dear reader, picture the scenes I will be describing over the next few hundred pages, think generally of the teens I refer to as "my kids" along the following lines: dark hair and dark eyes, golden skin. Most of my young people in the Marysville youth group were Mexican-American. Most of them were friends before they joined the group. They were a bright, outgoing bunch, laughing easily and loving to joke around. They had a lot of self-confidence; a certain sense, I guess, of their own worth, because in my interaction with them, I found them to be young people who expected to be loved, and who were abundantly ready to give love in return. I can, and do, thank their parents for these happy facts.

They mostly came from Linda and Olivehurst, the large and growing unincorporated communities south of Marysville. Whereas my alma mater is Marysville High, theirs is Lindhurst. Marysville is the oldest of the several communities clustered there where the Yuba and Feather rivers meet. It was established by survivors of the Donner Party, and for more than a decade after the start of the Gold Rush it had been, behind San Francisco and Sacramento, the state's third largest city. It was still among the state's largest cities at the end of the nineteenth century. Today, hemmed in by its levees, Marysville is smaller than any of its neighbors – Linda, Olivehurst, Yuba City, Plumas Lake. My kids came from Linda and Olivehurst. Some of them excelled academically at Lindhurst High, and others were star athletes, but most of them were content to sail through their high school years with no great achievement in view. Though I, in fact, believe them capable of great things, they were (and are) very typical young Californians, with all the usual concerns and preoccupations of youth, and wearing Guess and Tommy Hilfiger and Nike Airs and God-knows-what-all-awful-brand-nonsense-else. (I am no fan of designer-mania fashion.)

I had been to Rome, and I could see the kids, in my mind's eye, in the great squares and piazzas, could see them gazing upward at the ceiling of the Sistine Chapel, could see them bounding up the Spanish Steps and taking pictures among the classical ruins. It was easy to see my kids in Rome. It occurred to me that some of them might easily be mistaken for Italian, by the Italians – this has happened often enough to me, when in Italy. I did not doubt that my kids and Rome would hit it off.

I had never been to Medjugorje, but this fact did not for a minute stop me from "seeing" my kids there. I'd seen pictures, after all. I knew what St. James Church looked like, and I imagined my kids lined up in front of it, for a photo. I knew what the rocky pilgrim trails up the mountains in Medjugorje looked like. I imagined my kids trekking up those trails. I did not imagine them praying the Rosary or making the Stations of the Cross, as pilgrims do, climbing the mountain paths in Medjugorje. I had taught the kids about these devotions, but had not much tried to lead them in either. Good as my imagination was, that bright morning, it was not sufficiently fanciful to envision my kids – my happy, laughing, gently skeptical and slightly wild teens – praying five decades of the Rosary, or hanging in for all fourteen Stations. As I have said many, many times of my young men and women from Marysville, they have deep faith and joyful hearts. God can do a lot, a lot, with such a combination. But I have never made a claim of holiness for them. Though I know that many of them are capable of achieving sainthood IN THIS LIFE, the fact about my kids that summer of 1997, is that they were absolutely normal, regular American teens.

If I could not quite envision my kids praying a full Rosary as they made their way up Apparition Hill, I envisioned them plenty of other ways. I saw them with my mom, Sara, whom they all revered, and my sister Trudi, on this imaginary pilgrimage. Trudi lives in Marysville and got to know the kids the best of any of my seven siblings. I imagined Mom and Trudi on the pilgrimage, and extrapolated from that to see others on it, as well. My friend Marie Smith, for instance, who was on the Board of Advisors at the Dominican School at the GTU, and who led a weekly Rosary group that I frequented. Marie was, in Church parlance, one of my chief "formators," meaning, she was a major influence on me, spiritually and emotionally, as I prepared for priesthood. God sends such people into the lives of seminarians. Ask any seminarian. Marie had just that spring been described to me as an exteriorized conscience, and thinking about it, I had to smile and agree.

Marie and I had met in a class – my first – at the Dominican School, in the spring of 1995, a class called Mary, Mother of the Lord. Marie's devotion to Our Lady mirrored my own, and her straightforward, no-nonsense approach to living the life of a disciple had had an enormous influence on me. I had wanted my kids to have the benefit of some of Marie's counsel, but one way and another, had not yet gotten them together with her. I imagined Marie on the imaginary pilgrimage: I saw her walking with two or three of my boys, Oscar, maybe, Mikey and Fonz, maybe, in front of St. James Church in Medjugorje, and I imagined her talking to them the way she talked to me: "What do you care whether this or that effort of yours succeeds or fails? All that matters is that God's will be done, and don't buy into any of that 'see it be it' crap. Did the Crucifixion look like a success? What would the Gospel-of-Health-and-Wealth have to say to Joan of Arc? Sainthood comes at a price. Very few saints have looked like successes in this world." I saw Marie confidently evangelizing, her red hair ablaze in the Balkan sun, and imagined, and I stress that I was imagining this!, my boys fifteen, sixteen, seventeen as they were that summer of 1997, I imagined my boys listening to Marie with the same rapt attention that I gave her, when she would talk this way to me.

One of our cats, Iggy, maybe, named by my sister Flo for Iggy Pop, came ambling across the patio and brushed against my legs. I came out of my reverie and reached down to give the cat a little love. I do love cats. I like dogs, too. I have never bought into the idea that you must choose one or the other. But then, I like lizards and snakes, and wish I could train them to be pets, so take it for what it's worth. In any event, Iggy, or Bandit, or Crazy (Bandit's most appropriately-named mother) or Imperiatrix (our grey Russian, named for a title of Catherine the Great's) or whomever, came up against my boot-clad calf and distracted me. Or I should say, brought me gently back to reality. I had been daydreaming about this pilgrimage with the kids for maybe half an hour, maybe forty minutes.

I shook myself back into real time and real space. June, 1997. A serene summer morning on Mom's patio. Baby mockingbirds in the pyracantha, and the oleander a riot of color. June, 1997. My job at Cal behind me forever. Four classes left at the Dominican School. And a full year with the kids ahead. Obviously, there could be no pilgrimage to Europe. None of us could afford it. Not by a long, long shot. Nice to dream, very nice. I had enjoyed the reverie. But…get real, dude. You've got achievable goals for the kids to be thinking about. And you've got a whole wonderful year ahead, to achieve them. Get to work.

***

Among other things, getting to work that summer meant meeting with parents and parishioners supportive of my work with the kids. One of these was Alicia Haldeman, whose sons, Robert and Richard, were in the youth group. Alicia had once been in a convent in Spain; she was a serious and devout Catholic woman. She prayed a lot, and I trusted her insights and intuitions. She, the boys and I had a lunch date about a week after the morning I had spent daydreaming on the patio. We met at a Lyons in Yuba City, which lies immediately across the Feather River from Marysville. I do not remember the full agenda of that lunch meeting, though I know some of it had to do with fundraising. Some of it also had to do with faith-raising; with coming up with ways to help deepen and broaden the kids' experience of their faith. There was a point in the conversation when Alicia said, "Have you ever thought about taking the kids to Medjugorje?"

14

I think I stopped with my fork an inch or so from my mouth. I looked Alicia right in the eyes. She didn't blink. I put my fork down.

"Why do you ask?" I said.

"Because I think you are supposed to," she answered. "I think Our Blessed Mother wants it."

I looked down at my plate, shaking my head. I could feel Robert and Richard's gazes on me, waiting for me to respond. I can be pretty dense sometimes. I can miss some pretty obvious things. But I did not miss this. I knew in that instant that I had confirmation, from Heaven itself, that I was supposed to get my kids to Medjugorje. But…how?

I looked up, glancing from Alicia to the boys. "Alicia," I said. "A few years ago, my brother Dan and I looked into going to Medjugorje. It was over fifteen hundred dollars. It's going to be more than that, now. The kids do not come from wealthy families, and you and I make little better than minimum wage. How can we possibly get the kids to Medjugorje?"

"That's Our Lady's job, not yours," said Alicia. "Your job is to set the trip up, to put the plan in motion. Leave the rest to Heaven."

Robert and Richard were looking at me with expectant joy. Alicia was looking at me with absolute conviction. I absorbed both feelings, and I allowed myself to drift back to the reverie on the patio, six or seven mornings earlier. How happy that reverie had made me. I had asked myself, "If I could do anything for the kids this year, what would it be?"

I took a deep breath. "Let me tell you something," I said, and then related my daydreaming of a week before. Robert and Richard looked to one another, wide-eyed, smiling. Alicia sat back, satisfied.

"I'm game, if you are," I said, to Alicia. "We'll try to get the kids to Medjugorge and Rome, next summer."

"Not try," Alicia corrected. "Will. We will get them there. It is what Our Lady wants."

We left that lunch with our work divided between us. I would sit down and come up with a list of fundraisers for the coming year that would give us the best possible shot at earning the money we would need to pull such a plan off. Alicia would investigate pilgrimage operators, and start comparing tours and prices. We agreed that, to give us the longest possible lead-time, we would aim for an August, 1998 trip. "That's fourteen months," I remember telling Alicia. "If we can do this, we are going to need every day we've got."

***

The kids and I were already fundraising – fundraising had been an integral part of the ministry for me, since I had taken over in autumn, 1995. A lot of priests, and a lot of youth ministers, loathe fundraising, but I love it. It doesn't just fatten the bank account, it builds community. There was always a group of us at any fundraiser, and the first three letters of the word fundraiser describe what we had, raising money.

I remember that the summer of 1997 started with a special fundraiser, working the Cargill Company picnic, at the fairgrounds in Yuba City. It was a late afternoon-into-evening gig, a Saturday, and I remember that when I arrived, thinking I was twenty minutes early, a lot of the kids were already there. I pulled up near the dining pavilion to see Nelson and Omar, among others, unloading huge bags of crushed ice from a truck. The folks from Cargill found me and showed me how they were setting up. The kids would be handling concessions, making snow cones, cotton candy, pop corn, hot dogs and hamburgers, selling sodas, doing face-painting, running a bounce house and I don't remember what-all else.

I do remember Omar at the cotton candy machine, showing me how it worked, and how you could make the fluffy treat pink, lavender or pale blue, depending on what color sugar you used. He would turn fifteen that summer, but looked seventeen, and a lot of teen-aged daughters of Cargill employees were big fans of cotton candy, that afternoon. I also remember Fonz and Wally at the bounce house. Fonz and Wally are cousins, and they had been in my Confirmation class, along with Claudia, Wally's sister, the year I had taken over the youth group. The group's growth had occurred, in part, because of the way Fonz, Wally and Claudia had recruited members among their friends. Anyway, Fonz and Wally managed at one point to clear the bounce house of all Cargill children, and were in it themselves, creating more bounce than had fifteen little kids. I told them that if they broke it, they paid for it. I came upon them maybe an hour later, the bounce house full of tots, and watched, as the little ones wanted to come out, how carefully and gently Fonz got them

17

down to the ground, and I remember thinking, "He is going to be a great dad, one day." In the next instant, Fonz was looking into the bounce house, saying, "Does anyone else want to come out?" He and Wally couldn't wait to get back in.

Claudia, Alma and Elva were doing face-painting, at picnic tables under the trees, where it was shady and cool. Alejandra, who was one of my officers, and her sisters, Leticia and Vicky, were making snow cones. I think some of the other girls, Liz, Veronica, Talia, were at the soda stand. When it came time to get dinner going – steaks supplied by the company itself (Cargill is a meat-packing company) -- Bertha, mother of Claudia and Wally, and Gene and Gloria Harless, parishioners from St. Joseph's, joined me at the big open-air bbq, and we got down to the serious business of cooking several hundred steaks. A couple of the boys, Oscar and Pancho, helped out with this, as well.

Aside from the steaks, my job was largely to make the rounds of the concessions, and make sure the kids were manning their posts. There was a carnival at the fair grounds that weekend, with a number of rides. I found out that the kids had arranged their concession teams so that at any given time, several of them could be off at the carnival, being spun around on the Tilt-a-Whirl, and turned upside down on one of those horrible rides that does that. Although the kids were taking turns, going on the rides, it seemed to me that every time I asked for them, Matt, Mikey and Jorge were at the carnival.

I need to just say a couple things here, about Matt, Mikey and Jorge. First, they could not be purchased separately. Almost like the Holy Trinity, if one of them was there, all of them were. Second, Jorge's name is pronounced George. Third, Matt's last name is Nieschalk, and he has the blonde hair and blue eyes to prove it. Anyway, Matt, Mikey and Jorge: I don't know if one of the three of them did a lick of work the whole five or six hours we manned the picnic. They did show up at the concessions, though, when they wanted pop corn, a hot dog or a Coke, all of which Cargill was giving us for free.

We came home from the Cargill picnic with a lot of happy memories and six hundred to the good, at the bank. We also did car washes that summer at church. This had been the idea of Dave Offutt, the business manager for the parish, and who, with his wife Tish, was a steady backer of my efforts with the kids. Dave suggested we use the schoolyard, directly across the street from the church, and wash cars while people attended Sunday morning Mass. Dave suggested we adopt an every-other-week schedule, and from June to August, we held six Sunday car washes at the church.

We had a blast, at those car washes. I am even today impressed, thinking about the depth of my enthusiasm, my joy, those bright, already-hot Sunday mornings, joining the kids in the parking lot, setting up the hoses, the soap, the buckets, the cloths. I was forty-one. I had written five novels, and worked with several New York literary agents, trying to get published. I had a lot of good friends in the Bay Area and LA and New York, who were also pursuing careers in media and the arts, friends I would spend time with in trendy bars and restaurants, talking art, politics and culture. I had had a plan for my life, in my twenties, in my thirties, that simply was not consistent with washing cars in a school yard as a church fundraiser, with a bunch of teens. If you'd told me at twenty-one or thirty-one, that this was how I would spend six Sunday mornings the summer that I was forty-one, I would have been incredulous.

But I look back now on the summer of 1997, and revere it as one of the happiest times of my life. I was writing a big new novel that year, a novel I felt would surely and finally get my work into print (its title was GOLD COUNTRY). Though I had written my first novel in the summer of 1979, and had won the admiring approval, with that and later books, of several New York agents, I had yet to publish a word. I remember telling my sister Kathleen that GOLD COUNTRY at last would change that. Kathleen, herself an artist, had read all my earlier work, and could get indignant, at the fact that I was still unpublished. I assured her, that summer of 1997, that GOLD COUNTRY was going to turn the tide at last. I really believed it, and for that reason alone, my forty-first summer was a charmed one. But the summer of 1997 was not about my literary ambitions: it was about my kids. Not just the fundraisers, but the Great America trips (we took two, one at the start of the summer, and one at the end), the A's games, followed by ice cream at Fenton's in Oakland, the dinner-and-movie nights in Sacramento. When I think of the summer of 1997, I think of my kids.

Meanwhile, Alicia kept her end of the bargain. She had found a tour organizer in the East Bay, Maria Uribe, who worked for an Italian tour company, Ave Maria Azurra Tours. Maria had been in the business more than ten years, and had organized and led many pilgrimages to Catholic sites around the world. We met with Maria in Sacramento in July. She was relaxed, smiling, gracious. She was pretty and well-dressed, and she insisted on treating us to lunch. She was fluent in Spanish. She loved the idea of a largely Hispanic California youth group making a pilgrimage to Medjugorje and Rome.

We told Maria what we wanted, and told her as well that we could not afford to do it. She said she would find ways to bring the price down for us – among other things, she noted that she could trim probably a couple hundred off the price, simply by having us take a ferry from Italy to Croatia, rather than flying. Four-star hotels were not necessary, we all agreed. And Maria could give us one free ticket for every five paid. When I heard this, I actually began to think that maybe this could be done. If I had twenty-five paying passengers, and Maria could get five free tickets, and if I could make those, instead, ten half-price tickets, and if the price Maria got for us were under two grand...then I would need to come up with ten thousand in fundraising, to take ten kids.

And because I knew the Marysville parish, I believed I could raise ten thousand for the kids in the coming year. I just need to say this here, and then be done with it, because no one in Marysville wants this credit, but scores of people there deserve it, in fact, hundreds. The kids and I accomplished what we accomplished because the Marysville parish got behind us and stayed behind us. They stayed behind us for most of a decade.

There was a popular book out about this time, Hilary Clinton's IT TAKES A VILLAGE. I don't know if it takes a village to raise a child, but I do know that it takes a parish to raise a seminarian. From the Sunday in January, 1996, that I announced at all the Masses at St. Joseph's that I was studying for the priesthood, until May 20, 2006, when I was ordained, the Marysville parish was behind me all the way. And they got behind my work with the kids with a zeal and a joy that can bring a smile of heartfelt gratitude even today, years afterward. The people of St. Joseph's bought t-shirts, raffle tickets and bake sale goods; they supplied us with what we needed for our rummage sales, and then came out and rummaged; they sponsored lanes and teams at our bowlathons; left their cars for us to wash while they attended Mass; and so jammed our monthly breakfasts that we sometimes ran out of food. They came to call the kids "Jim's kids," and they adopted the youth group as THEIR youth group, their teens, their project. The kids and I went to Europe twice, because the people of St. Joseph's decided to get us there; because they got behind us and stayed behind us.

***

The summer ended with an Officers' Dinner, that is, the elected officers of the group and me, getting together to talk about plans for the coming year. It was Friday, August 29. (I have a good memory for such things, regardless, but I may also remember this date because it was the day before Princess Diana died.) I wanted to take the kids someplace nice, in Sacramento. I needed a second driver, so Bertha, mother of two of my officers (Wally and Claudia) helped out. We went to Cattlemen's in Arden, and I remember Bertha taking a look at the menu and asking if, with six teens, I had been prepared for the prices. I smiled. I had been prepared. I wanted the kids to get the idea, unmistakably, that I valued them. Years later, after many, many dinners out at the pricier chains, Ada (his full name is Adalberto, but no one calls him that) would tell me, "Jim, you could have taken us to McDonald's, and we would have been fine." I said that I understood that. But I was trying to make a point. MY kids were worth $25 and $30 entrees. I wanted them to understand that.

Besides, I am not a fan of fast food…

At that time I had three girl and three boy officers, but I will point out here that this was, while I was in charge, an overwhelmingly male group. At its height, when I had sometimes sixty-five teens in the Youth Hall at St. Joseph's, I had maybe forty-five boys and twenty girls. Typical meetings saw close to fifty teens in attendance, and about thirty-five of them were boys. This, I have come to learn, is somewhat unusual, among youth groups. But it was how things were, with us.

Anyway, five of my officers were able to make this dinner, and Claudia's then-boyfriend, Mario, also attended. I had already told the kids that I was aiming for us all to go to Europe the following summer. I do not know that they believed me. I mean, I am sure they believed that I meant to try to do it. I am not sure that even one of them really thought the idea possible, let alone probable. I explained to the kids that evening that our fundraising had to be focused on getting to Europe next summer. We could do other things, fun things (like the upcoming end-of-summer trip to Great America) but that we had to make getting to Europe our overriding priority, if we were to get there.

I don't think we talked about much else, in terms of plans, at that dinner. The kids were delighted with the menu – Fonz and Wally got surf and turf combos and Mikey got babyback ribs. Bertha and I had steaks; I think one of the girls, Claudia or Elva, actually got pasta, and took some kidding over it: pasta at Cattlemen's. These places tend to have great specialty drinks for the under-21 set, and I remember, too, the kids ordering exotic concoctions of soda water, lots of ice and brightly-colored syrups, some loaded as well with fruit: slices of orange or pineapple, maraschino cherries.

As we were winding up, the boys begged me to go to a movie. There was a major cinema complex across the parking lot. I remember being a little conflicted about it, as it had not been part of my plan for the evening: I had planned to be home relatively early. Bertha was not staying for a movie, and said she would take the girls, and Mario, home. I looked at my three boy officers – Wally, the president, Fonz, the treasurer, and Mikey, the secretary (who somehow always managed to leave the minute-taking to me, and only signed off on my notes, at each of our meetings). I looked at them as one might look at three puppies, right down to the pleading, big brown eyes, and I sighed and I said, "What movie do you want to see?"

We saw something truly silly but highly entertaining called MONEY TALKS, with Charlie Sheen. I remember getting the guys drinks and pop corn before we went in, marveling at what the teen-aged stomach can hold. We had just finished a BIG dinner, after all. We sat together in the very last row, and, as I say, we were very entertained by the movie.

I make a point of this night with the kids at the end of the summer of 1997, because it initiated an activity – dinner out and a movie – that would become a feature of my association with my kids, for the next half dozen years. We had many, many Wednesday nights together at the Youth Hall, at St. Joseph's. We had many weekend fundraisers. We held dances, and took fun daytrips to A's games and Great America. I attended many high school football and basketball games. Often as not, after our monthly parish breakfast fundraiser, several of the guys would go to my health club with me, and put in a good workout. But some of the deepest bonding between me and the kids happened in these informal arrangements – dinner and a movie on a weekend night, in Sacramento. And dinner at the upper-caste chains – Cattlemen's, Red Lobster, Black Angus, Chevy's and so on – because my kids were worth it.

I cannot remember how many times I came into one of these restaurants, three or four or five or six of the guys in tow, all of them laughing and joking and in great spirits, and the restaurant staff sort of sizing us up warily, as if to say, "What lucky waiter/ess is going to get THIS crew?" The next time I did a dinner out with the kids, that fall, was October 4, a Saturday. This was not an officers' dinner. This was the first official "Boys' Night Out." I took Fonz, Wally, Mikey and Jorge to the Roseville Black Angus. I remember that they put us in a booth that was circular, which had only a narrow opening to the rest of the restaurant. The booths at Black Angus are typically high. It may have been coincidence, or the restaurant staff may have been taking no chances. We were all but hidden from view.

The funny thing is, and this would continue for the next half dozen years: the guys charmed our waitress. She may have approached us thinking, "Oh boy, this is gonna be fun -- NOT," but by the time she was bringing the appetizers, she was one of the gang, laughing and bantering, and making jokes at our expense, which the guys always enjoyed. All my kids love a good laugh, but if it is on them, that doubles their pleasure in it. I remember that at one point that evening, Mikey laughed so hard that he fell out of the booth, which brought a roar of laughter from the other guys that must've been heard throughout the restaurant.

I always tipped our wait staff well, even very well, like thirty-five and forty percent. The guys would take me to task for this, but I did it largely BECAUSE of the guys, which they, uh, didn't get. "You're not the easiest customers," I'd tell them, which would invariably bring a protest along the lines of "What do you mean we're not the easiest customers? This place is lucky to have our business!" and so on.

But I would over-tip the waitresses as well, because I so much appreciated the way most of them would enter right into our energy and our space – giving at least as good as they got. I remember the waitress at this same Black Angus, some years later who, coming to the table twice and finding Jorge on his cell phone both times, told us that she understood: "He's talking to Johnny. Johnny's jealous and insecure." We all busted up. When Jorge finally had time to order, he asked us, "Why does the waitress think I'm gay?" I have photos of the hostesses at Peppermill, getting kisses from, and giving them to, Nelson and Omar. I have photos, too, of the gal at the Roseville Black Angus who played an imaginary violin, while Fonz explained why he had to change his order. These were fun evenings.

There was something more to it, too. There was my own conviction that if people, perhaps especially young people, are to be able to love well in life, they must first be well-loved. You cannot give what you do not have. I wanted my kids to know how much I valued them. Beyond that, I wanted them to come to glimpse how much God values them. I was not just the parish youth minister to my kids. I was not just their Confirmation teacher. I was a man preparing for priesthood. They all knew it, and most of them had never known a future priest before. In some real way, I WAS the Church to them, I WAS the faith to them, sort of a walking embodiment of it. I wanted them to associate the Church and the faith with an experience of joyful love. Where better than over a good meal at one of the pricier chains? Jesus himself enjoyed sharing a good meal with friends.

I suppose it was the same dynamic at work, in the fact that, once I had gotten my bearings as a new youth minister, in the spring of 1996, every meeting in the Youth Hall became a pizza party. The general format for the meetings had always been to start with the officers' meeting, proceed to the general meeting, have a teaching of some sort, and then have social time. The Youth Hall was equipped with pool and ping pong tables, and the gym, with its basketball court, was right next door (the Youth Hall was in the church basement). When I took over the youth ministry, in November, 1995, the free time at the end of the meetings included sodas and snacks. But at some point over that first winter and spring, I began to bring in pizza; every second or maybe third meeting, at first, but then, seeing the response of the kids to it, I was, by late spring, 1996, having pizza delivered at every meeting. Hot wings and those yummy Domino's soft bread sticks, too.

By the spring of 1996, I had sometimes as many as sixty-five young people at the meetings. That much pizza was not cheap, nor was it in our budget: I paid for it myself. I was working two jobs and had student loans; I managed. I remember Claudia saying years afterward, "Oh my gosh, Jim! Student loans for pizza! What did those pizzas end up costing, with the interest?" Not that much, even including the interest. I would do it all over again. I wanted my kids to know that the Church valued them.

***

The meetings, in any event, had always been much more than just a pizza party. This was especially true, in 1997-8, my last year as youth minister. By the time we reconvened on our regular meeting schedule in September, I had a slate of fundraisers lined up, aimed at Europe and pilgrimage; the most important of these being a bowlathon in January. I had as well an ambitious set of teaching goals. Mostly, I taught the kids through playing "Catholic Jeopardy." It is played just like the game on TV, except that, to include all the kids, I had them form teams of five or six persons, and

all the teams participated each night. We would run an autumn
series, maybe four or five weeks, and then a final round; a winter
series, and one in spring. The kids were playing for good prizes, too:
trips to Tahoe or Santa Cruz, to Kings' games at Arco Arena, or
baseball games in the Bay Area. They took it seriously. I still smile,
thinking of the time Elva asked if it would be okay to bring her Bible
to meetings, so that she and her team could search for answers in
Scripture.

"Is it all right?" I asked. "Elva! You get extra points just for
suggesting it!"

I was putting together a big weekend retreat, up at one of those rustic
resorts-on-a-lake that one finds in the northern California foothills.
The retreat's theme was going to be Christological – we were going
to dive headlong into the mystery of the Incarnation: God and Man
in the one Person, Jesus. Through Marie Smith, I had lined up a
great Dominican priest from Berkeley, Father Michael Carey, to be
our spiritual director on the retreat, and I had several speakers from
the parish's RCIA and Adult Faith Formation programs on deck, as
well. Marie was going to come up, from Berkeley, with Father
Michael. She had met some of the kids during the summer, when
she had been at St. Joseph's speaking on the Divine Mercy devotion;
now she would get to meet all of them. What's more, Maria Uribe
was going to attend the retreat, as well. She would talk about her
pilgrimage experiences, and in particular, about Medjugorge. I had
done retreats for the kids before, most recently, an overnight, just the
previous May; but this one was going to be special.

Additionally, I had spoken with Father Leon, pastor at St. Joseph's,
about preparing several of the guys for their Sacraments. Omar had

not yet been confirmed. And Oscar, Nelson, Jorge and Mikey had not yet received Reconciliation, Eucharist or Confirmation. I asked Father Leon if I could prepare these five teens in a special Sacraments class, to meet in the Youth Hall on Sunday mornings, as, frankly, they would be way out of place – and a substantial distraction! – with my eighth graders, whom I was teaching in the regular Confirmation class. (But for Oscar, who had just graduated from high school, the guys were sophomores.) Father was cool with the plan for the special class, and we began meeting in September, toward a late April date for Confirmation.

Although I sometimes had adult volunteers with me, in the Youth Hall, their presence was inconsistent. Because I valued both her experience and insights, and because I needed someone else over eighteen to be in the Youth Hall with me, I hired Heather Higgins, a student at Yuba College, in Marysville, to be my assistant. I could not pay Heather much, but I absolutely needed her, and in any event, she loved the ministry. Heather had been an officer in the youth group for a couple of years, just before I took over. Her younger brother Russell was still in the group, and a great favorite with everyone – with the guys because of his athletic ability, and with the girls because of his good looks (and, I suppose, because of his smiling and easy manner). Anyway, Heather also attended the Sunday morning Sacraments class. She said she did not know enough about her faith, and wanted to learn more. This is a remark I hear frequently, from the young.

It is hard for me to describe how happy this special class made me. I suppose that I am, maybe above all, a teacher of the faith, and the chance to design a special class, aimed at sacramental prep, for five teen agers who were as good as nephews to me, was a deep, deep joy. I remember putting together the weekly lessons, and including them in six separate folders, one for each of the boys, and one for Heather; I remember illustrating these lessons with photos, maps, art and so on, to engage the kids on all levels. I remember the easy, relaxed Sunday morning sessions themselves. The kids lapped up the faith; they were hungry for it – and they had a deep, a profound capacity for it. The morning I was explaining the Trinity to them, and using many images of how three can be one, including the image used by St. Patrick, to convert my own ancestors – the shamrock – one of the boys said he got the three leaves being one shamrock, but…what about the stem?

I stopped and thought about it, and…I did not have an answer. I suppose I was about to give my standard reply to such queries, along the lines that, ultimately, all human effort at explaining the Godhead must fall short, when Jorge chimed in with this: "Maybe the stem is the Church, bringing God down to earth." I have used Jorge's explanation, in discussions on the shamrock image, ever since.

***

So that was how things stacked up for the final year, this straight run at our almost unbelievable goal: getting to Europe on pilgrimage, the following summer. As maybe you can tell, my schedule that year was overwhelmed with the kids. I was technically still sharing a house in Oakland, with my sister Anne, but that entire year, I was never there more than two nights a week, depending on my class schedule at the Dominican School. Between the Wednesday night Youth Group meetings, the regular Confirmation class on Tuesday nights, the weekend fundraisers, the special Sacraments class on Sunday mornings, the dinner-and-movie nights, and all the prep work that was necessary, given such a set of priorities, I was

Marysville's youth minister, in a phrase just then coming into vogue among the young, "24/7."

This of course, is what I had wanted, dreaming on the patio, that bright June morning. I was deeply grateful not to have to be working my job at Cal, anymore; very grateful, too, that I had only four more classes to complete my MA, at the Dominican School. I took three classes each semester, regardless. I was hungry to soak up as much as I could from the GTU, while I was there.

And I was hungry to spend as much time with the kids as I could, not just to guide us toward success in our grand ambition, but to go deep with them, this year, knowing that it was my last with them. I felt an anticipatory wistfulness, off and on, all that year. At the same time that I was plunged into the ministry as never before, and truly, loving every minute of it, I was acutely aware that the minutes were ticking past, that when this year ended, so would my time with my kids. I was determined to make the most of it. I remember talking to my friend Ro about it, around Christmas sometime. Ro, a native of Manila, but a long-term parishioner at St. Joseph's, was one of my biggest supporters, with the kids – not just financially, either. She made time to be with the kids, in special situations, such as a two AM breakfast at Lyons in Yuba City, following the Midnight Mass at St. Joseph's. The guys loved Ro; she wasn't just attractive, she was downright glamorous, and what's more, she had their number, and they knew it. To this day, the guys love being given a bad time by Ro. Ro told me I should stick with the kids a couple more years – she pointed out that most of my kids were only sophomores; what would happen to the group, after I left? The argument that I should stay til 2000, when a large number of my kids would graduate from high school, had been made before, by the kids themselves. I would have liked to have stayed through to 2000. But I felt called to get to the seminary, in 1998. And so I felt a kind of urgency to go deep, this one last year, with the kids.

The year was an unprecedented success, by any measure, but there was one big disappointment: the great retreat I had planned for late October was cancelled following a devastating wildfire in the foothills northeast of Marysville. The fire raged for several days, burning up thousands of acres, including the rustic resort-on-the-lake where we had our reservation. I remember taking two or three afternoons out, in early October, looking for an appropriate venue to reschedule the retreat. I saw some lovely properties up in the Sierras, places where, if the retreat were held after mid-November, there would likely be snow on the ground.

But in the end, it was impossible to match our schedule, loaded as it was with fundraisers, and the kids' school commitments, with the availability of any of these other sites, and the retreat never came off. I remember how sad I felt, when the last weekend in October came, which would have been the retreat weekend, and the weather was perfect, sunny and in the seventies, and I saw in my mind's eye the kids on the beach at the lake, on the paddleboat which the center's staff had said would take us on a tour all around the lake; saw in my mind's eye Father Michael Carey, lifting the Host at Mass, before my kids; saw Maria Uribe telling the kids about pilgrimage; saw Marie Smith button-holing Mikey and Jorge, whom she knew from the summer, and asking them what they had done about their prayer life, since the last time we'd all been together. Here I am, a dozen years later, still able to feel wistful about what did not happen, that beautiful weekend at the end of October, 1997.

Something huge transpired in my personal life that autumn, as well. Uncle Jim died. Uncle Jim, that is Monsignor Poole, my mom's older brother, and my namesake uncle, had long been larger-than-life in my imagination. When I was a very little boy, I wanted to be a priest, and I think the biggest reason why is that I was named for Uncle Jim. I don't know that there was anything about being a priest per se that attracted me: I was never one of those kids who dressed in a sheet and played Mass at home. But I revered my namesake uncle.

He had not been, when I was young, my closest uncle. That honor went to Uncle Devore, who, a lifelong bachelor, lived with Grandma, in the home my grandfather had built, on land my great-grandfather had bought, in Marysville. I loved my grandmother's house, as a child, loved its high ceilings and quiet rooms, loved the spacious and well-planted yard. I had many, many overnights, at Grandma's, as a little boy, and Uncle Devore had a deep childhood influence on me. He was quiet and kind and faith-filled, and he was so devoted to the parish that when he died suddenly, in 1979, in his late fifties, the priests of Marysville made no effort to conceal their profound shock and deep grief.

Between Uncle Devore and Uncle Jim, there was Uncle Chuck, my mom's younger brother, a professor of Political Science at UCLA. Uncle Chuck was worldly, sophisticated and witty. He was a published author, and travelled the world as a speaker and consultant. His wife, Rita, was always my closest aunt, and their five children, my Los Angeles cousins, were almost like a second set of siblings. In my teens and throughout my twenties, Uncle Chuck was the man in the family I most wanted to pattern myself after.

Well, Uncle Chuck too died in his late fifties, in 1987. By that time I
had developed a real relationship, with Uncle Jim, the priest. When
Uncle Devore died, I owed him four hundred dollars. At my mom's
suggestion, I "paid" Uncle Devore back by sending twenty bucks a
month to Uncle Jim, to have a Mass said, for Uncle Devore. After
twenty months, obviously, I would have retired the debt, but I had
come to enjoy the business of writing Uncle Jim once a month, and
so continued to send him the checks, along with requests for Masses
for the family. After three or four years, I upped the monthly amount
to fifty bucks. This impressed Uncle Jim no end. I had during this
time also returned to the Sacraments, returned to the practice of my
faith, which gave me and my priest uncle just that much more to talk
about.

We agreed about a lot of things; we were also on opposite sides of
the fence on some issues. That didn't matter. Uncle Jim knew me,
"got" me, and respected me. And I found my childhood awe of him
now brought into close human focus; he was a man, not a god, and a
man who valued relationship with me. When Uncle Jim decided to
take his last "grand tour" (and his trips to Europe were always very
much that) in the fall of 1989, he offered to take me along, "as my
driver," he said, I think largely just to keep the other nephews and
nieces from feeling slighted. I never drove anywhere on that trip.
Uncle Jim and the rest of the party went for over six weeks – starting
with almost three weeks in Ireland. I could not get that much time
away from work, so I skipped Ireland, and joined them in London.
We went from London to Rome, and then both south and north, in
Italy: Naples and Ischia; Florence and Orvieto. We went to Spain for
ten days, and finished up in Lisbon, a city I had wanted to see for
several years, and which has become one of my favorite in the world.

There's a photo of Uncle Jim and me in St. Peter's Square, one of the fountains off to one side and the great façade of the basilica behind us, that may be my favorite photo of me with my priest uncle. I know for a fact that already, by autumn, 1989, Uncle Jim was suspecting my vocation. I may have suspected it, too, but I was not yet ready to discover it. When, however, in 1992, I heard the Lord's call unmistakably, and started investigating possibilities for priestly service, Uncle Jim became my first advisor.

He did not live to see me enter the seminary: that happened nine months after his death. But he saw my success at the Dominican School, and he saw my work with the youth, in Marysville. I was solidly on my way to priesthood, when Uncle Jim died, and my uncle knew it. He died November 10, the Feast of Pope St. Leo the Great, the feast, in other words, of a great man of the Church. When Sacramento's Bishop Weigand eulogized my uncle at the funeral, attended by more than a thousand people, he said, "Truly, a giant has fallen." My uncle was, indeed, one of the great men of the Church in Sacramento: he had in fact twice refused bishoprics, because he would not leave Sacramento. Uncle Jim's love for his native place is one of the things we held deeply in common.

I remember that the day of Uncle Jim's death, a Monday, I had a meeting in Berkeley, with Maria Uribe, to discuss how our pilgrimage plans were shaping up. I had been at the hospital in Sacramento, that morning, before my uncle died; he had slipped into a coma the previous night. I returned to Marysville, for some reason, and when I got back to the hospital, early in the afternoon, Uncle Jim had just died. At Mom's urging, I kept my meeting with Maria, and I am glad I did. I said a couple of rosaries, driving over to Berkeley that wet, windy, grey afternoon. When I met with Maria, at a north side coffee house, I felt almost as if Our Lady herself were consoling me, through this gentle and gracious woman, Maria, and through the promise of something very great to come: the promise of next summer's pilgrimage.

Uncle Jim's funeral was that Friday, at St. Charles Borromeo, the parish he had founded in Sacramento, in 1960. After the funeral, many family and friends came to Marysville, and were there at Mom's. There was a Lindhurst High School football game that night. Mikey and some of the other guys would be playing. Though only a sophomore, Mikey was playing varsity. It had been a cool, grey, blustery day, but it was dry, and so my sister Anne, my niece Lupe and I went over to the stadium to watch the game.

We ran into Jorge near the concession stand, and he asked about the funeral, and how we all were. Anne and Lupe both were impressed with him. We sat on the Lindhurst side, and at one point Mikey was close enough to the stands for Anne to call out his name. He heard and turned and looked up into the stands, but I do not think he knew it was us. The sight of him there in his uniform and helmet, the thought of him, playing with such skill and enthusiasm, just as my uncle had done, in his teens, in his twenties (for Uncle Jim had been a great athlete) consoled me on the loss of my uncle. I cannot analyze the feeling, so won't attempt it. I just throw it out there, as it is a feeling that resonates with me to this day: the comfort I took, seeing Mikey on the field, the day that I had tossed a white rose into my uncle's grave.

***

1997 became 1998. Our single biggest fundraiser, the January bowlathon, was a smashing success, all the way around. It was held Saturday the 24. We had a dozen lanes for the tournament in the morning, and twenty-two for the afternoon, after the winter league bowling ended. We had over one hundred-forty bowlers in all, divided up into teams of four; and the teams were not just composed of teens. A lot of middle-aged parishioners participated in the event. Seven teams took home trophies, as did individual bowlers for such accomplishments as men's and women's high game, high set, and also – just for fun, for the lowest single score achieved all day. I had been prepared to "win" that trophy, but was spared. Father Leon was there for the entire morning, which I greatly appreciated. My success as a youth minister was largely attributable to the way he supported me. Ro was also there: she won the high game trophy in the women's division. I had had no idea Ro could bowl. I'd have thought it an unlikely talent for her, simply because of the beauty, the elegance and the length, of her fingernails.

The next day, Sunday, January 25, was my birthday, and some of the guys wanted to take me to dinner and a movie in Sacramento. This was to be the first birthday dinner the guys would arrange for me, but not the last. They have taken me out on or near my birthday every year since, sometimes as many as a dozen of them. This first time was organized by Jorge. Matt, Mikey and Omar came along. We went to an all-you-can-eat Chinese buffet somewhere near Sacramento's K Street Mall. Then we went to the movie, and I remember that before we got there, I had to pull cash out of my wallet and slip it surreptitiously to both Matt and Mikey: they had spent all they had, buying me dinner. I think they were both a little abashed: they had really wanted to treat me, this time. I was so touched I wanted to hug them.

We saw TITANIC, which had already been number one at the box office for a month, but was to stay there three months more. I would see the film four times, that winter and spring: three times with various groupings of the kids. Fortunately, I am one of those people who have always been fascinated by the TITANIC, and it was no burden, seeing the film repeatedly.

Total income on the bowlathon was over eighty-two hundred dollars, and we cleared more than a five thousand dollar profit on it. We were doing land-office business at the monthly breakfasts, as well, sometimes pulling in over four hundred in profit. Maria Uribe came to Marysville one Saturday afternoon in February and spent the night, and worked the full breakfast with us, the next morning. I can still see her in one of her smart dresses, with an understated brooch and mid-height heels, carrying a still-hot tray, swimming with bacon grease, toward a back counter. She stayed through clean-up, early in the afternoon, and I thought how blessed we were to have met this woman. I felt very confident of Maria's capacities as a guide on pilgrimage, seeing how she was taking care of us right here in California.

The winter became the spring. The kids threw two hugely successful dances, one at Valentine's Day, and one at St. Patrick's; we actually made money on them, which any youth minister can tell you is a neat trick. The Valentine's dance was held at a youth venue in Marysville where the "Friday Night Live" program met. ("Friday Night Live" was a very good local teen program.) It was a great space, and the kids decorated it – not just Alejandra, Claudia, Veronica and Alma, but some of the guys, too – in a way that really gave it a club-like atmosphere. They were delighted with the result, and I have to admit to having been impressed myself. At the urgings of the guys, I "cut a rug" with one of the girls – Liz Quintero. Alejandra told me that when the rest of the girls saw the way I danced, that was it: they were leaving me to Liz. Liz was not intimidated by my mix of mid-seventies dance steps and late-sixties spasmodic gestures, sort of a "the-Hustle-Meets-the-Watusi" approach. She matched me shimmy for shimmy and shake for shake. Liz was never afraid of anything.

At the end of February, Oscar led a group of the guys in completely repainting the Youth Hall. One of the guys, Travis, was a real artist, albeit with a noticeable graffiti influence. When some of the parents saw the newly done walls, they admired the craftsmanship and originality of the murals, but added, with a laugh, "It's been tagged." The guys and I went to Chinatown for dinner, after they'd finished, and I remember that we talked about the trip. I had made several deposits for some of the kids, at this point: they were all able to believe, by February, that we just might really do it. We might really be in Europe, in six months. Some of them had begun to fill out their passport applications.

Early spring moved to mid-spring. We were fundraising every weekend – bake sales, t-shirt sales, car washes, a money raffle, the breakfast. Father Leon had committed to make the trip, a fact which encouraged a number of parishioners to seriously consider going. Brigitta Klug (the name is pronounced "clue" with a g) told me at one of the breakfasts that she was going, and bringing her teen-aged sons, Michael and Gabriel. They'd go on to Germany, after that, which is where Brigitta and her husband had been born. The Klugs were longtime friends of my family in Marysville, and the thought of having Brigitta, the mother of teens, on the trip, gave me extra confidence. I'd be glad to have lots of moms on this trip.

Karen Brown, at the parish office, got the trip advertised for me in
several other parishes, and we ran an ad in the diocesan newspaper in
April. Karen had been my biggest supporter with the youth group,
the whole first year I had been youth minister; it was Karen who
organized our first bowlathon, in 1996, a fundraiser which had set us
up for the whole next year. Karen's son, JD, was one of the kids
who would make the trip. I tried to convince Karen to come, too;
she was super-organized and had a great way with the teens. But she
did not want to go precisely because she wanted JD to have the
freedom of travelling safely in the group, but without having his
mom there. I could understand that.

The price Maria had gotten for us – just under two grand – was very
good for the itinerary, which amounted to two full weeks in Europe.
There was a little problem, but in April, and even in May, I was not
worried about it, yet: that problem was that we did not yet have an
itinerary. We knew only that we wanted a week in Medjugorje and
most of a week in Italy. Though she had a price for us, Maria had
not yet secured airline reservations or bookings on the ground, in
Europe. I was not worried, as I say, because Maria ran pilgrimages
for a living; if she was cool with letting it slide til late spring, that
must be okay. I had never been on the organizing end of a
pilgrimage, of course. That's my excuse, for what subsequently
happened, and I'm stickin' to it!

Confirmation happened in late April, a bright, breezy Sunday. A few
days before, the guys from the special Sacraments class and I went
over to St. Isidore's, in Yuba City, where they had mid-week,
evening confessions, and we all went to confession. For Oscar,
Nelson, Mikey and Jorge, it was the first time. For Omar, it may not
have been too much more than that! I remember when the guys
came out with their penances – Our Fathers and Hail Marys. They

asked me to pray with them, and we all knelt at one of the side altars there in that big, rather attractive modern church, the side altar to Our Lady of Guadalupe. We said our penance prayers together, a fact which made Mom smile, when I told her about it. And on Sunday, April 26, all five of my "graduates" from the special Sacraments class were confirmed, and received Eucharist, four of them for the first time.

Oscar and Jorge had asked me to be their sponsor. I had them sit next to each other, and as we went up to the bishop (it was Rich Garcia, then Sacramento's auxiliary) I stood first behind Oscar, then behind Jorge. That was, for me, a definitive moment.

Karen Brown had organized a nice reception, after the Mass, in the church hall, and we all went over. One of my favorite photos from those years was taken that afternoon. It's outside, with the breeze in the trees, and lifting my tie. I'm flanked by the guys from the special Sacraments class. I told the guys, as I always told all my students in the Confirmation class: this was one of the most important moments of their lives. It can be hard to get kids to see why Confirmation matters. But I am convinced that I only returned to the practice of the faith at the end of my twenties, after years away, because of the grace I received, the day I was confirmed.

I remember that Mikey and Jorge had no family plans after the reception, and so to mark the occasion, I took them to Daikoku, a Japanese restaurant in Marysville that was so authentic that friends from the Bay Area would come to Marysville, just to dine there. The boys had never seen teppan-style cooking before, and they loved it. We would get to Daikoku many times, over the next several years, and the waitresses there, gracious middle-aged women from Japan, came to know Mikey and Jorge, and some of the other guys, and they were always delighted to see us. More than once a couple of them told Jorge he belonged in movies, he was so handsome. They also assured the guys that they would love Japan, and Japan them. In any event, that Sunday evening with Mikey and Jorge at Daikoku ended my six years as Confirmation teacher/coordinator in the Marysville parish.

A couple weeks later, Ro threw a congratulations brunch at her townhouse for the guys. She and I took care over the menu and Ro put out silver, crystal and china: she made it very clear to the guys that she was proud of them. The guys watched me and Ro get this brunch together for them and said what they had said before: I needed to quit all this priest-stuff, marry Ro, become a deacon, and stay here in Marysville. Ro agreed it was an excellent idea: "We have to raise our kids!" she said, and indicated the guys. The attentions of parishioners such as Ro went a long way in helping the kids to grasp just how much we valued them. I am grateful to Ro, to Karen Brown, to Dave and Tish Offutt, and to so many others, at St. Joseph's, who made a point of paying attention to the kids. It was a vital aspect of their overall faith formation. (And perhaps it does take a village, to raise a youth group!)

***

On Tuesday, June 30, Maria Uribe came to Marysville for an informational meeting about the pilgrimage. This meeting took place in the evening, at the church hall, and was attended by forty-five people; all of whom were serious about making the pilgrimage. Dates had been set -- by Maria or by the tour company itself, which was located in Rome -- as August 3-16. These dates held a special resonance for Mom, Trudi and me: my dad was born August 16 and died August 3. When we heard the dates for the trip, we all assumed Dad was working on this project from Heaven (my dad had died four years earlier; he never knew any of my kids).

Though the meeting was immensely encouraging for the turn-out, and for the seriousness of the potential pilgrims – people wanted to write Maria checks then and there – all of us were rattled to learn that, though ground accommodations were settled, airline reservations had yet to be made. Asked specifically about this part of the package, Maria said that maybe we would go with Alitalia, or maybe Swissair – the company would decide that. The question left unanswered, of course, was WHEN would the company decide that? It was the last evening in June, and we were talking about leaving in 34 days.

Still, almost everyone there signed up for the trip. Some may have given Maria deposits; I don't remember. Maria was elated at the numbers, because it would mean so many free tickets to help get the kids onboard. Maria went away with a pilgrim manifest of forty-something names, and said she would be in touch in the coming week, with the specifics, about the airlines and a full itinerary.

The kids and I, meanwhile, had spent May and June fundraising feverishly. I remember that we held a rummage sale in late May. One of the women's organizations at the parish had suggested it: they used to do it, had not done it the past couple of years, and they guessed that we could make good money doing it that spring. They were right: over two days that weekend, we made upwards of $1100. I remember that on Saturday afternoon, after the initial rush of bargain hunters had tapered off, Mikey and Lilin both disappeared among the clothes racks and came out a few minutes later dressed as glamour girls. These guys never missed a chance to amuse themselves.

On June 13, which is a Fatima feast day, and that year, was a Saturday, we had a car wash at Sam's Club in Yuba City. I remember this car wash well, because I spent most of it filling out my application for St. Patrick's Seminary. I remember Ada at one point telling Wally to "get off your butt and get to work." Wally's response was unprintable. At which Pancho and Nelson responded to Wally, with, again, something unprintable. This provoked an unprintable rejoinder from Matt and Jorge. I at this point intervened, and asked them all to watch their language, as there were ladies present, and indicated Fonz and Oscar. Mikey turned the hose on me. Fortunately, I had finished the seminary application, at that point, and had stowed it safely in my car.

Every Sunday, late that spring, and into the summer, we had something going on at church, some kind of fundraiser. The parish was totally behind us; the parish intended to see us get to Europe. I remember coming home, late Sunday morning, week after week, sitting on the patio and counting the morning's proceeds. We were very close, and getting closer, but everything depended on getting several free tickets, which I could not know we had, until I had confirmation from Ave Maria Azurra Tours that a certain number of people had signed up.

Sometime in the first half of July, Maria Uribe left for a Rome-Holy Land pilgrimage. Because Maria was travelling, I was now in direct contact with Sergio Mortera, who was the president of Ave Maria Azurra, in Rome. I was…disconcerted by what Sergio had to report to me. He had a passenger manifest of over forty people, but had received only "some little checks" from Maria (I assume deposits that I, and others, had made over the past several months) and that he needed full payment from everyone and he needed it last week, last month; actually, he needed it in May, but let's not go there: "Jim, I need seventy-four thousand dollars from you and I need it now."

This was perfectly reasonable of Sergio. As a man who now leads pilgrimages a couple times a year, I know the business. For Sergio to have, at most, maybe five grand in deposits, for a trip where he was going to have to buy over forty air tickets, and secure land arrangements, and all in less than a month's time...well...Let's just say that I think Our Lady worked through Sergio to get it all done.

Sergio needed almost seventy-five grand from me. And he needed it yesterday. The kids and I had about ten thousand in the bank. I had, in theory, twenty-five or thirty pilgrims committed to go. At two grand apiece, that came to fifty or sixty thousand more. I looked at it, and my blood ran cold: we were going to come up short. And we had no time to make up the difference.

I got the word out to everyone on the list, that I was now in charge of getting the trip paid for, and that Ave Maria needed our checks NOW; please walk them into the parish office, where I would collect them each day, and overnight them to Sergio's Canadian office. And my pilgrims on this trip, who would prove to be an amazing group, got their checks in, and for the most part, promptly. Only after something like twenty thousand in checks had arrived at the Toronto office, did Sergio call and tell me that, as we were within three weeks of departure, he needed not checks but money orders; he needed paid funds. I had already sent, overnight, another maybe ten or twelve thousand to him, in checks, via the Toronto office. I told him I would get the rest in secured funds, and sent word to my remaining pilgrims that I had to have cashiers' checks or money orders.

Meanwhile, I was doing the math, and sweating it, on the free tickets. We had fifteen paid pilgrims, so three free; then we had twenty, so four. The kids and I had almost ten thousand in the bank. If I had four free tickets, that meant that I could make it a half-price trip for eight kids…but I had at least twelve kids committed to go, and I could not make it work, unless I got a couple additional free tickets…

It is hard now, more than a decade after the events, to convey the anxiety of July, 1998. Mine. Sergio's. Mom's. Some of the kids'. There was a Saturday in mid-July where I feel I was given assurance by the Blessed Mother herself that we were going to make it, even though I remained doubtful another ten or twelve days. There was a Saturday where, at the recommendation of Marie Smith in Berkeley, several of the boys and I went down to Stockton, a city south of Sacramento, to attend a Marian/Charismatic Mass presided over by Father Dean McFalls, a young and dynamic priest of the Stockton Diocese, whom Marie knew and much admired. I went down with Matt, Mikey, Fonz and Ada. Marie had alerted Father Dean that we would be there, and that we were on our way to Medjugorje, in August. Father Dean, just my age, had spent several months in Medjugorje before entering the seminary.

I remember that Father Dean introduced us at the Mass as "Jim Sullivan, who will start seminary for the Diocese of Sacramento in the fall, and several of the leaders of his youth group in Marysville, who are headed for Medjugorje, next month." I remember feeling unworthy of the introduction, because, though it was certainly true that I was going to start at St. Patrick's Seminary at the end of the summer, I could not have guaranteed anyone, that Saturday in the middle of July, that my boys and I would be on a flight to Europe, in just three weeks. The deal had not closed, and at that point, I just did not know if it would. But, for all my anxiety and doubts, I retained, in some quiet place in my soul, the ability to recognize reassurances from Heaven, and I felt that I had gotten exactly that from Dean McFalls.

Dean was (and I imagine is) a hard-working, high-energy, engaging and engaged priest. I remember watching him that day and thinking, "This is the kind of priesthood I want." Following the Mass, there was a healing service, and many prayer warriors came forward to offer me and the boys blessings and words from the Spirit. One woman told me, "The word I have for you is John Bosco. His mother was very close to him and his ministry to his young men. I see a woman behind you, in this ministry. I see her very clearly. She has red hair and she smiles easily. She has a lot of energy and she supports this ministry without question. Without her, you would not be able to do what you do." I told this lady that the woman she was seeing was my mom.

There was prayer for healing, as well, and we all lined up to be prayed over, and a lot, a lot of people were slain in the Spirit. All right, I will be honest with you, dear reader: I do not know that I was so much slain in the Spirit, as that I wanted to please the beautiful young Filipina who was praying for me. In any event, I went over backwards, at some point, and just lay there on the floor, with this lovely young disciple praying for my healing, my strength and my future priesthood. The boys, not one of whom had fallen over, watched this spectacle with some interest. We went to dinner there in Stockton, a bit later, and they all told me that they were sure I had fallen back just to keep the attractive young lady close to me. None of the kids had ever seen a Charismatic service before: when Mikey got home and told his mom about it, she told him, "That's not Catholic."

My friend Ruthanne, whom I had known since 1977 at Cal, was recovering from surgery that summer, in Manhattan, where she then lived, and I flew to New York to spend a few days with her. I remember calling Mikey from New York to assure him that the trip was going to work out. Though I had all along told each of the kids committed to going that they would need to come up with $500, not all of them did, or could. I remember being concerned that Mikey might feel that he was going to miss the trip, after all, because he had not yet gotten the full $500 together. I called him from Ruthanne's, in New York, and assured him that I had worked his ticket out. In fact, I was still short on the trip, but by the time I went to see Ruthanne, I was convinced that we were going to make it, and I did not want Mikey worrying about it.

I also went to Bermuda on that trip, to see my friend Joan. I had not been to Bermuda since the summer of 1995, just before I had become youth minister. It was largely because of my responsibilities with the kids, that I had not seen Joan in three years. Bermuda was and is one of my favorite places on earth, and I felt that I should not miss the chance to get there, being so close, in Manhattan. There was an afternoon when I was on the beach, in Bermuda, and saw a storm coming in, and so came back in early to Joan's. "Oh, thank God!" Joan said, as I came through the front door. "Call your Mom immediately! She needs to make a decision this afternoon. It's all about this trip to Europe with the kiddies."

I was gone a total of maybe five or six days, and had I had any idea of the scramble all of this was going to be, at the last minute, I do not know if I'd have made the trip. The thousand or so I spent on it, after all, could have paid for half of one of my kid's tickets. While I was in Bermuda, Mom basically closed the deal, with Neno, Sergio's father, who was also his Toronto rep, in a series of phone calls. I had left for New York and Bermuda, telling Mom that just a few details remained to be taken care of, and I gave her a list of things to be looking for, that week. I got home to hear from Mom that, she could not explain just how, but, one way and another, every single day that week had largely been absorbed, faxing Neno, sending checks and money orders overnight to Neno, talking to Neno on the phone, getting word out to pilgrims who had not yet paid, discovering that some folks had decided not to go after all, and God-knows-what-all-else.

"Honestly, Jimmy," Mom said, "I cannot tell you how it is that the whole week has been lost to this, but it has. I've been to the bank every day; FedEx, too." Mom told me as well that, at one point during the week, Neno told her that they needed to go to church and light candles.

During that week, which was the next to last in July, and just two weeks before we were to leave, Sergio had managed to get seats for us on Air Canada flights from San Francisco to Toronto and then Toronto to London. We would have an overnight in London, and then fly Alitalia to Rome. We would take a bus across central Italy and an overnight ferry across the Adriatic Sea to Croatia. Then we would take another bus to Medjugorje. We would be from Monday afternoon in California to Thursday afternoon, getting to Medjugorje. This was the best, given the last-minute crush of it all, that Sergio could do for us.

What was more, Maria Uribe, back from her trip to Rome and Israel, sent me word that she would not be accompanying us on the trip; I would be the pilgrimage leader. This at the time astounded me, and somewhat intimidated me. Today, of course, I see it as part of an overall design: I have led many pilgrimages since, and see it as ministry, as one of my deepest apostolates. I just needed to splash in and start, with this very first trip. Also, of course, given what I have since come to understand of the business, I believe that Maria was probably told by Sergio that she was not going with us, because his profit margin had already been shaved to such a thin line, with all these last-minute arrangements. Sergio was later to tell me that his profit on this trip was less than forty dollars a person. If that were true, then he would have lost money, sending Maria along with us.

It had, in any event, been a very trying week for Mom, and for Neno, in Toronto. I was sorry to hear it, as I really had thought that, before leaving for the East Coast, I had gotten most of the trip squared away. But in fact, much remained to be done, and in the end, Mom, who was flush that summer with her inheritance from Uncle Jim, stepped in and closed the deal, simply to have some peace of mind with it all.

"Your uncle supports this business," Mom said. "He does not object to my putting some of the money he left me toward getting our kids to Europe."

Mom, in other words, had stepped up to the plate, and when Mom steps up to the plate, she puts it in the bleachers. Risk-averse she ain't. It's all or nothing. I returned from the New York-Bermuda trip to find that the pilgrimage was paid for. I do not know if Mom ever has figured out how much she was out, closing the deal. It was certainly several thousand dollars. The amazing thing about my mom is that she does not care. Did not care then; does not care now. We had something we had to accomplish; she was committed to seeing it accomplished. From that time on, she acquired a new moniker among the kids, to whom she had been "mom" or Sara for a long time: from that time on, she was also known as Mama Warbucks.

With the trip paid for, the very last thing I had to do was get a general fund together, to make sure that if any of the kids ran out of money in Europe, I would have reserves. This was accomplished through a couple of final fundraisers at church, by an appeal to some of our supporters, and also by my last paycheck as youth minister. I was able to pull together a kitty of between three and four thousand dollars, which was to be used by me and the kids, as need arose, over the two weeks that we would be in Europe.

There was one last twist in this story's tale, before we were all good to go. Alicia Haldeman, who a year earlier had challenged me to make this trip happen, and who had been such a pro-active force in pursuing the pilgrimage, had, in the past few months, faded like a racehorse that starts out fast and then drops back, letting others set the pace. By May, Alicia was telling me that she and the boys, Robert and Richard, would not be going. I was upset by this, and now it was my turn to tell Alicia what Our Lady wanted, and I assured her Our Lady wanted her and the boys on this pilgrimage.

But Alicia was insistent, and she and the boys did not make the final passenger manifest that I sent in to Sergio via Maria Uribe, on June 30. However, sometime between June 30 and my trip to the East Coast, three pilgrims dropped out. News of these cancellations did not reach Sergio in Rome before he had reserved airline and hotel space for the original number. In other words, three spaces were available, on the flights and in the hotels. While I was in New York, Alicia turned up at Mom's door, grinning from ear to ear, and with six thousand dollars cash: she and the boys were going after all. It was early evening, when Alicia gave Mom the money. Mom could not get to the bank with it 'til the next day. Never having had so much cash in the house before, and wanting to make sure it was safe, Mom did something highly original: she hid it under her mattress. We still laugh about that.

With the Haldemans onboard and the trip paid for, just two weeks before we were leaving, all of us could finally exhale. We could finally sit back and relax. We had done it. We were going to Europe.

TWO

Monday, August 3, was a bright and hot day. It was the start, in fact, of an exceptional heat wave in northern California. Summer temperatures in the Sacramento Valley frequently hit 100, but a few days later, in Medjugorje, we would be hearing from friends and family back home that it was 110 and 112. These reports would make the 90-something degree heat in Medjugorje seem rather reasonable.

Though I remember vividly the afternoon and evening, that day of our departure, I do not have a clear memory of how Mom, Trudi and I spent the early part of the day. I suppose I was packing – in fact, I am sure I was: I do not think I have once in life packed for any trip as early as the evening before. I may even have been doing laundry, that morning, getting clothes I wanted to take with me ready to pack. I never feel rushed, getting ready for a trip at the last minute. I figure that is what the last minute is for.

I imagine, too, that I spent some time that morning, watering the garden. Several years earlier, I had begun a serious re-shaping of my mom's yard, putting in several new beds, a number of citrus trees, lining the patio with potted azaleas, camellias, and so forth. The impatiens out back were a new planting that summer, and I remember that they looked spectacular, backed as they were by bright subtropical greenery. That bed, in particular, needed regular watering, and I am sure I attended to it, before we left that day.

My sister Liz and my niece Marisol, who was thirteen that summer, arrived from Oakland sometime in the early afternoon. They were going to house-sit, while we were gone. Marisol made herself immediately at home at an umbrella table on the patio, reading a teen fan magazine. Mom and Trudi must have ridden up to church with other pilgrims, because I remember Liz and I driving over alone, in my car. I remember telling Liz that I was feeling almost envious of her and Marisol, having two weeks of quiet ahead of them, in Marysville. Liz smiled. She then reassured me that I was about to start one of the greatest adventures of my life, and so were the kids. Of course she was right, but I have often observed in myself a kind of reluctance, immediately before a trip, hard to describe because it is not an aversion to the trip itself. It has to do with leaving familiar surroundings, I guess; it has to do with leaving family and old friends; it has to do with realizing how much I have, right here at home, and why do I need to be going away from it? That's my best attempt at expressing this feeling, which as I say, often comes over me, shortly before I travel.

Liz and I turned onto C Street and saw the big tour bus, idling in front of the church. The kids were on the sidewalk, and up and down the many steps of St. Joseph's. They were all smiles, talking and laughing – we might have been headed to a Kings game, to watch them, and I said as much to Liz. The feeling of reluctance dissipated on the sound of my kids' laughter. I was going to get on the bus with them, and then on the plane with them, and we were all going to do this together, and though the trip would take us six or seven thousand miles from home, we would travel every foot of it together and…"You're right," I said to Liz. "This is gonna be one amazing adventure."

Liz smiled.

I got out and started doing something I would grow used to, in the next two weeks: I started counting heads. I must've been the last member of the pilgrimage to arrive – most of the adults were already on the bus; the driver had the engine running and the air conditioning was on. The kids, though mostly still outside, had also marked out their territory: several rows of seats near the back. The back of the bus would be their preference throughout Europe as well. Mom and Trudi sat together, as they would throughout the trip. Family members, especially moms and dads, were on and off the bus, saying good-bye and issuing last-minute instructions. Jorge's mom, for instance, wanted some dirt and pebbles from Medjugorje, to put in her own garden. Karen Brown was there. She had walked over from the office, carrying a clipboard and pen: she was still collecting the $35 per person for the bus. She smiled when she saw me and gave me a big hug, then handed me an envelope with money in it. "Dole this out judiciously to JD." I smiled and gave her a wink. As I watched Karen talking with the other pilgrims, and especially as I watched her easy and confident interactions with the kids, I found myself wishing yet again that she were going with us. In Karen's company, you feel as if you can handle anything. Angelica Klug, Brigitta's daughter, got on the bus at one point, her blonde hair down, and as I recall, and in spite of the heat, in something black; frankly, she looked like a movie star, and I remember that the guys were disappointed to learn that she was not going with us. Claudia told me that Alma was not here yet. A moment later, Alma's dad, Moises, was on the bus, explaining that they could not find Alma's passport, that Alma, her sister and their mom were home desperately looking for it, that he would drive Alma to SFO himself, and not to worry: she would make the flight.

This was alarming news. I could not imagine Alma missing the trip at this point, and wondered about her possibilities for a flight out the next day, if it came to it. Then I thought about all it had taken to get the tickets we had, and I just shook my head and decided to trust God -- and Alma's family -- with the whole business. It was more than two hours to the San Francisco airport, and what's more, we were likely to encounter some rush hour traffic, in the Bay Area. But we would have several hours, four or five, once there, before our flight. Mom and I had deliberately scheduled the bus to give us plenty of time at the airport. I could only hope that Alma's passport would turn up in time for Moises to get her to SFO. I looked at Claudia, who would be the only girl from the youth group on the trip, if Alma didn't make the Toronto plane.

"Don't worry, Claudia," I said. "Our Blessed Mother wants Alma on this trip, and she will get her to the airport on time."

Claudia looked reassured. That fact helped reassure me. But this business of Alma's passport was to be only the first of many, many worries and concerns, doubts and questions, over the next few days that I would simply have to…give to Our Lady, as they would be utterly beyond my capacity even to influence, let alone control.

What I remember above all about the bus ride down the valley was the brightness of it. The summer sunlight flooded through the big windows on my side of the bus, but the air conditioning kept us all comfortable. I remember watching the fields and orchards, and noting that the peach and nectarine trees were heavy with their red-gold fruit. I remember smiling at the endless row of oleander running along the median, blooming abundantly, white, cream, red and several shades of pink. Mom has more than once observed to me that oleander must take some kind of nourishment from exhaust fumes, so prodigiously does it grow along California's freeways.

I remember how I felt as we were leaving the valley behind, as the
Solano County hills began to encircle the freeway and we rose into
the Coast Range, golden and studded with California live oak.
Solano County in general, and the city of Fairfield in particular, have
always struck me as being among the state's most beautiful venues.
You get both, at Fairfield, the valley and the Bay Area. Jorge had
moved up to a seat near mine, toward the front of the bus, and he too
was staring out the big windows, watching our beautiful native state
roll by. I watched him for a moment and tried to imagine what this
must be for him: a seventeen year old Yuba County boy on his way
to Europe for the first time, and with a busload of his friends. I
couldn't imagine his thoughts, but was content with my own, and I
smiled. He turned and looked at me, caught me looking at him. He
smiled and gave me a thumbs-up. And that, I thought, pretty much
expressed it.

And that was the other reason for the afternoon's brightness. There
was a lot of smiling, a lot of happy conversation, a lot of laughter, on
that bus ride down through the southern Sacramento Valley, through
the Solano hills and into the East Bay. We said a Rosary, at some
point, along the way. I think it was suggested to me by Brigitta, and
we took turns leading the decades. I had bought a dozen rosaries in
Sacramento a few weeks before, for the kids, and distributed them
there on the bus – I wanted to make sure each of the kids had a
rosary on the trip. I remember the driver catching my eye in the
rearview mirror and smiling, while we prayed. He liked us. He
liked us so much that he arranged to come and pick us up at the end
of the trip. He, too, experienced the afternoon's brightness.

The traffic in the Bay Area was surprisingly light. It's true, of
course, that we were largely headed in the opposite direction of the
rush hour crush. We only slowed down south of San Francisco, at

which point we were just a few miles from the airport. We made very good time to SFO, and were off the bus, and through ticketing and check-in, with lots of time to spare. I made sure everyone knew which gate and when, and then we all fanned out across the terminal, with its many restaurants and shops.

I took charge of the kids, or anyway, most of them – I think it was eight or nine of the guys, and Claudia. We took stock of the restaurants and decided on an Italian place. Mikey and Nelson objected that it was too expensive. I told them I was paying, so shut up, sit down and enjoy a good Italian dinner – reminding them that we would actually BE in Italy, in just a couple of days. Claudia ordered a salad. She discovered a hair in it, somewhere along the way, and it upset her. The guys took off on this – you may use your imagination to guess at some of their suggestions as to how the hair got there. I quite insensitively laughed at this, really not thinking at all about the fact that Claudia was alone, without Alma.

When I saw that Claudia was blinking back tears, I felt awful. I told her she should order something else, but she didn't want to. The joking quickly subsided, but the attempts by the guys to reassure Claudia, though well-intentioned, missed the mark as completely as had my suggestion that she get something else to eat. She was sixteen years old. She was on her way to Europe for the first time. It is true she was with her brother and her cousin, and with a bunch of guys she'd known for years, but it was also true that, unless Alma made the flight, Claudia would be the only girl in this large and boisterous and less-than-sensitive crowd of teen-aged boys.

I only learned of this months after the fact, and from Bertha, but Claudia actually called home, shortly after dinner, and told her mom she didn't want to go. Bertha listened carefully and lovingly, the way only a mom can, which Claudia at that moment needed. She assured Claudia she would come and get her, if she really did not want to go, but meanwhile, she wanted Claudia to give it a little more thought – there were still two or three hours to our departure – and also, Bertha was hopeful that Alma would soon show up.

And Alma did show up, arriving at the airport with her passport, well in advance of the Toronto flight's boarding call. I remember asking Alma if she were hungry, but either she had eaten on the way down, with her dad, or she simply had no appetite – from the excitement, maybe. In any event, you may imagine my relief, and Claudia's, when we found Alma waiting for us, all smiles and happy anticipation, at the gate.

Paul Delaney also met us at the gate. Paul was my other chaperone for the trip. In all, we had seventeen teens on this trip, but five of them were travelling with adult relatives. I had a dozen I was directly responsible for, but in fact, three of them – Oscar, Pancho and Matt – were eighteen or nineteen, and so, strictly speaking, I had nine teens I needed to chaperone. Paul Delaney was a graduate student in physics at Berkeley, a native of Ireland with a lace-curtain accent, an easy smile and a gracious, gentlemanly manner. I knew Paul through – who else?! – Marie Smith. Paul often came to the Berkeley rosary group Marie ran on Thursday nights. Paul was slim, dark-haired, handsome, in his late twenties. He was an instant hit with the kids, who lost no time dubbing him "Little Jim."

It was dark by this time: I remember standing near the wall-to-wall windows and watching the bags going onto the plane. The older pilgrims were scattered in groups of three and four around the seating area; Mom and Trudi were laughing and talking with some of the boys.

"Gosh, Paul," I said, looking around the gate. "Can you believe it? My kids are about to start the journey to Medjugorje."

Paul smiled. "They started it when they joined the youth group," he said.

***

What I chiefly remember about the flight to Toronto was how quiet it was. It was a red-eye, and most people used the flight to sleep. The kids were awake the first hour or two, excited and talkative. I remember that JD went up front and was allowed into the cockpit – the captain knew he had a youth group on board, and sent word through the attendants that the kids could come up and see the cockpit, if they wanted to do so. Some of the other guys probably took the captain up on the invitation as well, but I remember in particular that JD did. This was 1998, of course, three innocent years before the horror of September 11.

Paul and I sat together and talked about what lay immediately beyond the trip for me: St. Patrick's Seminary. I had received my acceptance from the seminary just a few days earlier. I remember telling Paul that, seeing the seminary for the first time, in 1995, with its vast grounds, its huge swimming pool and many playing fields, its breath-taking chapel, its wide, quiet halls, its rich carpets and high ceilings, the first thing I asked myself was, "Gee, does the Church really need to be this rich?"

Paul said that he thought I should look at the four years I would be living there as a gift, a grace from God. He pointed out that I had worked tirelessly for the past three years, juggling a schedule that included not just the youth group and my studies at the Dominican School, but the Confirmation class, the Vocations Committee, my writing, and, for most of that time, my job at Cal. Eighty-hour weeks had become my norm. Paul added that he would not be surprised if I were similarly busy as a priest. He suggested that a period of deep quiet, and even of deep rest, such as the seminary could offer, might be very good preparation for my life as a parish priest. I had not thought about it this way. I liked the suggestion, though, and held onto it.

We arrived in Toronto and there was time for breakfast at the airport. Though they could not have gotten more than three or four hours' sleep on the plane, the kids were wide awake and full of energy. I remember some of them doing some shopping at the airport. I tried to dissuade them, simply because airport shops are so expensive, but though this was only Toronto, it was already "a foreign city" to them, and their excitement could not be contained.

I took a couple pictures of them as a group, at the gate, something I had not done in San Francisco. I remember that, as we were getting the group shots arranged, Jorge said, "Man, I can't believe this. We're on our way to Europe! All that time at youth group, I thought we were just coming to eat pizza!" There was laughter – and general agreement.

Though we on the whole arranged seating so that groups of pilgrims could sit together on all of our flights, one of the boys -- I don't remember which -- had somehow been placed by himself on the seven-hour Toronto-London leg of the trip. My seat was with a group of four or five of the kids, so I traded with him. I ended up next to a Canadian lady, flying to England to visit family, whose thirty-something son had died of AIDS a couple of years before, the same year my brother John had died of the same disease. What is more, she was Christian, and had had the usual struggles with her son's sexuality. She told me how much she loved and missed him. I told her about my brother. He had been my best friend from boyhood. I had been best man at his wedding. I dreamt regularly about him; my heart still ached, thinking of him. We talked most of the way across the Atlantic.

It was a sunny flight, all the way across Eastern Canada and the Atlantic. We came in at Heathrow well ahead of dusk: I remember that we could see the green English countryside from the windows. It would have made sense, given that we were to be only overnight in London, to stay at an airport hotel, but given the last-minute way in which Sergio had had to put this trip together, an airport hotel had not been an option. We were staying at the Royal International, in central London. It is a huge hotel, and though it was going on nine PM as we streamed into the lobby to register, there was a crowd at the reception desk, and we were most of an hour, getting into our rooms.

Since we were in the heart of the city – walking distance to Piccadilly Circus – I had suggested to the kids that we not worry about getting a lot of sleep, but instead, see a little of London at night. They did not need a lot of persuasion on this point. I checked in with Mom and Trudi, to make sure they were okay, and to let them know that I would be out for the next several hours. They had ordered room service, and Mom was having a glass of red wine, when I arrived at their room. They intended to have a nice evening in London as well, but from the comfort and safety of the hotel.

I had told the kids to shower and change and get back down to the lobby as soon as they could. Alma and Claudia did not come. I do not remember if it was because they didn't want to, or if it was because they did not know of the plan. In any event, it was just me and the boys when we went out that night. I had not been in London since my first visit, with Uncle Jim, in 1989. But I knew where we were in the city and I knew how to get the boys to Piccadilly. It was maybe a fifteen-minute walk. We were fortunate in the weather: it was dry, mild and breezy, a beautiful London night.

Nighttime London did not let the boys down. Piccadilly was brightly lit and thronged with people. I do not know just what I had in mind for the guys. We'd been able to change some money at the hotel, and I suppose I was planning to take them somewhere to eat. But they settled that question by buying from vendors in the square – I don't remember what they got, corn dogs or sandwiches or burgers, or maybe fish and chips, but they ate and ate, and then were satisfied. We walked about amid the crowds and the bright lights, considered going in at this club or that, looked, I suppose, a bit indecisive, and that was all it took for a club barker to approach us and promise the guys a fabulous time, at this wonderful venue, right across the square...

I remember that I mostly stood near the door. It was a teen dance club – I suppose there were twentysomethings there, as well. The music was what was popular at the end of the nineties – I remember hearing one of those annoying Spice Girls hits remixed for the dance floor. There were strobe lights and a mirror ball and a lot, a lot, of

young people, dancing, or milling about the tables and the bar. I
stood near the entrance and felt every day of my forty-two years.

After a while the guys all emerged at once from the teen maelstrom
in the inner and flashing darkness of the place, laughing and talking
boisterously and – ready to leave. I was surprised. Hadn't they liked
it? Liked it? They'd LOVED it. And, come on, did I think they
were only going to visit ONE club, tonight, in London?

I think we visited two. Maybe three. This is now more than ten
years ago, and I have the grey hair to prove it. I do not remember
going into the second (or any later) club. At some point, anyway, I
told the guys I would wait for them on a bench in the square. I
preferred the outdoor London night scene, which, crowded and
brightly lit as it was, was positively serene, compared to the
atmosphere in the youth clubs. I remember sitting there in SoHo,
watching the midnight crowds, glad to be out in the fresh air, and
smiling, smiling deeply, at the thought of my boys, my boys from
Linda and Olivehurst, whooping it up tonight, in London's clubs.

The walk back to the hotel, which happened after three AM, was all
taken up with their adventures in the clubs – there had evidently been
an Israeli girl, silver-sequined and amply endowed, who had caught
their attention as a group. Several of them had danced with her;
Mikey, at least, had actually talked with her, and all of them had, for
the night, anyway, fallen in love with her. There had been other
girls, too, of course – one from Hong Kong, two from Denmark, and
plenty of Brits. The girls had been disappointed to learn that the
guys would not be available tomorrow night: they would be on the
Adriatic Sea tomorrow night, en route to Croatia. The girls may
have been disappointed, but they were all the more fascinated with

these happy young Californians, precisely because they were going places. The air of exotic international panache which would surround my boys later on this pilgrimage had already begun to develop, that first night in Europe, in the London dance clubs.

***

I think most of the guys actually caught some sleep, between getting back to the hotel and coming downstairs for the bus at five-thirty in the morning. I did not bother. I came as quietly as I could into the room I was sharing with Paul, went into the bathroom to shower, shave and change clothes, then picked up my bags and went downstairs to the lobby. It was already past four. My pilgrims were, I hoped, sleeping deeply and well. I meanwhile had some work to attend to.

Sergio had sent the Alitalia tickets to the hotel and I had picked them up at the desk when we'd registered, but I had not yet looked at them. I went into a coffee bar off the lobby, but it was not open for business yet. I was disappointed not to be able to get a cup – several cups – of coffee, but the shower had refreshed me, and, amazingly enough, considering that I had had no more than three or four hours sleep in the last forty-plus hours, I was not tired. I was ready to get going with the next stage of our journey.

There were big windows in the coffee bar, and as I sat down at one of the little tables, my bags at my feet, and started looking through the Alitalia tickets, it was still dark out. By the time I had finished looking through the tickets, and finished thinking about what needed to be done, what could be done, to get us all to Italy, it was dawn beyond the windows, and my pilgrims were beginning to descend to the lobby. I smiled and waved at folks as they came into the coffee bar – most of them also disappointed, that there was as yet no service. When Mom came down, I waved her over to my table, and explained the problem to her.

I had forty-one r/t London-Rome tickets with Alitalia. That was good, that was as it should be. The problem was that three of the tickets were in the wrong names. They were for the three pilgrims who had decided not to make the trip, but who had been on the original pilgrim manifest. These three tickets should have been for the Haldemans, who booked at the last possible moment, and who had been able to get on the trip precisely because of the three cancellations. There had been no problem with the Air Canada tickets, and I had not anticipated this with Alitalia. Even in this pre-Sept. 11 era, you could not get on a plane with a ticket that said one name and a passport that said another. And I knew enough about airline ticketing to know that it was not simply a matter of issuing a new ticket, in the right name. Or well, yes it was that simple. You just had to pay all over again for the new ticket; that was all.

I do not remember what the Alitalia fare was. I think it was about $300, so to replace three tickets, something in the neighborhood of one thousand dollars. In any event, I could not fix this situation for the Haldemans. It would have eaten up close to one-third of the general kitty I had set aside for me and the kids. I knew we would need that money later. I had no credit cards: I was a broke graduate student. And it was not fair to Alicia, to ask her to pay for this mistake made by the tour company: she had paid the same two grand per person as everyone else on the trip. Mom agreed. "We'll put the new tickets on my American Express," she said. "But let's just buy them one-way. Sergio should be able to fix the return tickets, and I don't want to pay anymore than I have to." I sat back with considerable relief; Mama Warbucks to the rescue.

We arrived at Heathrow early enough to get the coffee, to get the juice and breakfast, we had all wanted at the hotel. The kids, despite even less sleep than they had had on the flight from San Francisco, were all wide awake, laughing and talking, and after breakfast, they were off once more to shop at the airport. I do not think most of them did much more than window-shop, but they did run about the big passenger concourse, looking at watches, sunglasses, leather goods, liquers – the sort of thing one finds in airport shops. We were together right up to the time when I announced that we needed to get to the gate. At that point, suddenly, Wally and Fonz were not with us. I had not seen them leave the group, and none of the kids could say where they were either, but at least a couple of the guys were sure they had already gone ahead to the gate. That was fine, I said, and hoped it was true.

It was not true, and when I got to the gate and did not find them, I went back out into the concourse, looking for them. I took twenty minutes or so, and did not find them. I began to feel worried, but consciously disallowed the feeling. After all, they were probably at the gate by now. I have often found that worry can be negated this way. We often worry without reason. Wait until you are certain that there is good reason, and then worry. Don't worry for nothing. I returned to the gate, passing through security a second time; in those days you didn't have to strip half naked to get through security. I got back to the gate, where the plane was now ready to board. No Wally. No Fonz.

Okay. NOW, worry.

I talked to Paul. He said the other guys had already assured him that Wally and Fonz knew the gate and the time, and not to sweat it; they would be here. I was not reassured, but as they called us for boarding, I got on, with the rest of the group. I alerted one of the attendants to the fact that two teens from my group were not yet at the gate. She smiled and told me not to worry, there was time.

I sat with Paul. The plane filled with passengers – Italians returning home from London, Brits on their way to Rome for business or pleasure. After a few minutes, one of the attendants asked me about the missing members of my group. I explained that they were American teens, and perhaps lost somewhere in the airport. Alitalia meanwhile, made an announcement out over the concourse, that the plane was boarding and urging Wally and Fonz to get to the gate.

I turned to Paul. "I will have to get off and stay here," I said. "When I find Fonz and Wally, I will get the next flight to Rome, and we'll just hope we can catch up with the group before the ferry, tonight, at Ancona." I said this knowing that I would have to use group cash to make up any difference in fares, which would likely be higher, given the circumstances.

Paul did not need to think before replying. "I'll stay," he said. "You are the tour leader. I am here to assist with the kids. I will get the three of us on the next available flight, and yes, we'll just hope that we can make it to Ancona in time for tonight's ferry. If we don't, then we will arrive in Medjugorje a day after you. I have a credit card, Jim. I will use it, if I have to."

I don't know if I sighed, smiled, or what; I do know I felt very grateful to Paul, and realized what a gem the Lord had sent me, in him. He could handle this. The boys already liked him: they'd be fine with him. It even went through my mind (and this is a good way to think, when unexpected things happen on pilgrimage) that for some reason Jesus wanted Wally and Fonz to spend most of the day in uncertain circumstances, with Paul. Who could say what might come of such a development, down the line? I firmly believed that any appreciable amount of time the kids might spend with Paul would be graced time for them.

Paul was getting up to retrieve his backpack from the overhead bin when Wally first, and Fonz behind, came panting onto the plane. I did not catch the look on Wally's face, but Fonz looked worried and apologetic. I wanted to ask what on earth they had been doing, but there was no time: they needed to get to their seats, because we needed to push back from the gate. They took some razzing from the other guys, who were seated around them, but in a couple of minutes, as we were pushing back, I heard them all laughing, and evidently, passing around whatever it was that Wally and Fonz had been so long buying. For some reason I want to say it was cologne. I do not know, though, that it was.

We were just two hours to Rome. For Americans used to vast distances, international flights in Europe seem surprisingly short. We saw the Alps from the air; always an impressive sight, and especially given that this was August, and there they were, still blanketed in snow. We've got some pretty impressive ranges in California, but by and large, the snow is, by August, gone from all but our highest peaks.

At Rome airport we transferred to the bus that was to take us to
Ancona, on the Adriatic Sea. Father Leon, who had flown over
separately from the rest of the group, was waiting for us. And
Sergio, the president of Ave Maria Azurra Tours, met us at the gate.
Neither Mom nor I had met him, of course, but after all that had
happened, pulling the trip together, the past several weeks, we all felt
like we knew each other. He assured Mom that she would be
reimbursed for the Haldemans' tickets, but he would have preferred
that she'd purchased them roundtrip, as that would have saved him
money. This fairly obvious fact had not occurred to either me or
Mom, that morning, without coffee, at the hotel, with dawn's early
light beyond the windows. In any event, it made no practical
difference, as Mom never did get reimbursed.

We liked Sergio, though – all of us. He was young, I'd have guessed
thirty-five, and quite good-looking, with curly, dark blonde hair
halfway to his shoulders, a white shirt left open at the neck, and I
think a gold chain; black jeans. He had a radiant smile and an easy,
confident air. I noticed some of my lady pilgrims watching Sergio,
as he and Mom talked ticket re-imbursement. Mom herself came
away from the encounter vastly pleased with Sergio: she is always
happy to do business with a young man who looks like a movie star,
or maybe, given Sergio's ancestry, like a Roman-copy-of-a-Greek-
original brought to life.

Sergio introduced us to Gino, who was to be our guide in Italy. Gino
was silver-almost-white haired, maybe somewhere in his fifties, with
dark glasses, a pastel shirt and khakis. He was relaxed almost to the
point of being phlegmatic. At first I didn't think he liked us, but
later I came to understand that his style was simply low-key and
understated, miles away from flashy and animated Sergio.

Sergio assured me that we had excellent accommodations both in Medjugorje, and here in Italy, on our return. He said that he had just one last detail to attend to – the last night of the trip, at Toronto airport: he could book us at either the Sheraton or the Comfort Inn, and did I have a preference. As the Sheraton was roughly twice the price of the Comfort Inn, and as the last night of the trip was on us, not included in the package, I opted for the Comfort Inn. Sergio waved us off and said he'd see us when we got back to Italy. I imagined him driving off from the airport in a silver Ferrari, a younger Gina Lollobrigida waiting for him at some romantic venue.

Once settled on the bus and on our way via the autostrada, I sat back with a sigh of real relief and said to Paul, "I think we are finally on firm ground." Paul smiled. I fell asleep. I had to have been physically exhausted; I had gotten almost no sleep yet, all the way from California. I do not know how long the bus trip across central Italy was. I do remember waking up when we stopped for a late lunch somewhere in the mountains. One of those autostrada-market-coffee-bar-cafeteria places. Most everybody got out to eat, but I stayed on the bus and slept.

I woke up as we were driving along the Adriatic coast. I felt refreshed from my long nap. I was glad to be awake, looking out the windows of the bus. I had not been on Italy's east coast with Uncle Jim in 1989, and was impressed with its palm-lined beaches, its subtropical flowers, its clean and attractive towns. The sea itself was beautiful: a sparkling deep blue.

We stopped at Loretto (it is also spelled Loreto), at Gino's recommendation. The story of the place is that angels carried the house of the Holy Family from Nazareth to Loretto, when the

Muslims invaded the Holy Land in the seventh century. It's the kind of story at which I smile and say, "How charming," and at which my sister Anne rolls her eyes and says, "Whatever." Historical facts and arguments aside, certainly the place has been made holy by the fact of countless pilgrims who have gone there to pray. I prayed at Loretto: it was August 5, a Marian feast day, a fact pointed out by one of my pilgrims, LaDonna. Having this fact pointed out to me made me smile: Our Lady was letting us know just how thoroughly this whole adventure was under her guidance and protection.

As to the shrine itself, there IS a very old and small house there, carefully preserved. We all went through it. There is an impressive basilica. There is a monastery. There is a gift shop. There are plenty of nice cafes in which to sit and have a drink, which the boys and I did. The views out toward the sea are spectacular. It was late afternoon when we got to Loretto. There were some high cirrus clouds that blocked the sun, so it was not hot. The place's beauty impressed the kids: we took pictures with the coast as backdrop. After eighty or ninety minutes, we got back on the bus, and drove to Ancona, where we would take the ferry to Croatia.

***

Now about the ferry. It was called the Sansovino, and its name shall live in infamy in the hearts and minds of forty pilgrims who crossed the Adriatic Sea on her the night of August 5, 1998. We arrived at the port at Ancona, a large industrial city on the central Adriatic coast, and proceeded past some impressive ferries, ships that looked like ocean liners. The boys were speculating as to which was ours, and what the staterooms would be like, whether there would be a pool, a Jacuzzi, a spa, a bar, a casino…

The bus came to a halt at a terminal building. It was near docks lined with some "down-market" ships, compared to the ones we had just been looking at, less impressive, clearly less luxurious, but in good repair and no doubt comfortable enough for a night's crossing. Gino and I got out and went into the terminal. It was crowded and noisy. High windows on the west wall let in the bright late afternoon light – no cirrus clouds here in Ancona. There were booths lining either side and I came to realize that these were the various ferry lines, Jadrolinea, a Croatian line, being the only name I now remember. Our ferry was with one of the Italian lines. Gino led me to our booth, and we waited in a fairly long line. There were long lines at all the booths, though, so I took it in stride.

What I could not take in stride was the conversation, all in rapid Italian, which transpired, when Gino reached the counter and started talking with the young Italian selling tickets for the Sansovino. It rapidly deteriorated from a conversation to an argument, and Gino was clearly getting mad. Given what I had observed of Gino's temperament up to this point, low-key and relaxed, I found this exchange alarming: I didn't need to understand the words, to know that we did not have tickets for the ferry. Gino waved his hand, at some point, and walked away, saying nothing to me. I followed him in worried silence.

I followed him all the way out of the terminal, into the bright, hot Anconan sun. Gino needed a phone to call Sergio, and I cannot now remember if the bus driver had a cell that he used, or if he went to a pay phone. There was a row of benches somewhere near the entrance to the terminal, and I took a seat on one. I watched Gino til he disappeared – not now, more than a decade later, remembering where he disappeared to. I could only hope he would soon reappear, with tickets for the ferry.

People on the bus, meanwhile, were watching from the windows. Mom later told me that Barbara Pauls saw Gino and me emerge from the terminal, and she said, "There's Jim! And oh dear – he does not look happy." Other pilgrims looked out the windows and soon shared Barbara's anxiety, a fact which, had I known of it, would have only deepened my own. I cannot stress enough how completely responsible I feel for the welfare and comfort of my pilgrims, and this sense of responsibility to them was already functioning at the top of my list of priorities, on that very first trip. I felt that they had already been asked to put up with a lot, just to get this far – it was almost forty-eight hours; it was three planes, two bus trips, and a not-enough-sleep night in London, since we had started from California, and we were only on the Italian coast. We had still a night at sea, and another bus ride tomorrow, to get to Medjugorje. I had written everyone just before we left, telling them that the trip to this point would be taxing, demanding, that it would try our patience and make us tired, but that, once we got to the ferry, and into our staterooms, we could relax; we would have a quiet night crossing with dinner and breakfast on board, and comfortable beds and very close to a full night's rest.

Now instead, here I was sitting on a bench outside the ferry terminal in the blazing Italian sun, not understanding a word of the unnerving conversation that had just taken place inside, and wondering where Gino was and how he was going to fix this. Sergio, after all, was off with Gina Lollobrigida in his silver Ferrari. This was, in fact, a real moment of truth for me. I have used this moment several times in homilies as illustrative of how we can betray faith, when we focus solely on what we see happening, and fail to give credit to what we do NOT see happening. Just because we do not see it does NOT mean that it is not happening.

Paul got off the bus, and came over to me. I think he was encouraged to do so by some of the other pilgrims, but I think they encouraged him at Our Lady's own urgings. He sat down next to me, not saying anything. I didn't say anything at first, either. Then I looked at him and said, "I don't know what's wrong. The guy at the counter and Gino just had a shouting match." I looked at the bus, thinking of my pilgrims. "Here we are on the Adriatic coast of Italy, Paul, and no way to get across. " I sighed deeply. "I just don't get it, I don't get it. This is messed up. And I don't know what I am going to do. I can't fix this. I can't even speak the language."

Paul said, "You don't have to fix it. This is not your problem, Jim."

I think I would have guffawed, but I didn't have the energy. "Paul. I have a busload of forty pilgrims sitting here at the docks, in Ancona. They have paid to cross the Adriatic Sea and spend a week in Medjugorje. We have no tickets to cross the sea, and we have no place to spend the night, here in Ancona. I think I have a problem."

"Our Lady has a problem," said Paul. "And Our Lady has a plan. Why do you not trust her plan? She has gotten you to the eastern coast of Italy. She has brought forty pilgrims with you, including a large group of your teens. She means for all of us to get to Medjugorje. It is now only a matter of crossing this sea. How can you look at that, and doubt that she already has this situation figured out?"

"Because we do not have tickets, Paul. Are the angels going to fly us over the sea, the way they did Mary's house?"

"Our Lady is very intelligent and careful in her planning," came Paul's calm reply. "She accomplishes a great deal with very little. She does not waste anything. She will get us all across this sea, Jim, and she will do it tonight. Wait and see. This is no time for doubt. Shall we show our trust in her plan, by saying a rosary?"

I could hardly argue with the suggestion. We needed all the prayers we could get. Paul and I said a rosary.

Gino meanwhile came back from where ever it was he had gone, and he went back into the ferry terminal. Paul and I followed him. We got in line once again for the Italian ferry line that we had waited for, earlier. But there was now a young woman at the counter. She and Gino exchanged a few sentences in rapid but calm and professional Italian. A moment later Gino was holding something that looked like a receipt. I was expecting tickets, but he explained that what we had instead was a voucher, because we were a group. He said we could now get on board. Our ship was the Sansovino, and it was docked almost immediately in front of us. I looked at Paul. He was smiling.

Gino was not smiling. He looked tired and annoyed. I shook his hand, thanked him, and said, "We'll see you when we get back, Gino!"

Gino waved the suggestion away. "No, no," he said. "It won't be me. I'm not coming back over here."

I was a little at a loss for words, but it didn't matter, as Gino turned and walked to the bus, where he let everyone know we could now board.

It was a few minutes before we were all off the bus with all our bags, and in line for the Sansovino. There was a short crowd (not a line by any means) ahead of us, for the ship. We stood around laughing and talking about the trip's near-misses so far. Everyone was very relieved to be getting on the ship.

We had to have waited close to an hour. As one of my pilgrims, Jane, pointed out to me, this was waiting for a ferry at Ancona, after all, not boarding a Carnival liner at San Francisco or Los Angeles. Customer service was no one's priority. Finally, the line, that is the swell, started moving forward. It took a while, even though we were near the front, because while we were all spread out in a crowd twenty passengers wide, we were boarding single file. We got to the guy taking the tickets soon enough to satisfy me though – which I guess should have tipped me off. He looked at the voucher and shook his head. He told me the voucher would not work. We needed individual tickets. He told me this in Italian, which of course, I had studied for years and years, in college and graduate school, precisely to be prepared for a moment such as this.

Not.

I looked from the young Italian to Paul. Paul somehow made himself understood to the ticket guy, and vice versa.

"Jim," Paul said. "We have to go back to the booth inside and exchange this voucher for individual tickets."

I sighed. "I thought that's what he said."

I asked, in my fluent Italian, if our people could just wait here, while Paul and I went back for the tickets. The line behind us was now not only wide, but quite long. (The Sansovino carried hundreds of people, maybe over a thousand.)

The young man shook his head.

I turned to everyone and apologized, and then explained the situation.

My pilgrims were simply amazing. I am convinced the Blessed Mother herself hand-picked them for their resilience and good nature. They got out of the line, that is, out of the crowd, with all their bags, and followed me and Paul back into the terminal. We went to our ferry line's booth. We exchanged the voucher for tickets, and as the kid at the counter looked at each passport, I understood why Paul and I could not have done this ourselves. Or anyway, at least not without everyone's passport.

Individual tickets in hand, we crossed back outside with all our bags, and resumed our places in the crowd – that is, we brought up the rear of what had become a long and fat line. It was certainly another half hour, before we were back up to the young man taking the tickets. As he took my ticket, he asked to see my passport. I showed it to him. He looked through it, shaking his head. He handed both passport and ticket back to me. Confident, at this point, in my fluent Italian, he explained to me that, as we were getting off this boat in Croatia, I had to have my passport stamped.

Somehow, I understood him. Resisting the many possible responses which suggested themselves to me, in both English and German, I simply asked the young man if he could tell me where I would go to get my passport stamped. He told me. He added that we needed to be quick about it, as the ferry was due to leave soon.

Back into the main building we all tramped, lugging our suitcases, and re-locating our passports, many of which had been safely tucked away for the voyage. There was a kiosk all the way down at the end of the terminal, Passport Control. There was a line, well, the Italian idea of a line, a fat crowd, waiting at Passport Control. By the grace of God, however, this line, this mob, moved quickly. I stood back and let all my pilgrims go through, then got my own passport stamped.

I followed the last members of the group back out to the ferry line, which was now non-existent, which consisted only of us. It had been bright and sunny when, maybe two and one-half hours earlier, we had first gotten into line for the Sansovino. It was now dusk. A lovely dusk, no doubt, there on the romantic Adriatic, but I, at least, was in no mood to appreciate it. There went up from my pilgrims a general cheer, when the young warden at the gate finally let a member of our group board. As we all passed safely through this post-modern Scylla-and-Charybdis-in-miniature, our spark and good humor began to return. My pilgrims were smiling and talking and laughing, as they made their way up the gangplank, and all of us, very, very much, were looking forward to dinner onboard and a good nights' sleep, in our staterooms.

Except that…We did not have staterooms. We found this out only as we came into a large sort of entry-way to the ship itself, and I asked a guy who looked like part of the crew where we would go, to get our stateroom assignments. He explained that the room number would be on the ticket. He looked at my ticket, shook his head (a gesture I was becoming very familiar with among the Italians), and explained that we did not have staterooms. He was speaking English, but he may as well have been speaking Farsi, so thoroughly did I not grasp what he was saying.

"Pontoon, pontoon," he was saying, pointing to my ticket. "Bridge, bridge. No staterooms. No seats. Bridge accommodations."

"Bridge accommodations?" I asked. Less asked, really, than simply numbly repeated.

"Anywhere you want, on the decks," he said.

"On the decks?"

"Benches, chairs, the floor, whatever you can find, and however you can make yourself comfortable."

For the first time, glancing about the big, open part of the ship we were in, I saw people spreading what looked like picnic blankets on the floor, unrolling sleeping bags, taking out pillows, and so on. Resisting the impulse to say a whole lot of things first in English and then in German, just in case I was not thoroughly understood, I explained carefully in English that we had paid for staterooms, expected staterooms, and…where were they?

He – to his great, great credit, in my view – looked a little abashed. He promised that he would do what he could to get me, as the tour leader, into a stateroom.

Now it was my turn to shake my head. "I will take a stateroom," I said, "after ALL my people have one."

The poor guy. None of this was his fault. He looked genuinely perplexed, and I could see that he would help us, if he could. He said, "All the staterooms are gone. I believe all the seats are sold, as well. But if I can get you some seats, that will be good. They are very good. Like first class, on the airlines. You can sleep comfortably in them. Please wait for me. I will be back shortly."

Everyone had heard this exchange, and so I did not need to tell my dear long-suffering pilgrims that we had no staterooms. They were just so amazing. No one blamed me. No one was angry. They were all, actually, a lot more resigned to, and ready for the situation, than I was.

Our conscientious crew member came back. There were no seats. It was to be bridge accommodations for the lot of us. Trudi had had, meanwhile, a flash of inspiration. She suggested to Father Leon that he put on his collar, and present himself to the folks behind an official-looking window nearby, and explain that we had an octogenarian couple travelling with us, in Alberto and Edelma Cruz, and couldn't the crew find beds for them, for the night? Father Leon did this, and came back with a stateroom for the Cruzes. You know those jokes about how a speeding priest can get out of the ticket, if he has his collar on? There just may be something to them.

As for the rest of us, it was catch-as-catch-can anywhere on the boat, and of course, the Europeans who had intended from the start to travel with "bridge accommodations" had already staked out all the "best" available places: benches and chairs not already claimed were few and far between, and almost all of them were located out on the open deck. That said, there was PLENTY of deck and floor space on the boat – no problem at all, finding a place to park ourselves for the night. SLEEPING was another matter, but simply in terms of room on the boat, oh well, there was gobs of room! Floors floors everywhere and more decks than we could count. In terms of space, our "accommodations" were positively luxurious.

By the time all of this was settled, the ship had slipped her dock, and we were making our way toward open water through Ancona's harbor. A bunch of us found our way to the main deck and were leaning on the railing, watching the lights of Ancona, as we left the city behind. Marge and Loyd Simeroth were setting up camp, so to speak, in a sort of alcove on the deck. "Look, Jim!" Marge said, in her crisp British accent. "Ocean-view rooms!" Marge's good humor typified the reaction of all my pilgrims to this situation. Carl and Lucy Cortez were likewise making the best of it. They were travelling with their teen-aged granddaughter Solana, who was helping them arrange their bags so as to have a bit of makeshift shelter. "Don't worry, Jim," Carl and Lucy told me. "We will make do."

I remember going to the railing and standing there, looking at the water thirty or so feet below. I must have looked forlorn, because one of my pilgrims, Vicky, came up alongside me and advised me not to jump. Other pilgrims, too, tried to reassure me. "It's only overnight," said Michelle, a beautiful girl in her early twenties, who had caught the attention of most of the guys. She was travelling with her aunt, Sara, and with their good family friend Bill, a retired professor of philosophy. Bill made some joke about the consolations of philosophy at moments such as these. "Look on the bright side," LaDonna said. "This is the Adriatic. At least we're not going to hit any ice bergs." "It's an adventure," said Jane.

Well, it was certainly that. After a few minutes, Mom was standing beside me. "I'm ready for the gin bottle," she said.

I laughed, and was glad to be able to do so. "Mom, I cannot believe this. I can't believe it."

I was worried, given this fiasco with the ferry, about what was waiting for us on the Croatian side. Would we find out that we had no accommodations in Medjugorje as well? Would we be sleeping on the floors there, too? I felt so bad. I can still feel how badly I felt. I had let these good pilgrims down. I had failed, somehow, in not being able to anticipate all of this.

My mom is an amazing woman. She was with me, in everything I was feeling. She did not need to have me explain it to her. She later told me that her thoughts at that very moment, as we were pulling away from Ancona, were, "Dear Lord, what more can go wrong?" And then she immediately followed up with, "Don't answer that!

We could sink to the bottom of the sea! THAT'S what more could go wrong tonight! So we'll just not go there, Lord. We'll thank and praise you, instead, for this marvelous vista, of Ancona, from the water."

And in the next minute, Mom did just that, calling my attention to the beauty of the city, rising into its hills, now lit up in the dusk, and under a large and bright moon. It was, in fact, a beautiful sight. The water, too, was beautiful. Light from the ship lit it up a translucent blue-green.

I shook my head. I had learned this gesture, this evening, from the Italians. I was not going to be consoled. I have observed this dynamic between my mom and myself, in tough situations in the past. She will recover her equanimity faster than I will recover mine. Several of my pilgrims had also reassured me on this score: "Jim," Vicky had said, "the day will come when we will look back on all of this and laugh."

In fact, that day was only the next morning off, but I can be quite self-indulgent with my moods, and the mood of failure and of having let good people down, which overtook me that night, did not subside.

There was a dinner, at some point, and we all went in for it, and sitting at our tables set with linen and silver and having a glass of wine as we waited for the soup, my pilgrims and I felt like normal human beings for an hour or so, rather than like refugees. After dinner, Mom, Trudi and I decided to look out for the kids, who wanted to go to the ship's bar and disco. In the disco, Mom found her gin bottle and I had a Heineken. I probably had two or three

Heinekens. The kids had a blast, drinking elaborate non-alcoholic concoctions that show up very glamorously in the few photos I took that night. The whole business of where we were to sleep was really not a problem to the kids, as they had not planned on sleeping anyway.

Mom, Trudi and I had been able to sit down in the bar, and it would have been nice, if the bar had stayed open all night, for just that reason. But it closed somewhere way out at sea (it is an eight-hour crossing) and we were forced back out onto the open deck. The Adriatic is called a flat and calm sea. You would not have guessed it from the waves that hit the ship that night. The boat lifted and dropped on the swells. The Sansovino is not a small ship. We were thirty or so feet above the water, yet the spray from the Adriatic was hitting us, where Mom, Trudi and I had tried to make a little shelter for ourselves, on a bench, on the main deck. We gave up – since it was no fun, getting wet – and went inside, where there was…floor floor everywhere, and to be honest with you, dear reader, I don't remember what happened to Mom and Trudi, for the rest of the night. I think they found a place to sleep sitting up, somewhere.

I meanwhile took charge of the kids' luggage. It was piled in one place, and arranging it creatively, I was able to – sit down! Wow. Awesome. What a concept! The kids had tried to sleep on deck for a short time, way up at the front of the boat, the prow, I guess you call it. Mom, Trudi and I had checked out their chosen sleeping venue, and guessed they would be all right. There was some shelter there, some kind of an overhang. But the sea-spray woke them up, despite this protection. Oscar had, before falling asleep himself, tied everyone's shoelaces together, so that as the kids awoke and tried to get up, they fell all over each other, which they thought hugely funny.

They got their shoelaces unentangled and came inside with all their bags, which is when they found me, looking like a zombie, and asked if I would watch their luggage. They spent the rest of the night, quite justifiably, in my opinion, exploring the ship and enjoying themselves. It was, in fact, an adventure. I only heard about this after the trip was over, but apparently at one point, while running about the ship with the others, Ada lost his footing and went sliding down the wet deck toward the railing, and toward a thirty-foot plunge into the sea. He literally caught himself at the railing. He came up from it laughing. First hearing this story weeks later, my blood ran cold. I know, I know, I know, dear properly concerned reader. I should have had all of the teens under lock and key from the get-go, on that cruise.

Well, I didn't. God was with us. Ada did not plunge into the Adriatic that night.

***

The first rays of dawn's light brought with them a most welcome sight: the Croatian coast. I had never been to Croatia, and had no idea what to expect. It is not possible to do justice to this coast, in words. The California coast is spectacular. But even a Californian is blown away, by the coast of Croatia.

I was really happy to be able to go out on the deck and see light, see land. Given our "ocean-view" accommodations, most of my pilgrims were up early, and were able to enjoy the long run in along the coast, to Split. The dawn was bright pink and pastel blue, and the color of the sea changed, as well, as we made our way in toward

Split. There were many islands. They looked a lot like California –
dry and steep. In fact, the Croatian islands are lush and subtropical,
but you do not necessarily get that impression from the sea.

I crossed up along the deck and saw Paul and Bill, leaning against
the railing, talking philosophy. They looked rested – God knows
how. Mike Czernecki was sitting on a bench with the Klug boys,
Gabriel and Michael, talking American football. The Cortezes, too,
were wide-awake and smiling; Solana had made it through the night
just fine. Lucy Cortez noted that the dawn's colors, pink and blue,
were Our Lady's colors.

The kids had scarcely slept all night. Amazingly enough,
considering that they had not slept much on the flight from San
Francisco, or the previous night, in London, they were wide awake
as we came in toward Split, and full of energy. I got a lot of great
photos, that dawn, of the kids with the Croatian coast behind them. I
noticed in particular the Split waterfront, lined with palms, and
wished that I could explore it.

It takes a couple hours, coming in along the coast, to get to Split. In
that time, breakfast was served. The whole group of us found one
another there in the ship's dining room, and everyone was
exchanging stories of how they had spent the night. The Cruzes
alone, Alberto and Edelma, had had a real night's rest, and thank
God, in the stateroom Father Leon had wangled for them. THEY
thought the Sansovino just peachy. As the boat docked, and we lined
– excuse me, mobbed – up, to get off, Vicky asked me if I wanted to
see the bedroom she and Jane had shared the night before, and
pointed to a space against a wall. She was laughing. I was thanking
God for such pilgrims.

Just as we had been a long time getting onto the Sansovino, we were a long time getting off. When at last the big gangway doors were opened and we were able, with the mob, to move, along came a couple of guys who said to me, "Grupo?" and I said, "Yes," thinking this must be the porterage which had been promised, but which, to this moment, had failed to materialize on the pilgrimage. These guys signaled maybe three or four other guys, who came over and started picking up our luggage. Carl Cortez had better sense than I did at this point. "Jim! We don't know who these guys are!" I was a deer in the headlights, and let's be charitable, here, dear reader, let's just chalk it up to lack of sleep (though I do sometimes wonder where I was when they were passing out the common sense). "Sara," Carl said, turning to Mom. "These guys could be anybody! We shouldn't entrust our luggage to them!"

Mom's reply makes me laugh to this day. "Carl, I am so sick of those bags that if I never see them again, it will be too soon!"

As it happened, though, Carl was 100% right. We got off the boat. I was looking anxiously for someone from Ave Maria Azurra Tours, to greet us, as Sergio had, in Rome. After the disaster with the ferry, I was fully prepared to find us stranded here on the Croatian coast, no bus, no guide, no nothing.

Miracle of miracles! There was a man with a sign that read, "Sullivan Group"! I leapt ten feet in the air. I did the Snoopy Dance around the disembarking passengers, to their great consternation and annoyance. I swung from the lower branches of the Mediterranean pines like Tarzan, and spoke in tongues, joyfully praising the Lord for all His benefits to me.

All right, all right…I walked over to the guy and introduced myself. I then indicated my group, behind me. The guide smiled. He was a gentle young Croatian with a dark mustache and big, soulful, dark brown eyes. He asked where our bags were. I said the porters had already picked them up. He looked at me, as if trying to size me up, and I felt…Oh crap.

We got to the bus and sure enough, our "porters" wanted five dollars a bag. I told them where to get off. They spoke no English, but they TOTALLY understood me. They had not carried the bags more than a couple hundred yards. I settled with them for two bucks a bag, and was only out forty, because many of my pilgrims had held onto their luggage. My advice: always have a Carl Cortez on your tour, and you will not have to deal with this sort of nonsense. There are times when suspicion IS the right response. Human nature is fallen. This is a lesson I occasionally have to re-learn.

***

It astonishes me now to realize that I completely missed the drive down the Dalmatian Coast. It astonishes me, because this drive has become one of my favorite in the world. But that first time I took it, dear reader, I was sound asleep. As with the crossing of central Italy, the day before, I remember the bus stopping somewhere, and everyone getting out and having something to eat and drink, and this time, I got out, too. It was pretty place, green, lots of flowers, some forested slopes above the terrace on which we all took our refreshment. I was sitting at a table with JD and a couple of the adult pilgrims; they were having lunch, but I wanted only a Coke. As soon as we got back on the bus, I went back to dreamland.

I remember waking up just as we were coming into Medjugorje. It was a bright, hot day. The surrounding countryside had a semi-arid look: hilly, stony, bare. But then suddenly there would be a tangerine or pomegranate grove, and the houses all had lush, semi-tropical gardens. Medjugorje itself was not too impressive, at least, not at first glance. It was small and dusty and had a lot of cinderblock construction. There was only one main street, the street on which the church is located. There were a lot of religious gift shops along this street, also a lot of cafes and restaurants. There was new construction everywhere; Medjugorje was clearly growing.

Our bus went down the street to the great square in front of the church, where the young man who had met the ferry got off, and Slaviska, our guide, got on. Slaviska was maybe thirty-four. She had short red hair. She had a rather athletic look, slim and graceful, and she carried herself with unmistakable self-confidence, which I am sure is an advantage in her business. The kids were immediately impressed with her, and indeed, she was to become a great favorite with them over the next six days. Slaviska said that we would go to our hotel first, get our rooms and get settled in, then meet up with her in the lobby at five PM, for a general orientation. This gave us almost two hours to freshen up.

In Medjugorje, they call the hotels pansions. You will read that pilgrims "stay in private homes" of host families in Medjugorje. This creates a false impression. Typically, the pansions include the residence of the family which owns the hotel. But you never see the family's living quarters, and where you are staying in no way resembles "a private home." It resembles, in most cases, a retreat house: the rooms are Spartan and bare. There may be a public meeting room/lounge on the ground floor; there may be a prayer room or chapel. The dining room is set up like a refectory, with long

90

tables for group seating. It is all very new, very clean and very simple. There are no four-star accommodations in Medjugorje.

We were staying at Pansion Primorac. It faced the main street, but was set back by a palm-lined driveway and an expanse of lawn. I remember that there were a couple of crepe myrtle trees, very popular in Hercegovina, and that they were in riotous mid-summer bloom. I have only been to Medjugorje in the summer, so cannot say what it looks like the rest of the year, but in the summer, the gardens are ablaze with color.

The Primorac, in any event, was a good-sized pansion, over thirty rooms on four floors, with a light-filled dining room and a couple of public rooms on the second floor, one for meetings and one for prayer. The construction, like most new construction in Medjugorje, was solid: a wide marble staircase, shining hardwood floors, a stone-and-tile front porch. Our group had three single rooms – one each for me, Paul and Father Leon; everyone else was sharing a double. The accommodations, as I say, were very spare, but they met every need. The "shower" was a hand-held spray-nozzle hose, without walls or curtains, and you couldn't help but get the whole bathroom wet while using it. But after the three days we'd just come through, none of us were about to complain. This was also before the advent of air-conditioning in the Medjugorje pansions. Indeed, many of them still do not have air conditioning. There are frequent breezes in Medjugorje on summer days, however, and with windows left open, the lack of air conditioning was not a problem for most of us.

We got our room assignments and our keys, and as Mom, Trudi and some of the others made their way toward the stairs, several of the kids barreled past them, running up the stairs, laughing and talking, excited. Mom has several times told me how impressed she was with Mikey, who, realizing that it might have looked rude, six or eight teens rushing ahead of everyone that way, turned on the stairs, hands out as if to plead, and said, "You'll have to forgive them. This is their first trip to Europe, and they are very excited." Then he turned and dashed from sight, up the stairs.

Slaviska was in the lobby at five, but only about two-thirds of us were. Those who were not coming down had sent word through roommates: they were going to sleep til dinner at eight. This group included Oscar and Pancho, among the kids. In fact, I did not see Oscar or Pancho until almost lunchtime, the next day. All of us were simply exhausted, but most of us dutifully followed Slaviska down the main street to the plaza in front of St. James, where there were many benches in the shade. Here, for the next hour or so, Slaviska familiarized us with the main outline of the events of Medjugorje, from the first apparition June 24, 1981, to the present time. She gave us an idea of how our own tour would proceed, what we would do when, and so on. She gave us practical information on such things as Mass times, meal times, the exchange rate on the Bosnian mark and the Croatian kuna, and so forth.

We drifted back to the pansion in groups, some of us stopping in at gift shops along the way. I do not know how many of us made it out to the Croatian Mass that evening at seven. I know I did not make it. I was too tired. I knew better than to let myself fall asleep, but I needed to rest, and did so, the couple of hours between the orientation, and dinner. The kids were in and out of my room, and around eight-thirty, a couple of them came up looking for me, as dinner was being served, and I was not there.

The meals at Primorac were really good. The chef (who was a member of the family) had studied culinary arts in Switzerland, and it showed. What's more, while we had assumed that we were only getting breakfast and dinner, at Primorac, the staff understood that we were full board; Slaviska just shrugged and said, "If they make you lunch, eat it," and so, we got three great meals a day, at the pansion. As soon as we arrived in Medjugorje, things started looking up.

After dinner, probably half the adult pilgrims went to bed. But a lot of us, and almost all the kids, our energy at least temporarily refueled by dinner, decided to go out and see some of Medjugorje. This was the end of the Youth Festival, the last couple nights. The city was jammed with teens and twentysomethings from all over Europe and America. As we made our way down the street in the direction of the church, I heard the kids striking up conversations with other young people. There was a play that night, I forget where, that some of the other young people told my kids about, and they asked if they could go. Some of the adults in the group decided to go with them, so I was free to simply wander Medjugorje, which I did, with the remaining members of my party.

We stopped for a drink at one of the streetside cafes. It felt good, just to be able to sit down, sip a cold beer, and watch the evening scene, there, within sight of the twin towers of St. James. The bells rang out the hour – I suppose it was ten. After a while, Mike Czernecki and I were the only ones from the group left. Mike, already past eighty, but looking sixty-five and acting fifty, asked if I wanted to walk a little more, before going back to the pansion. I said "Sure."

We did not know where we were going, of course, and in a short
time found ourselves outside of town altogether – the street we had
followed looped around through several acres of vineyards, and then
brought you back to the main drag. Today, this whole area is built
up, but in 1998, that was how close Medjugorje's main street was to
open country. Mike and I never lost sight of the buildings along the
main street, of course, and after twenty minutes or so, found
ourselves back on it. We turned in the direction of the pansion.
Mike reached two hundred dollar bills from his wallet and handed
them to me, saying he imagined that, before the trip was over, the
kids and I would need it. Mike was always a big backer of my work
with the kids.

We reached the pansion, and I went up to my room. I was not long,
getting into bed. It was just a slim mattress, two sheets and a pillow
(there were blankets in the closet, but there was no need for them). It
was monastery-simple, but to be able to slip between those sheets
and put my head on that pillow, after the last three days, felt
luxurious. I thanked the Blessed Mother for bringing us to
Medjugorje. I asked her to bless and guide our time here. I prayed
for each of my pilgrims by name. Then I got my first full night's
sleep since California.

THREE

The routine in Medjugorje was established the first full day, Friday, that we were there, and it's a routine I have followed on every subsequent trip—so deeply but *easily* prayerful that Mom and I have agreed, Medjugorje is like a spiritual beach.

Rise when you want, and if you miss the breakfast at the pansion, so what? For the equivalent of $3 or $4 you can get a full American-style breakfast at one of the restaurants along the main drag. The English Mass is at ten. In addition to the scheduled events for our group, there are always lots of opportunities for talks, by the visionaries, or priests of the parish, or others closely associated with the apparitions. There are special events such as rallies or concerts or testimonies. There is both private and public prayer, at the church, and in other venues, such as the Oasis of Peace, the orphanange or one of the convents. There are the mountains, and their respective climbs. There's no shortage of good restaurants for lunch, or a mid-afternoon snack. There are the gift shops and the bookstore. You can be as busy or as unbusy as you like, in Medjugorje.

Paul had suggested the breviary for the kids—in fact, I myself did not know how to use it, didn't even have a copy. This was, after all, just before my entrance at the seminary, where, of course, I would pray the breviary every day. We decided on a morning Rosary.

I had a meeting with the kids in the prayer room with which the pansion was equipped. This was a large, airy room on the second floor with big windows overlooking the main street toward St.

James. Nelson had his camcorder with him, and captured part of this meeting on video. We went over the schedule for that day, plans for the next couple of days, and we agreed on a buddy-system and on a curfew.

I am a little surprised, now, watching this video, at the "teacher"-like tone I took with the kids. I mean, strict-old-school teacher-like. I know that in my early days as a Confirmation teacher, I was badge-heavy, and rode the kids a little too hard. But those days were six years in the past, by the morning we were all assembled there in the prayer room at Pansion Primorac. I suppose I was anxious simply for the kids' safety. This anxiousness was, as I say, only recalled to mind, watching Nelson's video years later. My own memories of the kids on the trip are relaxed and happy – with one glaring exception.

After the meeting, we went to Mass and after that, the guys took off as a group to explore Medjugorje. I was not worried. It was broad daylight; this was a small place; this was a place, I firmly believed, guarded by grace. Besides, I wanted my kids to enjoy themselves, to flex their muscles a bit, so to speak, in terms of freedom and responsibility, on this, their first trip to Europe. I wanted them to be open to the experience and the possibilities the pilgrimage would offer.

No need to worry on that score. These guys hit Medjugorje like rock stars. It's almost as if they created their own atmosphere—buoyant, good-natured, laughing, confident, open to the world, open to experience. Nelson's video shows this in ways I cannot describe— but I'll try, anyway. You see it in the surprised looks, and ready smiles, of the girls working the cash registers at the gift shops. You see it in the impromptu conversations with other young people –

more often than not, female – on the street. Most of the young in Medjugorje have at least some familiarity with English. The guys, of course, all but Matt and JD, were fluent in Spanish as well, not that that helped them much with Swedes, Hungarians or Croatians. But it did help them with girls from Spain – and Italy. We always hear how alike Spanish and Portuguese are, and to be sure, they are linguistic cousins. But for my money, Italian bears a closer resemblance to Spanish than does any other language. Speak Spanish slowly and clearly, and the Italians will understand you.

But language was not much of an impediment to the guys, in any event. Smiles, laughter and an open, confident attitude make themselves understood universally. Time and again, as they are leaving a gift shop, or a restaurant, Nelson's video records the boys leaving on a wave of returned joy: every young woman working in Medjugorje that morning was, I would bet, smiling. I know all of this from Nelson's video. I had spent the morning with the Klugs, with Alma and Claudia, first at St. James, then later along the main drag, checking out rosaries, crucifixes, books and so on, at the many gift shops along the street.

The guys were back at the pansion for lunch. The plan for the afternoon was to climb Apparition Hill. We would leave late in the afternoon and have the climb accomplished well ahead of dinner at eight. Some of the kids went back out to explore the town; others went upstairs to take a nap. I had made up room assignments before we left, two kids to a room, but the boys were very casual about it. Their rooms were all on the same floor, and it was as if they felt they had a five-room suite. I came in one morning to find four guys sleeping all over one room. Often, on trips with them since, both to Europe and to Venezuela, where I now travel regularly with them, I have observed this sort of my-room-is-your-room attitude and approach among them. They are as close as brothers to one another, as many people have pointed out to me.

***

Apparition Hill is one of the two holy mountains in Medjugorje. It is the hill on which the visionaries first saw Our Lady, the afternoon of June 24, 1981. According to the story, Our Lady appeared about two thirds of the way up the hill, at a place where there is a natural plateau. She was seen by two of the visionaries, one of whom said, "Look! It's Our Lady!" and the other replied, "Don't be ridiculous. Why would Our Lady appear to us?" The visionaries have always laid great stress on the fact that as teens, their age when Our Lady started appearing to them, they were hardly holy. Indeed, they make no claim to holiness today: only the desire for it.

For a time in the summer of 1981, the visionaries saw Our Lady every day on Apparition Hill. As the crowds swelled with the reports, however, the then-communist regime got nervous and closed off the hill. Apparitions later occurred in other sites, including, for a long while, the parish church.

In any event, the climb up Apparition Hill is on every pilgrim's agenda in Medjugorje. Slaviska met us at the pansion and after some discussion with me and Father Leon, she recommended that the Cruzes, who were well into their eighties, take a cab to the foot of the hill as it was a moderately long walk. Pilar Perron, who had been to Medjugorje several times before, and knew her way around, went with them.

The rest of us crossed the fields and vineyards to Podbrdo. No, that's not a typo. That is the spelling of the name of one of the five villages that make up St. James Parish, and through which you pass to get to Apparition Hill. Although it had been bright and sunny and hot, earlier, some high, thin summer clouds had since formed, and they blocked the sun intermittently, which made the walk comfortable. We were mostly crossing through vineyards; we could see the bunches of grapes, not yet ripe, among the leaves.

Slaviska was always teaching us. She explained about the first apparitions, as we made our way toward the hill. Some of the guys, meanwhile, had stopped at a last-chance-for-water-or-soda market at the edge of town, and I was waiting for them. As we fell behind, these kids and I – Fonz and Ada, Matt, Mikey and Jorge – took pictures of ourselves, along the dusty, red dirt path; a couple of these are among my favorites from the trip.

At the base of the hill, we found no sign of the Cruzes and Pilar. We considered it, and decided that they must have started up ahead of us; Pilar, after all, knew the hill. So we started up, Father Leon leading us in the Rosary, as we went. I had nothing to compare it to, of course, never having been to Medjugorje before, but the hill was very empty that Friday afternoon. At the time we started up, ours was the only group making the ascent. This was a true grace for us, as the way up is along a wide goat trail that, while not too steep, is littered with stones. The stones are, for the most part, part of Apparition Hill itself; they emerge from the ground; they are not lying on it. It is not as if you could bring in a bulldozer and clear the path. I figured we would soon catch up with Pilar and the Cruzes. They could not possibly be moving very quickly, along such a path.

The path is marked out with stone-carved stations for each of the original fifteen decades of the Rosary. We were saying the Joyful Mysteries as we climbed. At the second or third mystery, when we still had not caught up with the Cruzes, Father Leon asked me to take one of the boys and go back down, looking for them. Mikey and Jorge both volunteered. The three of us went back down.

We got to the bottom of the hill -- no sign of Pilar and her elderly charges. We looked all over down there, where the village ends and the path up the mountain begins, knowing that Pilar knew where things were, so it was unlikely they'd gotten lost. They were not in any gift shop, nor in any restaurant near the bottom of the hill.

Mikey, Jorge and I returned to the foot of the hill. Meanwhile, a large Italian group had assembled there, and was just moving up. There was a woman at the back of this group. She was maybe fifty. She had red hair and wore a yellow-print sundress. I do not remember if she was carrying her shoes or had handed them to someone else. I do remember that she was barefoot. I watched her as she carefully made her way amid the rocky protrusions of the path, looking for places of smooth rock, or the red dirt, to place her feet. I was impressed with her – so much so that I can see her in my mind's eye today, more than a decade later.

I quietly pointed her out to the guys. They looked at her, looked at her bare feet. "What the hell is she doing that for?" asked Jorge. "To win grace for herself and for the whole world," I said.

The guys exchanged an excited glance, and all of a sudden I thought, "Oh crap."

100

We went up the hill barefoot. Jorge and I were tenderfoots, but Mikey climbed as fast barefoot as he did in his shoes. He quickly crossed through the Italian group and was lost to sight to us somewhere up the hill. Jorge and I got through the Italian group as they paused to say the second decade of the Rosary. We did not know the way and kept right on climbing, right past the point after the fifth Joyful Mystery where you turn sharply right and go along the side of the hill, rather than continuing further up. The whole group, guided by Slaviska, of course, had turned here, to get to the original apparition site. Mikey, too, had turned here. I don't know how he knew to do so – maybe he caught up with the group as they made the turn; that would have been a possibility, given his mountain-lion capacities on that path. Jorge and I kept climbing, passing the stations for the Sorrowful Mysteries, to a point several hundred feet above the apparition site, where we found -- Pilar and the Cruzes!

They were not the least bit tired. They were praying the decades of the Rosary, and they had wondered what on earth was taking the rest of us so long, catching up to them. The path came back around to the apparition site, but by the time the five of us got there, the group was already starting back down.

Brigitta and the Klug boys, Michael and Gabriel, were still there, and they joined up with us, to help the Cruzes down. Most of the kids had not yet left the plateau of the apparitions either, and, on seeing Mikey barefoot, all of them had taken off their shoes. I looked at the bunch of them there, barefoot, and smiled, and was a little more sanguine about my own bare feet, and the discomfort I had endured, in the climb. The kids and I were in this together.

Jorge and I stayed with the Cruzes, with Pilar and the Klugs, while most of the other kids bounded barefoot down the hill ahead of us. Somewhere, though, on the way down, something happened. Something happened, I should say, for the kids ahead of us. Somewhere on the way down, the kids started noticing the sun. I was not with them when this happened and only heard about it later that day. But most of the kids saw it. They were able to look straight at the sun, and to keep looking at it. They did not want to look away, because what they were seeing was so beautiful.

The sun was covered, they would later tell me, by a sort of disc; "Like a Host," an adult pilgrim was later to relate to me. "It is as if the Eucharist moves in front of the sun, so that you can look right at it." Then the sun began to vibrate, began to spin, began to turn various colors and to throw off colored light. This "dance of the sun" is, of course, one of the several mystical phenomena associated with Medjugorje. I have never seen it, and ask no one to believe in it, if they can't. I am simply reporting what happened.

Claudia said it was so beautiful that she began to cry, and that she kept crying, afterward, on the walk back through the fields to Medjugorje. Wally said he was way up on the side of the hill, when he started looking at the sun, and then, next thing he knew, he was down on the red dirt path among the vineyards, not really knowing how he'd gotten there. All the kids were awed by the spectacle. They said it was serene and beautiful and filled them with joy. They could not do the experience justice, in words.

As I say, our group – Jorge, Pilar, the Cruzes, the Klugs and I – did not witness the miracle of the sun that afternoon. But many others in our group did, including my mom and Matt, who were somewhere along the path together, not with anyone else from the group. Both Mom and Matt stopped and stared and stared at the sun. And both Mom and Matt said the same thing to me about it, afterward: they had both thought to themselves, or maybe even said aloud to one another, I do not remember which, "I suppose I really should not be doing this; I am risking my eyesight."

I wanted to slap them. Here Our Lady gives you this – miracle – and rather than simply releasing yourself to it, as Claudia did, you reserve a section of the rational mind to yourself, and argue the merits of witnessing it! Oh all right, I didn't really want to slap them. I love Matt and I obey the Fourth Commandment. All the same…In seven trips to Medjugorje I have never witnessed the dance of the sun. Mom and Matt did, and employed rational argument with the experience, WHILE experiencing it! Must be the German in them.

In any event, we got down. I remember that Jorge and I walked barefoot all the way back into town—that cool, red, dusty path felt so good after the stones and pebbles of the hillside. Almost like Heaven, maybe, after Purgatory.

***

We were barely back at the pansion, showered and changed for dinner, when Slaviska came in with the news that there was to be a public apparition that night – at the original site, on Apparition Hill. Public apparitions are just that: the visionary has the apparition in a place where pilgrims are able to gather and watch. They happen with some frequency, in Medjugorje.

103

So, we all went back up Apparition Hill after dinner, and as it was getting dark. And this time, the path up the hill was very crowded, nothing at all like our quiet climb late in the afternoon. I was with Mom and Trudi. Various members of our group were near us in the crowd, others were spread out well ahead or behind. Veteran Medjugorje pilgrims were equipped with flashlights, which helped a lot: this was before the hill was illuminated at night.

We reached the plateau, where there was a hush of whispers in many languages. The valley or plain, or whatever it is that Medjugorje lies in, spread below us -- lights delineated the extent of each of the five villages. We were a huge crowd, but we were very quiet. A dog barked somewhere down in the valley, and its sound was solitary. There are many crickets in Medjugorje, but up on the hill, we could not hear them. The stars were myriad and bright, as they almost never are in California, simply because of our urban haze. Marysville and Yuba City are very urban, compared to Medjugorje.

The visionary was Ivan. He arrived sometime after most of us, was escorted to a roped off area that was illuminated – I don't know by what means. I could see the light where he was, but not Ivan himself. I was told that he knelt immediately in prayer, and waited in that posture for some time. Then at once he looked up smiling in raptly attentive joy. After a couple of minutes he was seen to be saying something, though no one heard it. There was an absolute hush all across the mountain. I do not know if I have ever "heard" such silence.

Then it was over. I knew it was over because of the rustle, the wave of hushed whispering that spread through the crowd, eventually reaching me and Mom and Trudi. After a few moments came the translations of the message in language after language -- Croatian, German, Hungarian, Italian, Spanish, French, English… I don't know how many other languages it was translated into. The message was not particularly remarkable – I mean, it contained nothing that those familiar with Medjugorje would not have expected to hear. It was one of the simple, direct, and profound messages Our Lady regularly delivers via these visionaries: a call to greater prayer, greater trust, greater self-abandonment to God in all aspects of our lives. I do remember that one of the things Our Lady asked for was prayer for a plan of hers, a special plan she was hoping to be able to move forward with. She thanked us, as she always does, for having responded to her call. Then she was gone.

Some people saw things, up there on the hill. Trudi saw flashes of light as Our Lady arrived, and as the apparition ended. Lucy Cortez, at the window of her room in the pansion, with Solana, saw a vision of Our Lady coming to the hill from the starlit sky. I saw nothing extraordinary, and that was fine with me.

Mom and I still marvel at the silence on the hill that night. And the simple fact of the crowd, all those pilgrims, so hungry for God, so dedicated in their search for grace, that simple fact deeply impressed me. Like Loretto, I thought; Apparition Hill is holy in part simply because of the countless pilgrims who have streamed to it, praying, hoping and believing all the way.

We all tended to start back down after we'd heard the message in our own language, which must have been a little annoying for those whose translations came toward the end. English was one of the first three or four languages in the long series of translations, though, and so we were heading down the hill shortly after the apparition had

ended. As it was dark, the boys helped Mom down, Pancho and
Matt. I watched them, loving them. They all called Mom "Mom,"
and they really knew how to be good sons.

The cafes and bars at the foot of Apparition Hill were packed, and
above all with the young: it was the last night of that year's Youth
Festival, and there were thousands of teens and twentysomethings in
Medjugorje that evening. The contrast with this scene of joyous
youthful celebration and the deep silence, even in the midst of the
crowd, atop the hill, was impressive.

The boys fanned out amid the cafes and bars there at the foot of the
hill, mixing it up with girls from all over—the States and Europe.
Mom, Trudi, some of the other pilgrims and I walked back to
Medjugorje through the moonlit vineyards. Some of the pilgrims
went to bed, but some of us went for ein Bier, at the Dubrovnik Club,
a nice outdoor restaurant almost directly across from St. James. It
was to become our unofficial headquarters the rest of the stay. At
the suggestion of Brigitta and Rose (Rose was also German, and
Brigitta's roommate) we ordered Kaltenberg, which I had never had
in the States: it's a good substitute for Heineken. Trudi doubtless got
a Coke and Mom probably ordered red wine. Whatever we were
drinking, we enjoyed the festive atmosphere of the restaurant, and
toasted our first out-of-this-world day, in Medjugorje.

***

The next day was Saturday, not that that made much difference given
the typical pilgrim's routine in Medjugorje. Some of the guys were
up too late for breakfast, so I took them down to the Dubrovnik Club,

106

where I had a couple cappuccinos while they had ham-and-cheese omelettes or eggs and cevapcicci (the delicious little Croatian sausages).

That afternoon, we went to hear Father Jozo in Sroki Brjeg (I have likely misspelled that); he had been pastor at St. James when the apparitions began. He had gone to prison, rather than deny the apparitions, and is properly a hero to all of Medjugorje's millions of pilgrims. It was a thirty-five minute bus ride through a spectacular countryside of cliffs and gorges, but also of the level and fertile Neretva River Valley, with its vineyards and pomegranate orchards.

Slaviska translated Father Jozo's message. It was a fiery and impassioned call to conversion. After he had finished speaking, Father Jozo came around blessing people a la the healing Mass with Dean McFalls, in Stockton. Folks started being slain in the Spirit, going right over backward at the touch of the priest's hand. Mikey laughed. "Not this again!" he said, keeping his voice low. I couldn't help but smile. My kids from the get-go in 1996 had displayed a deep and joyful faith at the same time that they evidenced a sort of cheerful cynicism, a worldly and street-smart skepticism well beyond their teen-aged years. It was a combination that perhaps more than anything else, really made them MY kids.

I could never have been a "typical" youth minister. I came to it too late in life – just months short of my fortieth birthday. I was what I was, at that point – and a lot of what I was, was worldly and cynical, not surprised by much. I have many times said that God was clearing the bench, to send me into youth ministry. There had to have been better candidates, but for whatever reason, they had not shown up. So the Lord sent me – almost forty, with a lot of sophisticated and worldly friends and a resume of life experiences that was, well, atypical, for a youth minister. But when I think about the emotional resonance between me and the kids, I do sometimes wonder if, maybe after all, I was not just EXACTLY the man God wanted for this job. The kids say they would not have hung around, if I had been on their case, for instance, over rap music. They say my relaxed approach is what made them feel at home and accepted; that it is what enticed them to listen to me.

In any event, I had to smile, when Mikey joked "Not this again!" about the folks being slain in the Spirit. I firmly believe in the phenomenon, but I wasn't going to insist that Mikey believe in it. I had long before seen the depth of his faith; he might one day come to an appreciation of the Charismatic movement. Or he might not. Meanwhile his good-natured skepticism struck a responsive chord in me.

We were back at the pansion by mid-afternoon, and I remember that a group of us were sitting out front, on the porch and along the low stone wall that ran to the street. Pilar, who had been with me and the Cruzes, and who had not heard about the kids' experience on the mountainside, the previous afternoon, said to me, "Jim, what I am praying for is that Our Lady will show your boys the dance of the sun. When I first saw it here, I was moved to tears. It is so beautiful, and you feel it so deeply. My hope and prayer for your kids is that Our Lady will show them this miracle."

"She's doing it now."

Pilar and I looked toward Ada, who had spoken. He was leaning against a car in the drive, and apparently, staring straight at the sun.

Pilar looked at the sun. I looked at Pilar.

"Oh!" Pilar said. "Oh! She is doing it! She is doing it! Oh, it is so beautiful! Our Lady is so good! She loves us so much!" Tears came into Pilar's eyes, as she spoke.

I looked from Pilar to the others in the group – everyone was looking at the sun: all the boys, Barbara, Marge and Loyd, Father Leon. They were all seeing the miracle of the sun.

I looked at the sun.

That is, I tried to look at it. I couldn't. When has anyone ever been able to look at the sun? I tried again. I couldn't. People were exchanging happy exclamations, and someone asked me if I had just seen that – whatever "that" was. I answered that I could not look at the sun. I was not seeing anything.

"Jim," Ada said, not turning from the spectacle. "You have to give it a moment. You have to turn slowly toward the sun and let the disk come in front of it, before you look directly at it."

I tried to follow Ada's instructions. I saw no disk. What I did see is our own brilliant local star. (Did you know, by the way, that of the three thousand stars in our celestial neighborhood, the sun is the sixth brightest? I forget where I read that, but I thought it was a cool fact, so I pass it along. Our sun is truly a shining star.)

I tried four times to see the dance of the sun, that afternoon. I did not see it. And I feel compelled to add here that NO ONE must ever demand this grace from God. We have all heard stories, apocryphal perhaps, but all the same, sobering, of people looking at the sun in an EXPECTATION of this miracle, and damaging their sight as a result. You know the phrase, "Don't try this at home?" Apply it one thousand times over, here.

After two or three minutes, it was all over. Everyone turned away from the sun at the same time, and everyone had the same look on their faces – a kind of quiet and inward joy. People felt sorry for me, not being able to witness it. I did not feel sorry. Although I believe in miracles, my faith neither needs nor seeks them. I felt that I had been given a rare gift, that afternoon. I witnessed over a dozen of my pilgrims witnessing the dance of the sun. It certainly looked to me as if they were looking right at the sun. I could testify with some objectivity, about their claim; I was something of a scientific "control" for the experience of a miracle. How cool was that?

That evening there was a wild thunderstorm—lightning, rain and wind -- and we sat out on the porch at the pansion and were enthralled for more than an hour. It cleared off completely, leaving a mild, breezy night. I don't know where everyone went after dinner that night, but I do know that a group of us wound up at the Dubrovnik Club. Brigitta, Rose and I practiced unser Deutsch, while Claudia and Alma talked it up with the Klug boys. Mom observed that the four of them made for two cute couples, and in fact, Claudia and Alma spent as much time on the trip with Michael and Gabriel as they did with the guys from the youth group; maybe more. Michael and Gabriel were just as much fun, but they were a lot quieter, a lot less inclined to attract or grab the spotlight, than were the guys from the group.

As I had done the first night, I sat up downstairs at the pansion, making sure the guys were all in for the night. I had given them a liberal curfew: 1 AM. By 1:15, all my kids were in. This was the second night in a row that they had not let me down. I was satisfied. I knew my kids and they knew me, pardon the Biblical paraphrase. I had imagined myself having to make the rounds of the clubs and restaurants, up and down the street, ordering the boys to come in for the night: no such thing. I was proud of them, and pleased with the arrangement we had all agreed to, in the curfew. Plenty of time for them to make whoopee with the international youth set out there on the street, but also a reasonably early hour for them to be in by. I went to bed that night feeling deep satisfaction and gratitude at how this pilgrimage was turning out.

***

The next morning, Sunday, I was in the prayer room saying the Rosary by myself when suddenly Nelson burst in — wearing a sheet from his bed as if it were a Roman toga — he was so excited he hadn't waited to put his clothes on.

"Jim!" he said. "Look at this! Look at my rosary!"

The silver chain of his deep-yellow glass rosary, which I'd bought him in Sacramento, a few weeks before the trip, had turned gold.

All right, all right already. Let's talk about this gold rosary thing. The first thing I have to say about it is that my sister Anne, a notorious skeptic, has a rosary that turned gold. So there. That proves it.

Okay, maybe not. The fact that I have half a dozen rosaries that once had silver chains, which are now gold, does not, I imagine, prove anything to the genuine skeptic, either. And I will put it to you straight: I honestly don't care whether people believe in the mystical elements of Medjugorje or not. Medjugorje is Our Lady's gift, not mine. The Church compels no one to accept private revelation, not even fully-approved visions, such as Guadalupe, Fatima and Lourdes. I'm not trying to prove anything in relating this part of the story. I am simply telling you what happened. Let's just observe a few facts about the business, and my own experience with it, and then move on with our story.

Fact number one, this is a Medjugorje thing. Prior to the apparitions at Medjugorje, no one ever had a rosary turn from silver to gold. Fact number two, when a rosary turns, it often does so instantaneously, which pretty much debunks the oft-heard "oxidation" theory. Fact number three, God created the physical universe, and ex nihilo, from nothing. If God can do that, God can turn a rosary's chain from silver to gold. Fact number four, we should be rightly grateful for the miraculous gift of a rosary that has turned gold, but the Medjugorje visionaries themselves do not attach much importance to it. Our Lady has said at Medjugorje, "I have come to remind the world that God exists." Miracles help us to remember that God exists. This gold rosary thing is not the parting of the Red Sea, but it is undoubtedly miraculous. To the extent that it can be an aid to faith, well and good. But it is God, not the rosary, that matters.

The first rosary of mine to turn from silver to gold did so in May, 1997. I was up at my foothill rosary group, northeast of Marysville. Before the group started praying that afternoon, one of the ladies, Nina, a former Army captain, and the mother of a Sacramento priest, showed me her gold rosary and asked if I had ever seen one before. I told her no, though I had heard of the phenomenon. Nina told me how hers had turned one afternoon, as she had prayed with it. I thought, "How charming."

The group of us prayed the Rosary. We followed it with the Chaplet of Divine Mercy. We followed that with petitions for, I think, every human being who lives in the Yuba County foothills. We followed that with the ladies asking me to tell them about "my boys." These gracious churchwomen had taken up my kids as a special cause; they prayed for them regularly and they had come down to Marysville a couple of times, to attend our breakfast, and see the kids for themselves. While I was telling the ladies about Oscar, Omar, Nelson, Fonz, Wally, Pancho, Ada, Mikey, Jorge, Matt, Robert, Richard, Russell, Jason, Angel, Cruz, Jerry, Ravi, Timmy, Lilin, Rafael, Alvaro, Travis, JD, JT, Junior, Juan, Mike, John and so on…I looked at my rosary and thought, "Gee, the chain looks different, almost golden. Must be the slant of the afternoon sun."

It was not the slant of the afternoon sun. And as I kept talking about my boys – and girls – and kept glancing at my rosary, it became more and more evident that my sterling silver, Austrian crystal rosary, bought in Boston at the St. Francis Chapel in the Prudential Center, three years before, had turned gold. When this happens, only the chain changes color. The crucifix and medal remain silver, and the beads remain whatever color they were. There was a point where I nudged Louise, seated next to me, and said, "Louise, when we started talking about the kids, my rosary was sterling silver…"

Louise took one look, smiled with deep satisfaction, and said, "Ladies, I think we all want to take a minute, to have a look at Jim's rosary."

I eventually gave that rosary to Omar. As I say, I have had five more turn gold, since. If you have trouble believing in the gold rosary business, I can hardly blame you. I'm telling you about it because it happened; it is part of this story. I will say as well that I believe that rosaries turn gold for one reason: to remind us that God exists.

I had my camera with me, that Sunday morning in the prayer room at Primorac, and I took pictures of Nelson holding his rosary against the white toga-wrap of his sheet, the better to show up the gold color of the chain. The whole rosary, really, was now gold, given the almost-amber glass beads.

What is more, Oscar's sparkling green rosary had also changed. And Mikey's red rosary changed that morning as we said our group rosary. Mikey's rosary changed, however, while Ada was praying with it. I don't know why, but for some reason, Mikey lent Ada his rosary, that morning, for the group rosary. The fact that his rosary now had a golden chain made Mikey very happy at the same time that it troubled him because the miracle had occurred while Ada was praying with the rosary. Had Our Lady meant the miracle for Ada? Ada himself was more than satisfied simply to have been holding the rosary when grace manifestly touched it: he handed it back to Mikey with a joke about how much better it was, now that he had prayed on it. The whole group thought this was great – the whole group but Mikey, that is. The rosary broke, later on in the trip – teen-aged boys are hard on rosaries. This fact did not console Mikey any, either. I bought Mikey a new red rosary later; meanwhile, he still has the pieces of the one that broke in Medjugorge.

I remember well our group rosaries there at Pansion Primorac. We took turns leading the decades and we prayed the Rosary in English, Spanish, Polish, German, Tagalog and Gaelic, the languages of our group. I remember the time that Jorge offered to lead one of the decades. It was on the bus. (We would say a second group rosary on days when we were taking a bus somewhere.) Jorge's offer to lead was a first among the kids, and the whole bus sat up and paid attention. Well, I mean, not that we weren't paying attention to our prayers before! Just that now one of the kids, "our kids" as we all now called them, was leading us in prayer. Jorge has a good voice, and he was reverent, confident and calm. We were all so pleased with him that I think we might have applauded, except that it would have embarrassed him. I sat back and wondered at my own under-estimation of the kids – I had never tried to lead them in more than a decade of the Rosary before, because I did not think their attention spans would allow it.

***

On Sunday we went up Mt. Krizevac. For some reason I am not sure of, we went up in the afternoon, which is unusual. Though on subsequent visits I have come to prefer mid-day because the mountain is empty of the throngs of pilgrims who climb it early morning and at dusk, it was definitely out of the ordinary for a large pilgrim group to be ascending Krizevac at three in the afternoon. The more so, given that a fair number of our pilgrims were over 70.

For some reason I no longer remember, I was late getting to the base, that is, the start-point for the climb. Oscar, Wally and Jorge were with me and the four of us went up alone, well behind the larger group. I was going to go barefoot but the boys talked me out of it -- it would slow us considerably and we were already well behind Father Leon and the rest.

Krizevac is over 2000 feet high but at the base you are already several hundred feet up, so that the climb isn't all that bad. It's similar to Apparition Hill in its stoniness, but I have noticed, taking both of them barefoot over the years, that Krizevac is actually a less tortuous climb, because it has more big rocks, more flat rocks, more places where there is a smooth surface large enough to land your foot. It's not the real rocks that make these climbs so hard, barefoot — it's the many pebbles, and Apparition Hill, in my experience, is the tougher barefoot climb, on account of its abundance of pebbles.

The path winds up the face of the slope, lined with pomegranate trees, just like Apparition Hill. The hundreds of pomegranate trees on the hills surrounding Medjugorje make me wonder if the tree is simply a native species that has taken possession of its environment, or if they are actually orchards — owned by locals and harvested in the autumn for commercial sale. We have peach and nectarine orchards, also walnut, almond and olive, all over the Sacramento Valley. But the trees grow on flat alluvial land, and hard as summer work in California's orchards is, it would be a lark, compared to the work that would be involved in harvesting the pomegranates of Medjugorje from these steep, stony slopes.

You make the Stations of the Cross on Mt. Krizevac. I went up with my three sons, so to speak, Oscar, Wally and Jorge, stopping at each stone relief to talk to the boys about the Way of the Cross, and Jesus' Passion.

I have always loved best the Jesus of Good Friday. Since I was a little boy, since I was five or six years old, and first able to know what Good Friday was all about, it has always been my favorite day of the year. I've had friends react with surprise at this, but to me, Christmas and Easter find meaning through Good Friday. The Lord as *the* Superhero: that was pretty much my feeling for the Christ of Good Friday, when I was a boy. This is also truly the Eucharistic Lord -- offering his body and his blood -- I mean, this is when he did it, literally. How are we saved? By his body and blood. Good Friday is the day he gave both up utterly for us. Good Friday is the day that salvation was won; the day that the sin and curse of Adam were reversed; the day that the whole course of human history changed forever. The Man nailed to the Cross on Good Friday is Jesus at once at his most vulnerable and at his strongest, his most utterly heroic, and as a little boy, I simply fell in love with him.

So up the side of Krizevac with Oscar, Jorge and Wally. We were well over an hour getting up the mountain and the afternoon sun was bright and hot. At one point, Oscar took a swig from the big plastic bottle he carried -- then suddenly spit it all out. I looked at him with a questioning concern: "Is something wrong?" "I told Jesus I wouldn't take a drink until we got to the top. I was so thirsty just now, I didn't think of it -- it was like a reflex." He meant taking the drink. "So, as soon as I remembered, I spit it out." I could hardly have been more proud of Oscar. I had sometimes talked to the kids about Our Lord's own terrible thirst, on His way to the Cross, and as He hung on the Cross. "It was at once a real, physical thirst, like none we can imagine," I would say, "and at the same time, it was His deep thirst for souls, for our salvation, for our eternal happiness.

There was literally nothing He would not give, to ensure that happiness for us." Oscar had evidently been listening, as I had spoken thus. He didn't take a drink from his bottled water, until we reached the summit.

This kind of penitential piety -- the bare feet up Apparition Hill on Friday, for instance, which was no plan of mine -- is one of the things that I really revere in my kids. They "get" their lovability. They also get their sinfulness. We emphasize one at the expense of the other, in my view. Times were when some in the Church laid excessive emphasis on sin and guilt; times are, in my opinion, when a great many are doing exactly the opposite. Sure, God is love. But God hates sin, and for the same reasons we hate cancer. God aims to separate us from our sins, IF we will let him. We can only do this if we are first able to acknowledge sinfulness and repent of it, that is, turn away from it. Our repentance, God's forgiveness. That's the dynamic. We need to hold the tension of the dynamic and not relax or deny it. We need to do this because salvation itself is at stake.

The boys and I reached the rest of the group near the top, maybe the 11th or 12th Station. I was having a pretty serious catechism session with the guys on the Passion and didn't want to stop the lesson to join the more general devotional approach the larger group was taking, so we tarried, let the group go on ahead of us, and I continued with my talks. I noted, meanwhile, how the boys, Pancho and Matt, JD and the Klugs, were helping older members of the group, along the stony climb. Father Leon and Carl Cortez took the lead, while Paul and Mike Czernecki brought up the rear: we were almost like a family on the move; there was something beautiful in it, something touching.

Oscar, Jorge, Wally and I were the last members of our group to reach the summit—where we all took lots of pictures. The view from the summit is panoramic, and we were favored with a bright and clear afternoon.

Slaviska told us she'd meet us down at the base, where there was a café that sold ice cream. The kids' eyes lit up. She said she knew a short cut down, off the main path, and could be at the café in just fifteen minutes, and Oscar, Jorge and a couple of the other guys opted to go down with her. I came down with the main group, and in fact, you *can* get down Krizevac much faster than you can get up. Maybe twenty-five minutes. Though we made it down quickly, sure enough, Slaviska had come down even faster — she and Oscar and the other guys were sitting at an outside table under a canopy of grapevines, with their ice cream. The whole group flocked to the counter, some for ice cream: some, like me, for something brisk, clean and COLD; I think I got a bottled iced tea.

***

One of the mornings that we were there I got a knock on my door at about 6:00 a.m. The bright Bosnian sunshine was already pouring through my window and I could see it was a beautiful morning, but I *never* like being awakened at 6:00 a.m. The knock was followed by a falsetto and fake-accented voice: "Housekeeping." There followed a little rhyme which cannot be printed here, and then the promise "I love you longtime." Snickers and excited whispers, rather than outright laughter, followed. There was then the sound of footsteps—several pairs—hurrying away. I rolled my eyes and went back to sleep.

Later, maybe 8:00 or 8:30, as I was showering, it occurred to me that the boys had gotten up *awfully* early this morning. I came down to breakfast intending to ask them about it, but didn't have to. I was bombarded with information from several of them at once. It was not that they had been up early; rather, they'd never gone to bed last night. Instead, they'd been assured by "the Irish girls" that Krizevac was awesome at night, and that they needed to go up with them, at three in the morning.

Now as a matter of fact, all kinds of weird things are said to happen on Krizevac at night. There are stories of people seeing burning vegetation (that nonetheless is NOT burned – does that sound familiar?), of people witnessing ethereal multi-colored lights, seeing auras around others, encountering their guardian angels and even Jesus and so on. I had heard all these stories about Krizevac at night, but I was not in mind of them on this trip. I had not come to Medjugorje looking for mystical experience, and in any event, no one in our group had any plan to go up Krizevac at night.

There were, on the other hand, "the Irish girls." Among the many young ladies encountered by the boys on this trip were several lovely lasses from the Emerald Isle, at least one of whom, I was later to learn, could drink any of the boys under the table. These impressive young women took it upon themselves to take several of my boys up Krizevac at night. I no longer remember how many of the guys went up, but I know Mikey, Ada and Fonz were among them. They not only went up Krizevac at two or three in the morning, they stayed there til the sun came up. With the Irish girls.

"Jim! NOTHING happened! There were a bunch of kids up there all night!" Mikey, pleading his innocence, that morning at breakfast at the pansion.

"We talked about God, Jim!" Ada, trying to soothe my fears and anger.

"We didn't drink up there, or nuthin'," Fonz, the realist, looking for a bottom line, in this conversation.

"Right," I said. "What DID you do up there?"

"I told you," said Ada. "We talked about God!"

"Ada," I said. "I was born in 1956, and in case you need to be reminded, 1956 is NOT yesterday."

"I can prove it to you!" said Mikey. "I learned the Creed by heart."

I looked at him. "You learned the Creed…"

"I learned the Creed!" Mikey shot back, indignant. Mikey was always expert at knowing when to display indignation, and so gain the moral advantage in an argument.

I'd taught the kids the Creed, but I hadn't made them memorize it. The idea, frankly, of Mikey memorizing the Creed while spending the night on Mt. Krizevac with three hearty Irish lasses—

"Say it," I said.

"Apostles' or Nicene?"

Mikey was good. I've always given him that. I smirked. "You choose," I said, expecting him to fall back into playful banter along the lines of "Jim! NOTHING happened," instead of which. . .

He first recited the Apostles' Creed, line for line and word for word; *then* the Nicene. I need to tell you something: sometimes leading the Rosary *I* can get these two mixed up. Here Mikey was, sixteen years very young, with perfect recitation of both creeds. Whatever ELSE may have happened on Mt. Krizevac that night, the Irish girls had taught Mikey the creeds.

Now another youth minister may have had a very different response here, and I know it. I'm thinking of a guy with a teen group I saw at a Giants' game in May, 1996, a game at which I also had my kids. I can still see and hear him. "TAKE YOUR SEAT AND STAY IN IT. NO TRADING. NO GOING TO THE CONCESSION STAND. NO ONE GOES TO THE BATHROOM ALONE. TAKE A CHAPERONE." I remember hearing that, letting out a long sigh and… looking at my kids and saying, "Go to the bathroom when you need to go. You don't need a chaperone to take a whiz." We had a buddy system. I brought all my kids home safe and sound.

Look, I am not unaware of the kind of world we live in. "Monsters," my friend Vera, from my office at Cal, likes to put it. "Some people are just monsters. Gotta be on the lookout for monsters." Vera's right. But—

Number one, this nocturnal climb up Krizevac was over before I knew it had happened.

Two, the boys were safe.

Three, I believed the boys to the extent that I was sure they had, in fact, spent the night on the mountain.

Four, I told them it was okay if they wanted to do it again, but that I *had* to go with them, in that case. They understood what I meant; it wasn't a matter of trust. It was a matter of my responsibility to them and to their parents.

Five, I trust the action of grace at Medjugorje. The way I saw it, happening as it had, while I slept innocent of all details, thinking my boys were also asleep in their rooms, what could I have done to stop it? I was willing to believe it happened because there was something good in it for my boys. Nothing bad was going to happen to my kids here; of that I was sure. And the way this happened seemed to me stamped with grace. I was not angry at the guys. But I had to make sure they understood that I came with them, if they went up again at night. I had NO desire to do any such thing and doubted it would happen, but on the off-chance that it did, then, because I owed it to their parents, I HAD to be included in the night climb and stay, on Krizevac.

I was satisfied that the matter was happily closed.

***

Monday morning we were preparing to leave for a day trip to Dubrovnik. I no longer remember how I found this out; no longer remember who told me that the boys had been breaking curfew since Friday and *not* just to go up Mt. Krizevac. The previous night, at least, all of them had been clubbing in Citluk.

Citluk is a city, well, really, a large town, so near Medjugorje that if you had to, you could walk there in an hour's time. It is a city with many, many restaurants, bars and youth clubs. It is, for the young pilgrim in Medjugorje, an oasis of worldly delights; like a smaller, Bosnian version of Piccadilly Circus, and as far as my boys were concerned, the place to be, after curfew. They had been there every night since Friday.

It was easy enough to see how this happened. These guys, the charmers of waitresses in Marysville and Sacramento, had been an instant hit in Medjugorje, from Thursday night on. They were rather exotic, for that part of the world: at once, American and Mexican. They could have been Spaniards, Italians or Brazilians, but they were Californian, Mexican Californian -- ten of them -- all good-looking, all fun and funny, not one unsure of himself, though some were less forward than others -- great dancers, great talkers, great partyers. They were fun. They were exotic fun. The girls -- Irish, Portuguese, German, Polish, Italian, Hungarian, Croatian, and North American -- were *very* taken and wanted to spend the evenings with them, and the place to spend the evening, that is to say, the early morning hours, as my boys evidently found out, their first day in town, was Citluk.

Yes, they were all in the pansion at 1:00 or 1:15 every night. No, they were *not s*till there at 1:30. I'd go up to bed praising God and thanking Mary for these wonderful teens -- and ten minutes later, dressed to kill and ready to rock, the boys were back on the street, taking cabs, getting picked up by pre-arrangement, sometimes walking, a couple times *hitchhiking* to Citluk.

I hit the roof. The guys never saw the dad in me, like they saw him that morning, as we were leaving for Dubrovnik. I ordered all the seventeen-and-unders off the bus, stood them up alongside the curb and read them the riot act.

"What the HELL do you think you were doing? I have LEGAL responsibility for you! I have parental rights, signed over BY YOUR PARENTS! Your parents trust me, and I TRUSTED YOU! I gave you a LONG leash here – a ONE A.M. CURFEW! Because I wanted you to be free to enjoy yourselves. But I also wanted you to be safe, because I love you. This is how you repay me?!"

They did not protest. Not one of them. They understood perfectly and in fact, to a boy, looked ashamed. Nelson told me I was right and apologized. I was impressed, because Nelson and Ada had been in a sort of eh-eh category because their brothers were over 18. I was willing to consider letting them do things Mikey, Jorge, Fonz, etc. could not do—be out later or go places, so long as Oscar and Pancho took full charge. This may sound lenient, and no doubt it was, but it was leniency based on experience; I'd seen how Oscar and Pancho policed their younger brothers. They did a better job of it than I did. Nelson apologized. His instinct for justice had been touched by my anger.

Several of the other boys apologized as well, but I was too angry to do anything but continue to glower. I told them to get on the bus. They did. I told Pancho, Oscar and Matt (the 18 and up crowd) that I was really disappointed in them. None of them offered an excuse. All three looked dejected. We set off for Dubrovnik.

The drive down the coast to Dubrovnik is gorgeous, and I have many times since taken real pleasure in it. That morning, I was so caught up in my disappointment and anger at the boys that I could only manage a cursory appreciation for the spectacular Dalmatian coast.

We got to Dubrovnik and had a quick tour of the old city by a very nice and well-educated lady whom I tipped generously, maybe in part because I was feeling bad about my anger toward the boys. After the tour, we had lunch and after that a little time for shopping and some exploring of the old city area. The city was not just hot that day, it was sweltering. Dubrovnik's walls block off the sea breezes, and the dazzling white pavements throw the sunlight back up as residual heat: it is a hot, hot city in the summer -- hot even by Sacramento standards.

It is also an immensely fashionable city with more beautiful women — of all ages — than the boys had ever seen anywhere. Several of the guys pointed this out to me, and I agreed, but did little more than that. I was with the guys like a hawk, but I was hardly speaking to them, I was so deeply burdened by their disobedience. I was worried with a dad's burden of worry—guilt and disappointment and love and fear and all mixed up. This first visit to Dubrovnik we did not go up on the walls, and I remember little more than surface impressions of the city itself. What I most remember of my first visit to Dubrovnik is my anger at my boys.

Slaviska had been completely unaware of the situation between me and the boys, all day. But her pleasure in their company began to win through and by the time we were on the bus, mid-afternoon, she said, "Jim, we're all hot, and you're tired. The boys couldn't swim here this afternoon, but up the road about an hour is a nice beach with a good restaurant. We'll stop there and everyone can have iced tea or a beer or ice cream, and enjoy the view, and the boys can take off their shoes and socks and wade into the water to cool off a bit."

It was a nice restaurant and a beautiful creamy-sand beach against blue-green water, an Adriatic lagoon. There was a short cement dock down the beach a bit, which the boys quickly gravitated toward. The beauty of Dubrovnik had mitigated my anger a bit; maybe, too, it was my exhaustion from the heat. I was still not in a good mood, but. . . Down to the dock, because the boys were there, and after all, I did love them, and I had PARENTAL responsibility for them, signed over to me before a notary.

The water off the dock was deep enough to dive into. By the time I got there, most of the boys had already stripped to their shorts, and ever the group, they were arranging a collective splash-in. So much for Slaviska's suggestion that they "wade barefoot into the water…" Their ease and confidence in the situation made me smile in spite of myself. "Here, let me take a picture, first." I took five, and they are memorable. Loyd Simeroth was standing nearby, and he got the best shot, one where all of the guys are mid-flight between the dock and the blue-green water – they look, as Mom has said, like something out of Greek mythology. Mom to this day has a blow-up of Loyd's photo on her refrigerator in Marysville.

I stood watch on the dock, still really troubled by the boys' deception. I remember pacing back and forth, intensely conscious of the boys in the water, and at the same time intensely conscious of my mental image of them, sneaking out of the pansion at one-thirty, night after night after night after night. I loved them. I was angry at them. I was afraid for them. Afraid that their very strengths would be their undoing. Two nights left in Medjugorje — but then, Italy, Rome. Good God, I thought. Help me. Keep my boys safe.

"Jim," they shouted. "Come in!"

"No way."

"Come on! It's great!"

"Salty as hell. But it's still great!"

"Come on, Jimmy; come in!"

"Forget it."

Nelson said, "Jim, I feel so *free*."

I looked at him and smiled. After all, Nelson really had felt contrition. "So you should," I said. "You're swimming with all your best buddies in the Adriatic Sea!"

"I feel so free," he repeated, and up in a twirl over his head came his shorts.

"Nelson! Do you want to wind up in a Croatian jail? Put your shorts back on."

At which point one of the guys mooned me. I yelled again. "This is a *foreign country*! If you get in trouble with the cops here, I *can't help you*!!! Put your shorts back on — NOW!"

At which point an old Croatian man who'd observed all this, sunning himself nearby, crossed toward me on the short dock: "Young man," he said, in that wonderful Balkan accent, "don't be upset at the boys. Let them swim naked, if they want. This is Croatia. It's okay, in Croatia, for the young people to enjoy themselves."

I don't remember if I said anything at all; if I did, I don't remember what it was. I felt like a middle-aged Puritan, a feeling, I assure you, gentle reader, I have only very rarely experienced in life. I turned back to the guys, who were frolicking regardless, unaware of their vindication.

"COME IN!" they insisted, absolutely certain of my approbation, of my love and esteem for them.

129

I stalked the dock, watching, answering their entreaties with maybe some responses I do not want to include here, though the boys were not at all offended. I looked up the beach and saw Carl going in, saw Michelle in the water, along with some of the other ladies from our group.

"Jim! Come in!"

I thought, "When am I ever again going to have the chance to swim in the Adriatic Sea with my boys?" To thunderous cheers from the boys that brought looks from up and down the beach, I started unbuttoning my shirt.

***

When we got back to Medjugorje, I went straight to the statue of Mary in front of the plaza at St. James and knelt there, in the bright, hot light, saying rosaries for the boys, asking for help, for insight, and above all, asking that they be kept safe. In fact, over the years, this became my first prayer for the young people in Marysville and I have kept it since: Just get them safely into adulthood, Lord, and then let's worry about praying for their spiritual maturation, their sainthood. I never hesitated to tell the teens in my Confirmation classes that they should aim at sainthood, *in this life*. I would argue that after all, if you aim at Heaven and miss, there's a net— Purgatory. If you aim at Purgatory and miss…there's the big barbeque.

I think that one of the things we've missed in our de-emphasis the last few decades on the possibility of damnation is the human dignity implied by free will. God is no bully. He respects our free will. He respects the way we are made, and does not force us to choose him. We have a right to damnation, if we want it. And as C.S. Lewis has pointed out, in a manner of speaking, the damned are real successes: rebels to the end. They have their horrible freedom — the freedom, in fact, to choose slavery to some sin. Flannery O'Connor made the same point in her fiction: short stories and novels both. "He threw the whole thing off," her character The Misfit says, of Jesus, in A GOOD MAN IS HARD TO FIND, "and ever since, there ain't nothin' for it, but to follow Him, or find some meanness."

What's more, though we are free to choose them, the meannesses are limited and limiting. As a priest professor of mine at the Dominican School once put it, "Jim, after years of hearing confessions, you come to realize that there are only so many ways to be bad. But there is an infinite variety of ways to be good."

People have sometimes told me that one of the fears they have is that Heaven, or anyway, commitment to Christ in this life, is going to rob them of their individuality. A good example of this fear was provided by Mother Angelica who related the story of a woman who said she didn't want to come any closer to Christ because she was afraid God was going to want her to give up her house. Mother Angelica's smiling answer: "God doesn't want your house. He wants *you*."

And I'll add, he wants you as YOU. He has blessed you with your particular gifts, with your temperament, family background, friends, educational and employment experience: it is the person in and of these circumstances whom God wants to make a saint of. He is not asking you to sell all you have and give it to the poor. He is asking you to let him shine through you in the circumstances of your life, at once transforming both you and your circumstances, and not at all coincidentally, drawing others toward his light, through you. No one else has your life and no one else has your particular mission; no one else can reflect God at your particular point on the spectrum. No two gemstones are exactly alike, but they all refract light and shine with sparkling beauty. It's the same with us.

.

Muriel Spark, as long as I am quoting some of my favorite writers here, calls this process, this realization, the transfiguration of the commonplace. It is the recognition, the flash of insight that grace flows and surges through our daily lives, lighting up ordinary events with God's own love, so that everyday interactions become opportunities for sainthood itself. All reality changes in an instant, and yet, in fact, nothing has changed: we are still where we are, doing what we must do, but now, with Heaven itself shining through all of it, making it at once transparent and vibrant with new lights, with new colors, and with eternal meaning. This realization, once achieved, changes lives. It is the beginning of our own sainthood.

In any event, we got back from Dubrovnik late Monday afternoon, and I went straight down to St. James, and knelt before the statue of Our Lady, in the square, and prayed for my boys. It was hot. There was no shade, and there was little or no breeze. Pretty soon I was sweating, but I was glad to sweat; pretty soon my knees were tired of the cement, but I wanted to be uncomfortable. Good old Catholic penitential piety.

I am not one for suffering (who is?) but in that moment, I would have accepted a cross of some sort, for the good of the boys, for their safety and for their salvation. Six years later I was to ask for a cross on their behalf – and I got one! The details of that event are beyond the scope of this book, but I'll observe here that we must be very, very careful, asking for sufferings, no matter how much we want to help those we are asking to suffer for. Peter Kreeft has given some good advice on this question, in one or two of his books, and I am sure other Catholic authors have as well. It is absolutely true that great grace can be won, for ourselves and others, by patient and loving suffering, but in fact, most of us encounter crosses enough in life as is, without needing to ask for more. At any rate, that hot afternoon in Medjugorje, I was content with sore knees and, by the time I was done, an all-body sweat, on behalf of my boys.

An amusing anecdote from the trip, connected to the business of the nights in Citluk, was brought to my attention by some of the boys themselves. One of my pilgrims, Marge Simeroth, had worked as a yard supervisor at Lindhurst High for many years. The kids all knew, and respected, Marge. Marge spent some time every afternoon, sitting in the cool shade of the porch, at the pansion, and so was there when people would enter or exit. On one occasion, some of the boys showed up with several European girls. Marge shook her finger and said, in her authoritative (and British-accented) yard-supe tones: "Oh no you don't, young ladies. You can just wait right here in the lobby, while the young men go upstairs and freshen up." The boys later complained to me that Marge was "hating on us." I smiled. "Good for Marge," I said. "And don't even think about bringing girls to your rooms."

***

It was still early, an hour to the Croatian Mass at seven, and when I got back to the pansion, LaDonna told me that a bunch of the boys had gone to confession. There are always priests hearing confession in the square in front of St. James, before the Croatian Mass. They have signs which let people know which languages they speak, and some of the priests evidently can hear confessions in three or four languages.

The kids had to go to priests they did not know, as Father Leon had left the group at Dubrovnik, in order to fly to Rome that afternoon. We would meet up with him again, in Rome, toward the end of the week, but he needed to fly over early, because he wanted to see an old seminary professor, who would be leaving the city on Wednesday. The professor's name was Karol Wojtyla. Father Leon had been a new seminarian in Cracow, when Professor Wojtyla became John Paul II. Father Leon later told us that, when he told the Pope that he had just come from Medjugorje, the Pope smiled and said, "Ah! Medjugorje! A holy place. A holy place." John Paul II evidently expressed many times his desire to visit Medjugorje, which he called "the fulfillment and continuation of Fatima." He could not visit it, of course. I was, in any event, relieved to see how quickly my prayers for the guys were being attended to, in learning that most of them had gone up to the church for confession.

That night there was another public apparition on the hillside. We all went out after dinner and made the climb with the crowds, along the stony path. An American lady named Myrna, whom we had met during the week, took Mom's arm to offer to help her. Mom did not need Myrna's help, but wanted to be gracious, so let Myrna take her arm. About a fourth of the way up, Myrna, who had asthma, could not go any further, as she'd forgotten her inhaler. "This girl needs to sit down, Sara," Myrna said. "How about right here?" she continued, and directed Mom to a smooth, flat boulder sheltered by a couple of pomegranate trees, just off the path.

Mom was about to say that she would go up on her own, but something in Myrna's enthusiasm for her company, and in her confidence that that enthusiasm was returned, made Mom stay with her. They took seat on the boulder and watched as the pilgrims streamed past them. A couple of the boys, seeing Mom seated off to the side, crossed over and offered to help her up. Mom waved them on, smiling, and assuring them that this boulder was as far as she intended to go, tonight. Mom later told me that she and Myrna "felt" the time of the apparition, and that they "heard" it, too: that is, they knew it was happening when the utter hush came over the slope. Then came the murmurs of multi-lingual conversations, and the first pilgrims starting down.

We all caught up with each other at the Dubrovnik Club. We took up several tables. It was a nice, breezy night, perfect for an outdoor café, and the restaurant was packed. Slaviska had hurt her ankle coming down, and had been helped to level ground by Oscar and Pancho. She was with us at the restaurant. At one point, she turned to me and said something surprising, intending to be heard not just by me, but by the whole group, and especially the boys.

"Jim, tell your boys they are not putting anything over on me. I have heard all about them, all over town. I know every place they've been. I know everything they've done. I know who they sat with, who they danced with, who they drank with, what they drank and who paid for their drinks. They're famous, you know. Everyone looks for them, every night, at every club. When they show up, the party starts. Where ever they are, that is the place to be. I'm glad they are enjoying themselves. All Medjugorje's glad. Just tell them they aren't fooling me. Not for one minute."

Slaviska still knew nothing of my fury with the guys. I looked from her to the boys, who looked at once proud of themselves and a little abashed. Mom and Trudi were laughing. I laughed, too.

***

We spent Tuesday morning at Vicka's, under the grape trellises. Vicka is one of the six Medjugorje visionaries. She is gregarious and good-natured, and people are very drawn to her. She was giving a talk from the stone terrace of her family's house up near the base of Apparition Hill, and a couple hundred people gathered to listen. It seemed a good-sized crowd, but it was nothing at all like the crowds I have encountered on subsequent trips to Medjugorje. I mean, we could all see and hear Vicka easily. She was not more than a few dozen feet from any of us. (Of course, this was just a talk to the English-speaking pilgrims who happened to be in Medjugorje that morning. The visionaries give many such talks, throughout the week.)

I was with Claudia, Alma and Mikey. The four of us sat on a stone wall, maybe four feet above the street, and we were under the grapes that Vicka's family grew over the terrace. It was a fresh and cool morning. The pictures of Alma and Claudia under the leafy canopy, with bunches of grapes hanging here and there, are among my favorite from the trip.

Vicka's translator was a striking young redhead. I could not have known it at the time, but this young woman was someone "from my future." Her name was Slavenka; she was (and is) a guide, in Medjugorje; she is good friends with Slaviska, and starting the following June, when I would return to Medjugorje, and on every trip since, Slavenka would guide my pilgrims. She has become a good friend, and is an ardent fan of both my mom, and my boys.

I'm going to take a moment here for another philosophical observation: I would hold that people are "in our future" just as surely as they are "in our past." There are people we are meant to meet, in this life, and I have a faith that one way or another, depending on present and future actions, ours and theirs, we will link up. The timing and circumstances may have to be almost infinitely flexible, given the operation of free will, but I do believe that if we are meant to meet someone, assuming that neither of us simply digs in his/her heels and refuses to cooperate with grace, then, one way or another, we will meet that person.

The Prayer to St. Raphael is a Catholic prayer for guidance, where the people in our future are concerned. It starts off, "O Raphael, lead us to those we are waiting for, those who are waiting for us…" The prayer is taken from the story of Tobit in the Old Testament, in which the Archangel Raphael guides a young man to his future bride. I first encountered this prayer in the collected letters of Flannery O'Connor, THE HABIT OF BEING. O'Connor prayed the prayer daily, and I have, too, for more than a quarter of a century, now. There was a long time there, when I prayed to be led to my future editor, to my publisher. I smile now, thinking about that, and realizing that my future editor was all along looking back at me from the mirror, and that my future publisher and I had shared a bedroom, growing up together, in Marysville. At any rate, though I do not buy into fate or pre-destination, I am a believer in a non-random future. Choices we make today will influence how the future develops, but there are people waiting there in the future, for us, who, as long as grace is not utterly thwarted, will one day or another step into our lives. Slavenka Jelavic was such a person for me. I did not know her, that bright, fresh morning under the grape leaves at Vicka's, but simply in both of us being there, Slavenka and I had set the stage for our meeting ten months later.

Tuesday afternoon the kids were mostly shopping along the main street; it was our last day and they needed to buy whatever they wanted to take home with them, if they had not done so already. Some of us went back to Apparition Hill. I was in that party, and we found the slope almost empty, which made for a serene and prayerful climb. It was a relaxed afternoon for all of us; we had "done" Medjugorje, and we were all filled with gratitude and satisfaction with our stay there.

That evening, Fonz and Mikey got drunk at a Medjugorje bar with "the Irish girls." To my real satisfaction, they resisted going off to Citluk and came back to the pansion. I had never seen any of my boys drunk before and I remember thinking what a grace it was that they trusted me enough to show up at the pansion inebriated. We had all been at the Croatian Mass together, and when they did not show up for dinner at the pansion, after it, I went out looking for them along the main street. It was still light. I assumed they were doing some last-minute shopping. I did not find them, and came back to the pansion thinking they had probably since returned, which they had. They were waiting outside my room, laughing and talking in a way that told me immediately that they had been drinking. They blamed the Irish girls, who, after getting them drunk, had evidently sent them home for safekeeping. I suppose I was grateful to the Irish girls. Matt was with them, but I am no longer clear on the details of his presence – whether he had been at the bar with them, or not. I do remember that Matt was stone cold sober; he was their "designated driver," so to speak.

There was some talk of going to Citluk. I told Mikey and Fonz they were not going anywhere. Fonz was cool with that, but Mikey, annoyed, went off to his room. Sometime later, I found myself sitting on the curb in front of the pansion, with Fonz, Matt, Ada and Paul. It was dark by then, probably past nine. We were talking about the trip. The subject of Citluk came up again. Matt volunteered that Oscar and Pancho had gone back over, after dinner. I reiterated what I had said from the start: Oscar and Pancho (and Matt) could do as they saw fit: they were all legal adults, and I did not have to take official responsibility for them. I told Matt he was free to go, if he wanted, but unless I am mistaken, he stayed with us til we all went in.

That was my response to the suggestion of Citluk. This was Paul's: "I understand that you have a lot of fun in Citluk, with all the other young people. But think about where you are, right now. You are in Medjugorje, where the Blessed Mother herself appears every day. She is the one who brought you here. I know you know that. And this is your last night in town. Perhaps the Blessed Mother would like to have you close to her, tonight, making a little sacrifice in not going to the clubs. If she were to ask you to do that, you would do it, wouldn't you?"

I looked from Paul to the guys, a slow smile playing at the corners of my mouth. Damn, I was glad for Paul. He had a gentleness and a gravity that the kids really responded to. He was no pushover, but at the same time, and unlike me, he *never* had to raise his voice, to impress the kids with his seriousness. Ada said he'd really wanted to go to Citluk, but now was glad he'd stayed. It is an indication of who my boys are that they respond readily to this kind of suggestion. It was like going up Apparition Hill barefoot, Friday afternoon -- call the kids to something higher, challenge them to better things, call forth spiritual strength and they will provide it, they will show you what they can do. "Little Jim" was better at this than I was, and I watched with real gratitude as my boys calmed down and let thoughts of Citluk and its noise dissipate on the quiet night air.

***

The next morning, my unease about travel arrangements, absent the last six days, returned. Gino had said he would not be there to meet us; would anyone else be at Ancona for us? Did we have a place to stay in Assisi? In London, I'd been given the vouchers for the trip through Medjugorje; I had nothing for the Italian hotels, didn't even know the name of the place we'd be staying in Assisi. There was also the thought of the ferry – of course we would have no seats again, but at least it would be daylight, and the bar and restaurant would be open; there would be places to sit and no one would need to sleep.

I decided to deal with these anxieties one at a time, and only as the need for dealing with each arose. There was no need to worry about the bus to Split, where we would catch the ferry, and as Slaviska was going to the terminal with us, there was no need to worry about actually boarding the ferry. The worries lay on the Italian shore – I would deal with them, when we got there. Meanwhile, we had a magnificent Adriatic summer day for our journey.

I had missed the Dalmatian coast on the drive down from Split, because I had slept almost all the way. I had not been able to really appreciate the coast further south, on the way to Dubrovnik, because I was focused on my anger at the boys. This morning, on the way to

Split, I was fully able to drink in the beauty of the Croatian coast. I remember that Mikey, sitting behind me, said, at one point: "I want to come back here, Jim. I want to come back to Medjugorje. But first, I want to come to these beaches, commit lots of sins, and then go to Medjugorje, go to confession, go to Mass, climb Krizevac barefoot..." I laughed.

Slaviska was impressed that we had come on the ferry. American pilgrims did not arrive by ferry. "I knew this was a special group," Slaviska said. "I could tell from the first afternoon. You are real disciples and you are having a real pilgrimage, not a vacation. You are a spiritual group, and that's all of you including you guys back there. Are you listening?" she called over the mike to the boys, gathered, as always, toward the back of the bus. "Do you hear me, young men of California? I think there are five future priests on this bus—maybe a future sister or two, also."

The whole bus erupted with cheers given this stunning confirmation of what I had said about the boys all along. I jumped out of my seat and ran up the aisle to give Slaviska a hug. I am not sure the trip held a happier moment for me; surely it held no more inspiring one. I really felt Slaviska was speaking in the Spirit. She "got" my kids. She saw them exactly as they were and, like me, thought they were wonderful, just for being who they were in 1998. And like me, she sensed who they might become.

The Sansovino was waiting for us at the ferry terminal at Split. All I had was the return-trip deck accommodation voucher, so I went straight to the cashier's window and asked about seats. They had plenty available. I bought forty-one. It was about $6 a person, and I paid for it myself; not about to ask my people to pay for something that should have come with their ticket to begin with.

Our group spread out happily and comfortably across our great block of seats. Some were content to stay there most of the eight-hour trip; Marge slept most of the way, so did Mikey and Ada. But many of us were all over the boat, all day long. It was about as perfect as a day at sea can get: bright, sunny, warm, with cool sea breezes. Paul went to the bar and came back with a Coke for Trudi, white wine for Mom and himself, and the three of them took seat on an open-air bench, and toasted the day. But for Mikey and Ada, the boys were all over. There was a Jacuzzi and sundeck, and the restaurant was open. A number of the group had lunch, and some lingered afterward at the tables, playing cards, having a drink. Claudia and Michael Klug stayed awake all day, clowning around with pictures of some of the guys, as they slept. At some point, most of the kids did nap.

It is a long time, leaving the Croatian coast and its islands behind. We had been at sea close to two hours, before they disappeared from view. It was then maybe five hours or so, before Italy appeared on the western horizon. By the time we were approaching the Italian coast, all the guys were awake and back on deck, and I was glad, as the views were nice. The Italian hills looked blue in the late afternoon light, rising above a sparkling blue sea; I got a lot of photos of the guys on deck, with the Italian coast behind.

The crossing that afternoon had been wonderful. Now, here we were back on the Italian side. Gino had assured me he would not be here to meet us. Would anyone?

FOUR

We came ashore at Ancona and were surprised -- and relieved -- to find Gino there to greet us. We went to dinner at a nice restaurant near the wharves and then got onto the bus for the drive to Assisi. Most of my pilgrims slept -- it was a couple hours' drive. We arrived in Assisi after midnight and were put up at two hotels side-by-side in the "new" part of town, below the medieval (actually, Roman-era) city on the hill. Most of the adults were in the other hotel. The kids and I were at a place called the "Fratre Sol" ("Brother Sun"). It was a nice place, comfortable, clean, quiet, and it had a great breakfast the next morning in its bright and sunny, many-windowed dining room.

Getting in that night, Mikey had come to my room to ask me what Assisi was all about. He'd heard from me about St. Francis, but had not connected the "saint of the animals" with this city. The door was open and I heard a lot of noise from the other guys. I had to go to their rooms and tell them to be quiet; it was, in fact, the only time on the trip that I had to ask the kids to keep it down. Of course, this was due in no small part to the fact that, most nights in Medjugorje, the kids were nowhere near their rooms...

Anyway, I spent some time talking to Mikey about St. Francis. Then I took a shower, getting all the salt from the day at sea off me, and went to bed, for the first time assured that the rest of the trip was secure. It really was a major relief, to land at Ancona and find Gino waiting for us, to have gone to such a good restaurant that evening, and then to find ourselves here in Assisi at two attractive and comfortable hotels. I was thanking the Blessed Mother for our smooth arrival in Italy, and really was no longer worried about the rest of the trip.

I woke up the next morning thinking about my sister Liz. It was powerful, how much I was thinking about her, almost as if experiencing her presence. It occurred again in the hotel's sunny breakfast room, where the spread was so good that I regretted that I am just not a breakfast kind of guy. My stomach is the last part of me to wake up: I like lunch at two and dinner at ten, and I do not eat breakfast at all, even though I love most breakfast food. Anyway, sitting there with my coffee and watching with a smile as the kids loaded up their plates at the expansive buffet, I thought of Liz again, saw her in my mind's eye fighting for farm workers in the fields of the Sacramento Valley, saw her organizing parents and teachers in poor neighborhoods in Oakland. It did not yet occur to me why my sister might be coming to mind so powerfully.

Our first stop was the immense baroque Cathedral in the lower, modern city. This church is named for Our Lady, Queen of the Angels, and its name underscores just how deeply Franciscan California's heritage is. Obviously, San Francisco was named for Francis, Santa Clara, for St. Claire, Ventura County for St. Bonaventure and so on. But Los Angeles was named for THIS CHURCH. The church itself is a knock-out, if you go for baroque, which I do. Many, if not most pilgrims, however, are drawn to the cathedral for the "Little Chapel" of Francis which sits inside the great church, the Portiuncula. In Francis' time, there had been no lower city, and the area where the cathedral now stands was open countryside. When the cathedral was built, the chapel was simply incorporated into it. The chapel is very small; maybe twenty people can stand in it at once, shoulder to shoulder. I remember that on a later pilgrimage we once celebrated Mass at the

Portiuncula, but I and maybe half of my pilgrims had to stand out in the main cathedral; there simply was not room for all of us inside.

The place was swarming with priests -- okay, okay, that doesn't quite sound right -- there were many priests at the cathedral that morning, and quite a few of them were hearing confession in various languages. Claudia went, as did a couple of the boys. I remember watching them lining up. I smiled. We were on pilgrimage, all right!

The cathedral contains other beautiful chapels and it is the home of the famous thornless roses of Assisi. This is a variety of rose which apparently will not grow beyond the district of Assisi, and which has no thorns. The story is that Francis, tempted by sexual desire, said to his body, "I will give you sensation!" and threw himself into a bunch of rose bushes, intending to make himself bleed and hurt. Instead, the thorns disappeared as the saint landed amid the branches and blooms, and they never have reappeared on this variety of rose. "How charming," I would say; "Whatever," my sister Anne would say.

The main church at the Basilica of St. Francis was inaccessible, because of the 1997 earthquake. Much of the upper city, in fact, was under scaffolding -- indeed, there were construction cranes and scaffolding as late as summer, 2000, when I would return to Assisi several times. We couldn't get into the Basilica of St. Clare at all, but we were able to visit the tomb chapel at the bottom of the Basilica of St. Francis. Here again, Liz came to mind, and while I was down there I realized why I had been thinking so much of her. I was in Assisi. Francis was *her* saint. She'd loved him from very early in life -- had wanted to take his name in Confirmation, and she meant *his* name, not "Frances," which all the same, she was forced (by some well-meaning nun) to settle for. Her whole life had been driven by her concern for the poor, for the marginalized, for those who experience racism, sexism and poverty.

The first real memories I have of my sister the activist date to the 1968 presidential contest. I was 12 and Liz 13, and we both wanted Bobby Kennedy 'til June 6, when we wanted McCarthy. Then came the Democrat National Convention in Chicago -- a watershed moment in my own political consciousness. I can still see Abe Ribicoff shaming Mayor Daley for his tactics from the podium. I can still hear the chant from the angry street crowds, "The whole world is watching!" Liz came away a reluctant but reliable supporter of Hubert Humphrey. But after Chicago, I wanted Nixon. And I wanted him again in 1972, when Liz walked precincts for McGovern. Her work with Cesar Chavez came later, when she was in college: she quit school, in fact, to organize for the farm workers fulltime (fulltime meaning seventy- and eighty-hour weeks). She did this for several years. She finished school in her early thirties and became a kindergarten teacher precisely because she felt that if kids could be reached at an early-enough age, their lives could be changed for the better. By the summer being written about here, Liz was organizing parents and teachers for educational reform in Oakland. As Mom once put it, in taking on the problems of the city of Oakland, Liz finally had a cause big enough for her energies.

Anyway, here I was in Assisi -- and my sister simply came to mind again and again and again, and finally, there at the tomb in the dark and quiet crypt church, I figured it out. It's Francis! He wants you to let Liz know how grateful he is for all she

does; he wants you to tell Liz how much he loves her. When I
got back to California, I did just that.

It would not be going too far to say that the spirit of Francis --
peaceful, irenic, joyful, reverent, but playful -- lingers over
Assisi. Several people I know who've been there agree; as one
of my priests on a later pilgrimage was to observe, "the power
of the saint's personality has transformed the local geography."
He was speaking actually, of Anthony and Padua, but this is a
good way to describe Francis and Assisi.

We had lunch on the hill. Many of the group headed toward
the quick-lunch vendors at the big bus parking lot a little way
down the hill, but I saw from that lot a terrace restaurant that
looked really attractive and suggested it to Mom and Trudi.
The restaurant was in the Subasio Hotel. Robert Haldeman,
Alicia's older son, joined us. The restaurant, open-air, offered
cool shade under a dense canopy of grape vines. It looked out
over the lower city and the surrounding countryside, by turns
green and summer-gold. The shade made for a nice contrast
with the sundrenched panorama beyond the wrought-iron rail.
The sense of cool retreat was underscored by a plashing
fountain.

"Wow," Trudi said, as we crossed the stone terrace toward our
table. "Good choice, Jim!"

I remember that the lunch menu included eggs and -- finally
ready to eat breakfast, though it was probably one in the
afternoon -- that's what I had. I got some great shots from our

table, not just of Assisi, but of that lovely garden-like restaurant, as well. On several subsequent trips to Assisi, I have only once found the restaurant open. I would have lunch there every time I am in Assisi, if I could.

It was in Assisi, up on the hill, among the medieval buildings and the great churches, that I watched my kids, laughing and talking and taking photos and shopping, and I thought how blessed I was to be witnessing their first experience of Europe. It occurred to me what a unique joy this was, and I wished that their parents could have been blessed with it, as well. It is hard to describe feelings of the deepest gratitude. That is the sort of feeling I had, in that moment.

At some point that afternoon, we got on the bus to head for Rome, driving through southern Umbria with its gentle hills, its olive orchards and vineyards. We saw several gorgeous villas and many handsome farm houses, along the way. It was bright, warm, sunny -- this is a beautiful region of Italy. The vegetation was a bit thicker, and more subtropical, as we drew near the coast. In less than two hours, we came into Lazio, the region of Rome.

***

The Marco Aurelio, we discovered, was a good tourist-class hotel somewhat left to seed. The pool had no water and the grounds had been left to nature, with the result that things which could thrive unaided in the long, dry Mediterranean summer—oleander and certain flowering vines—were overgrown and riotous, and everything else was dead. The rooms were fine and everyone had a private bath. The lobby and bar downstairs were a nice place to gather late in the day or at night. The dining room in the basement had all the charm of an Army mess -- though the food was good enough. The staff in the dining room was so rude that they became a source of amusement to us. In any event, our time at the hotel was limited.

And the first night there, I was deeply pleased to discover, by going out and walking with some of the guys, that we were too far from anywhere for the boys to get into any trouble, or to be out late. They didn't know the bus lines (and neither did I) and cabs were too expensive: we still had four days to go and the guys didn't want to run out of money, so the safety and quiet of our nights in Rome was pretty much assured. Especially after Citluk, I had been worried, about the boys, at night, in Rome. Roman nightlife was legendary centuries before Anita Ekberg's nocturnal frolic in Trevi Fountain in LA DOLCE VIDA, after all. On the one hand, I wanted my kids to really see and experience Rome. On the other, if anything at all was going to be happening "after hours," here in Rome, I was determined to see to it that it happened with me in charge. The boys were not only cool with this, they were on my case for never partying with them in Medjugorje...

Well, as I say, that first night in Rome, the boys and I did what we had done in London, except that we came up empty. The nightlife districts of Rome (Trastevere, Piazza Navona, the Via Veneto) were simply too far away for us to walk to them. There was a tobacconist across the street from our hotel and I mean, it was a store and semi-cafe kind of place, with beer and wine and sidewalk tables, and after we had determined that we were nowhere near any nightlife district, we spent the better part of that first night there. We sat at the streetside tables, with Coronas, which greatly pleased the kids who were old enough to drink in Italy: Mexican beer in Rome.

The next morning we toured the patristic basilicas -- well, no we didn't. We saw two of these four famous churches that morning: St. John Lateran and St. Mary Major. I'd seen all of the patristic basilicas in 1989, with Uncle Jim, and remembered loving St. John Lateran the best. It was the same thing through this time and, in fact, it has been the same thing, every time since. They are all magnificent, but for my money, St. John Lateran is the stand-out. I can't point to any one or two reasons why without demeaning five or six other reasons why: it is simply my favorite church in Rome. It is, in fact, the most important church in the Catholic world -- more important than St. Peter's, which is simply the Pope's residence. St. John Lateran is the Pope's cathedral, it is the ecclesial seat of the Diocese of Rome, and as such, it is considered the Mother Church of all Catholic churches throughout the world (and don't you still hate Saddam Hussein for calling Desert Storm the "Mother of All Wars" and so forever cheapening the power of that expression?).

In any event, a full tour of the major basilicas of Rome includes not just St. John Lateran and St. Mary Major, but St. Paul-Outside-the-Walls and, oh yeah!, St. Peter's. Well, on our morning excursion, our young Roman guide showed us only John Lateran and Mary Major (they are quite close to one another), explaining that she had only been hired for the morning and going to St. Paul and St. Peter would have required her being with us into the afternoon. Sergio's cost-cutting, which angered some of us, but honestly, knowing what I did of how this trip had been patched together at the very last possible moment, I was okay with it.

We were dropped off at St. Peter's and left to see it on our own. I had no problem with that, as I knew St. Peter's, and so did Mom, and anyway, I'd found our guide obnoxious with her incessant references to "the great aristocratic families of Rome," to families which could trace their ancestry back to the Roman Senate, to ducal and baronial estates which in recent decades had been surrendered (sadly, if we were to infer anything from her tone) to the people and/or the city of Rome. This young lady seemed really enamoured of Rome's wealth, and in particular of antique Roman wealth, a fascination I thought shallow and uncritical. I am naturally unimpressed with great wealth and naturally suspicious of inherited privilege, and in any event, ours was a Catholic pilgrimage: we weren't interested in hearing about the great aristocratic hunting parties sponsored by the Barberinis on their vast looted estates around the city of Rome. Our guide evidently thought we'd find the Vatican Post Office and gift shop more interesting than St. Peter's itself, and took us there for forty or more minutes, though I must admit, the time we spent there was mostly because people were going to the bathroom, getting bottled water or coffee, or buying postcards.

Although I have never held that it is important to have an opinion on everything, I do in fact have some strong opinions. But I more often than not keep them to myself, and in any event, have always been able to talk to almost anyone about almost anything. I found myself on the sunny sidewalk with our guide, waiting for people to be done at the gift shop, and made some pleasant comment about how much I loved Rome, and she told me that she couldn't live anywhere else. This remark went some way in endearing her to me. It is a great thing, I think, to love your native place. When I was first looking into priesthood, I told the Lord he could send me anywhere. I told him I would leave California, if he wanted me to.

I know I could happily live in many places other than California --
Manhattan, New Orleans, London, Lisbon, Caracas, and in fact,
Rome -- but I also have come, over the years, to revere California
and am glad that God did not ask me to give up the Golden State.

Paul and I had opportunity to discuss our guide later that day. As
always, he was gentler than I in his judgment, or at least in how he
expressed it: "She's very young," he observed (she was, I suppose,
about Paul's own age, not yet 30). "She is very young and she is
idealistic; she loves the antiquities and the history of civilization
itself which exists so palpably here in Rome. That is all quite
laudable. There can be, however, a subtle influence that creeps in
with these attachments." Paul equated this influence with
Freemasonry, and if this association freaks you out, or causes you
to scratch your head and ask, "What's wrong with the Masons?"
let me assure you, inquiring reader, I once did the same thing.
What's wrong with the Masons? Consult the thirteen Papal
documents since 1738, condemning their philosophy as being a
variant of naturalism: materialistic and in essence, anti-Christian.

In any event, we got to St. Peter's on our own. Dumped at the
Vatican Post Office, we really were already there. We just
needed to cross the Square, to enter Catholicism's grandest and
most famous church. I can still remember my own first reaction
to St Peter's, when I was there with Uncle Jim, in 1989. I walked
through the place (as so many first time visitors do) with my
mouth open. But unlike so many others, including good friends of
mine who are not Catholic, I was NOT favorably impressed. My
first reaction to St. Peter's was, "My God. Martin Luther was
right." Let's just say I have issues with ecclesiastical displays of
great wealth, and nowhere on earth is the Church's wealth so
impressively on display as it is, at St. Peter's.

Over the years, I have mellowed somewhat, in that first reaction. I understand that the art treasures at the Vatican belong to no one. I have heard the argument -- from atheists and Protestants alike -- that the Vatican should sell all its art and give the money to feed the poor. You know what? If the Vatican sold all of its art treasures, which are available for the world to see, the poor would eat for a day, and the art would disappear forever from view, into the private collections of billionaires.

And do consider the art. The Pieta. The Apollo Belvedere. The Sistine Chapel. The side chapels. The mosaics. The high altar and baldacchino. The colossal statues. My favorite is the one of St. Helena. If Helena were in the private collection of some titled and fabulously wealthy dude in Austria or Argentina, I would never have seen her. So, as far as I am concerned, end of argument. Leave the art just where it is. Is it perhaps a little disconcerting that the Church established by Jesus Christ has a headquarters that outshines Buckingham Palace, in terms of being just absolutely fabulous? Damn straight, it is. But you know what? That is the situation as it has come down to us. Let's try to be sensible about it. No one is gonna inherit the Vatican. The treasures there really are for all humanity. And the fact is, they offer a testament to the Church's own claim: in sponsoring, rescuing and preserving for posterity so much art down through the ages, the Church shows herself to be the friend of man, the supporter and ally of our many noble instincts and passions: she is no mean-spirited sect, destroying icons and burning books. The Church extols artistic genius, and commends and supports art's loftiest ambitions.

Having said that, let's say this. I have to laugh, every time I think about the panels in the floor of St. Peter's that tell you where the other great churches of the Christian world measure up. Here, one-third, maybe, of the way in to the high altar, is where St. Patrick's in New York ends. Here, maybe half the way in, is where Notre Dame Paris ends. Here, maybe three-fifths of the way in, is where St. Paul's, London ends. (I am just throwing these out -- I do not know the actual distances, for any of these churches.) I mean, come on. Are we impressed with ourselves, or what? On this one, with my sister Anne, imagine my eyes rolling heavenward: "Whatever."

In any event, my pilgrims and I crossed the Square, and visited the Vatican. And the kids loved it. I have many pictures of them at St. Peter's, and you can see how impressed they were. I have always been very ready to admit that my initial take on St. Peter's is NOT typical. Typically, people are blown away. The kids loved St. Peter's. They loved St. John Lateran and St. Mary Major, especially, in the latter, the crib chapel.

Nelson got a lot of video inside the basilica. Some of it is watchable. (The guys had a tendency to do fast pans with the camcorder, creating a spinning sensation that could leave you feeling slightly sea-sick. But Nelson's video inside the Vatican included some good, long, steady shots.) We took pictures outside as well as in, and I have several favorites of the kids in the colonnade. There is one in particular in which six of the guys are spaced naturally -- it was not posed -- among the columns, and as Liz put it, when she saw the photo, "the young men are like pillars themselves, there among the pillars of stone." There's also a shot of nine of them lined up by one of the fountains in the Square that I really love.

We didn't go to Peter's Tomb and we didn't go to the top of the dome, which I know the kids would've loved. By the time we got to St. Peter's it was almost noon, and meanwhile Brigitta had heard an upsetting rumor: because of the holiday (Feast of the Assumption) next day, the Vatican museums, including the Sistine Chapel, were closing early; at 1 p.m. It was already going on one. We couldn't walk the distance to the Vatican museum entrance, and be there before one. I was disappointed; in 1989, we had not gotten to the Chapel, either. I had assumed I would finally see it, this trip. I was disappointed, but practical: the kids are starving, let's get lunch. Then we can come back here, to the basilica. There's still plenty to see here. But Mom disagreed, and she was adamant: "After lunch, we take our chances on the Sistine Chapel being open. I want our kids to see it. This is Rome, this is the Vatican, this is Michelangelo; this is the heritage and the right of our kids. After lunch, the Sistine Chapel. Jimmy, we simply canNOT not go there."

I let out an exaggerated sigh. "Okay, Mom. Fine. Lunch first."

Out in the bright Roman noonday sun, one of those smart 30-ish Italian women who represent restaurants found us and experienced absolutely NO sales resistance to her pitch. Smart, contemporary decor, air-conditioning and comfortable seating, great pizza, salads and Roman specialties, modest prices. We followed her to the nearby restaurant and found her to be truthful in her advertising. About a quarter after two, everyone relaxed and refreshed, we set off toward the Vatican museums and the Sistine chapel. I really thought this was a wild goose chase, but along the way noted the many vendors -- with brightly colored Roma t-shirts, rosaries, medals, calendars, post cards, picture books in eight or ten languages, prayer cards, devotional booklets -- we could, at least, get in some good shopping, on our inevitable disappointed walk back to the basilica.

Well, lo and behold: the museums were open. They were open all afternoon. I was deeply surprised, as was Brigitta, and we were all very grateful to Mom, for *insisting* that we go, go for the sake of the kids, if nothing else. I turned to Mom with big eyes that said, "Okay. Thank you!!!" Mom paid for the tickets for all the kids. Individually, the tickets were not expensive, but we, the kids and I, were beginning to reach that point in the trip where we were counting our remaining lire and travelers checks.

The long, long walk through the galleries to the Sistine Chapel, as anyone who has taken it knows, is a treasure in itself. Those long, spacious corridors hung with tapestries, crowded with Greco-Roman statuary, medieval maps of Italy and so on. Among other things, we passed the tomb of St. Helena, the first Christian Roman Empress and mother of Constantine; Helena also happened to be the first Christian pilgrim in history. She left Constantinople at or near age eighty, to tour the Holy Land, and she loved it there so much, she never returned. She died in Palestine some six or seven years later, having erected churches, monasteries and shrines commemorating the great events of Christ's life and ministry. It is because of Helena that we have any certainty as to the sites of the Crucifixion, of the Resurrection, of the Annunciation, and so forth. Helena had become my patroness, in fact, when I realized that I, and not Maria Uribe, was in charge of this trip. Helena has ever since been one of my favorite saints, and I consult with her regularly, on matters pertaining to my pilgrimages.

We got to the Sistine Chapel at last. By 1998, of course, the long restoration was completed. I stepped down into the chapel, looked up and...gasped. This time, I did *not* invoke the name of Martin Luther. This wasn't opulence. This was something I could relate to: it was heroic art. It was genius. I stood looking up, just in awe. There were a good number of people there that afternoon, but it wasn't just packed, as it would be two years later, during the Jubilee Year, and when I would visit the Chapel five or six times. You could move around comfortably, sit down along the benches, as many of the older folks did. I wandered slowly through the chapel end-to-end, admiring and...admiring and...admiring. Nothing could have prepared me for it. I was with some of the kids, off and on, and explaining various sections of the painting to them, the Last Judgment at one end and Judith and Holofernes at the other: "Who's that naked dude on the bed?" asked Fonz. "Holofernes, the Assyrian Commander-in-Chief." "She cut off his head?" "That's what the Bible says." "Did he really reach for it like that, after it was gone?" "Scripture is mute on that point."

Fonz was told twice to stop videotaping. The third time, he was escorted out. I found out about this after the fact, as we were all gathering at the far end, to leave. I asked where Fonz was, and JD told me he'd gotten the boot. I was upset for Fonz, but needn't have been. First off, he got plenty of great video to show at home, and to treasure indefinitely. Second off, consider Fonz's cool and unruffled attitude about being booted from the Vatican...

"It's just Sony and their copyright," he explained to me, out on the street. "They paid for the restoration, and they want to be able to sell any video of the place themselves." He then suggested what

Sony could go do with themselves and their high-priced videos, a suggestion I shall refrain from quoting here.

"Whatever," I said. "You're lucky they didn't pull your tape out."

"They're lucky they didn't try," Fonz answered.

The kids, finding Mom, could not thank her enough. Nor could I. I can still see Mom, her red hair ablaze in the Roman sun, with the kids around her, thanking her, thanking her, for her insistence that we go to the Sistine Chapel, despite the report that it was closed. I want to think that all my kids will see the Sistine Chapel again, but to date, not one of them has. We all owed Mom a huge debt of gratitude.

After the Sistine Chapel, we decided to take some time to just look around at the Vatican. Some of us went back into St. Peter's, some went to the gift shop, some tarried among the many, many street vendors. I remember that about six or six-thirty that afternoon, I was hailing cabs out at the edge of the Square, to get us back, in groups of three and four, to the hotel. We had done the Vatican. We were satisfied.

That evening, just before dinner, the guys decided to play an American-youth-in-Rome version of the old `50s stunt of how many college boys could you squeeze into a telephone booth. The rickety and slow elevators at the Marco Aurelio had signs denoting their capacity: four persons. Eight of the guys crowded into one of them and closed the doors and started up and promptly got stuck between floors. I was going up and down the stairs at the hotel because, even though my room was on the sixth floor, it was so much faster than the elevators. I came out from the stairwell into the corridor on my floor and Barbara Pauls told me, "Jim, some of the boys crowded into one of the elevators, and now it is stuck between floors."

I was tired. Not in the mood. In need of a shower, and maybe some adult company before dinner. My plan had been to shower, change, go find Mom and Trudi and go down to the bar for a beer or two. I remember that I said to Barbara, "Well, I guess that's a lesson for them."

She looked surprised.

"Barbara," I said, "there's only so much I can take responsibility for."

"I understand," she said. All the same, I think Barbara was disappointed in me.

I got to my room, and of course, thought better of it. I looked sadly at the shower, where I wanted to go, and instead, took up my key, and went back out. I crossed down the six flights of stairs. Mom was there, and Trudi, and Barbara, and several others from our party, all concerned about the safety of "our kids." Barbara saw me as I came through the stairwell door. She smiled.

The guys had apparently been laughing earlier. They'd been stuck for maybe four or five minutes, laughing, and at the same time yelling, "We're stuck! Help!" and pressing the emergency bell. In the few minutes that they had been caught, however, they had apparently begun to realize that they might be stuck a while, and --

"Can you hear them?" said Mom.

"Hear them what?" I said.

Mom just indicated the elevator doors, through which, now that I was listening, I could hear the strong, happy, confident sound of eight teen-aged boys -- praying the Rosary.

"Holy steer manure," I said. Actually, I said something else, but it comes to the same thing.

The hotel staff was on it, and they had the guys safely down within another three or four minutes. The sound of the elevator moving was accompanied by two sets of cheers -- one from us on the ground, and one from within the elevator.

The elevator reached ground, the doors opened, and the guys streamed out -- all eight of them bare-chested. They'd taken their shirts off as the stuffiness and heat in the elevator climbed. They glowed like a bunch of young Olympians and smiled with the joy of released captives -- "Whoa, Jim! That was scary, man!" "Did you hear us?" "We were praying, man! You should be proud of your boys!" "We asked Our Lady to help us, and she did!"

I turned to Mom. "I'm ready for a drink," I said. "How about you?"

After our dinner in the basement, liberally spiced and seasoned with insults from the dining room staff, most of the group went across the street to the tobacconist's, and had coffee or a soda or a Mexican beer. When the tobacconist closed, we came back to the hotel bar, and had a couple more drinks there. It was a very relaxed and enjoyable evening; all the pilgrims, from the kids to the Cruzes, simply enjoying one another's company, and the fact that we were in Rome. I suppose, too, that that Friday night had this going for it: we had now done the main events of the pilgrimage. We had thoroughly explored Medjugorje, and we had, today, really seen the Vatican. These were, of course, the main points of our trip. We had another full day in Rome, and we had a plan for it, but whatever happened from here on out, we had accomplished our pilgrimage goals. We were a happy and contented lot, and we raised a toast to the fact.

***

Saturday, we were on our own, in Rome. Most of the group wanted to return to the Vatican, where there were major festivities, given that this was August 15, the Feast of the Assumption. Paul, Brigitta and I were agreed, though, that the kids should see some of classical and secular Rome. We decided, after consulting a map, that many of the must-see places were an easy walk for a bunch of teen-agers, it was just a matter of getting down to those areas of the city, and so, arranging for several cabs with the hotel desk...

We were dropped off at the Coliseum. I was astounded to see the fabled Roman arena covered in scaffolding, as had been the facade of St. Peter's, the day before. Rome was determined to give itself a face-lift, for the Jubilee. There was a long, slow-moving line to get into to the Coliseum, and we decided to pass. The guys could look through the barred entrances and get a sense of the interior of the Coliseum, in any event. The kids got a kick out of the Roman soldiers and gladiators, posing for pictures with tourists. A year later, when the film GLADIATOR came out, the guys were very pleased with the fact that they had actually been to the Coliseum and so were able to make a personal connection with this fact of classical Roman history and a brand new American hit film.

The Arch of Constantine is right next to the Coliseum, of course, and we took a lot of pictures in front of it. After that, we walked alongside the Forum. We could not enter it, as it was closed for Jubilee renovation, but again, you could peer in and get a good look at the many stone monuments, cultic statues, columned temples and pagan shrines: the glory that was Rome. The kids got a good idea of it, all right.

We crossed up past the "Wedding Cake" monument of Victor Emmanuel, and I gave the kids a thumbnail sketch of nineteenth century Italian history. We walked on to Trevi Fountain. It was a bright, hot morning, going on noon. The Via del Corso is, of course, a busy, heavily-travelled city thoroughfare. Trevi, in contrast, was a cool, translucent lake. I think we'd all have been glad, standing or sitting by its cool spray, to pull an "Adriatic" -- strip to our shorts and dive in, girls included. I know that I thought once again of Marcello Mastroianni and Anita Ekberg, in that famous scene from LA DOLCE VITA. We posed for pictures and, despite the many places at Trevi for food, drink and ice cream, at my insistence, we pressed on. "We'll have lunch at the Spanish Steps," I promised the kids. "They are not far away."

Boy, were the kids glad that I had made them wait. We arrived at the Piazza de Espana to find something rather exciting going on -- at a cafe with a large outside seating area, a film was being shot; here was modern, secular Rome right up front. The kids were so taken with the movie set that they ignored the Egyptian obelisk marking the entrance to the Piazza until I pointed it out to them, trying all the while to tell them about Imperial Rome's fascination with Egypt, which was already vastly more ancient, in Caesar's day, than is Caesar, in ours.

We all were, I'll admit, fascinated with the film in progress, and so I was unprepared when --

"Jim! Jim!" Fonz, running across the Piazza to us. "We found a McDonald's! WE FOUND A MCDONALD'S!"

Alma and Claudia were with him. "Jim!" Alma said. "You have to SEE this McDonald's!"

I am not sure that the kids had a happier moment on the trip. Oh, they'd been good. They had been very cosmopolitan and open, with regard to the food, in London, in Medjugorje, in Italy. Their satisfaction with varied cuisines had made me smile; they were the sort of young Americans who ought to travel. (And in fact, the food had been great, the whole trip.) But it had been almost two weeks since they had had American food of any kind, let alone a hamburger, let alone still more a MCDONALD'S hamburger. They were practically leaping for joy. Paul, Brigitta and I looked at each other; shrugged and smiled. Then we called the rest of the guys to attention, and followed Fonz and the girls across the Piazza to --

The most outrageous and opulent McDonald's I have ever seen. Moorish arches that (however incongruously) bring to mind the cathedrals of central Spain. Black-and-white tiled floors. Fountains and potted palms. Framed photos of famous Roman sites. It was so unreal that I had to look twice at the big-board menu, to make sure this really was a McDonald's. But sure enough, and to the absolute delight of all of the kids, there it was: the universal McDonald's menu, right down to the Big Macs and super-sized fries. The kids ordered happily, and I paid happily -- we were now, after the shopping blitz yesterday, at the Vatican, really beginning to run low on money. McDonald's fit our budget perfectly.

After lunch, we climbed the Spanish Steps to the Church of Trinita dei Monti. The kids mostly took a quick glance around this beautiful church, then went back out and sat along the wall lining the steps, watching the in-progress filming of the movie. I stayed inside the cool, quiet church for some minutes. There is in the vestibule a statue of Christ, the Christ of the Passion, that I particularly love. His wrists are tied and he has a look of surrender to what is to come which deeply touched me, the first time I saw it, with Uncle Jim, in 1989. That same feeling came over me, seeing it again, now, nine years later. I just stood there gazing at the statue, and feeling close to him. This was one of the trip's most serene moments for me. I can feel its serenity even today.

I came back out into the bright light of the Roman summer afternoon. I saw the kids along the wall above the steps, saw the crowd in the Piazza, saw the movie being filmed, and I smiled. The view from the top of the steps is unrivalled. I crossed to Paul, Brigitta and the kids and suggested that we move it along -- to the Piazza Navona. But first, a stop at the Pantheon.

I had taken a class at the Graduate Theological Union, the previous semester, offered by the Greek Orthodox faculty, called "Encountering the Holy." It was, basically, a class about pilgrimage. I had done two papers, in this class, on Roman sites: St. Mary Major and the Pantheon. I had seen St. Mary Major in 1989, with Uncle Jim. It had impressed me a great deal more, of course, this time around, as I now knew so much more about it.

St. Mary Major is dedicated to the Mother of God. It was erected in 432 to coincide with the Council of Ephesus' 431 decree that Mary, the God-bearer, or Theotokos, was not simply the mother, as Nestorius claimed, of Jesus' human nature -- no one is the "mother" of a "nature." Women are mothers of persons. And Jesus' Person was at one and the same time human and divine: therefore, Mary, Mother of God. This great church stood on the Esquiline Hill, on the site of the ancient Temple of Juno Lucina. Juno, Mother of the Gods. The Church knew what it was doing -- inculturating Roman mythic understandings so as to assist the people in their grasp of the Catholic faith.

The other great Roman monument to inculturation that I wrote on was the Pantheon. Built originally while Christ walked the earth, in 26 AD, it was damaged in a fire and then expanded and made into the grand temple of all the gods and goddesses by Hadrian in the early second century. It was probably the most opulent temple of the Imperial era, with real diamonds and sapphires in the jewelry of the goddesses, walls of onyx, pink marble, carnelian and so on.

It was given to the Pope by the Byzantine Emperor Phocas in the early seventh century, by that time something of a derelict shadow of its former self, in terms of ornamentation, but structurally as sound and as grand as ever. It was consecrated as a Catholic Church and named for Mary and All the Saints -- all those niches and altars built for Venus, Apollo and Mars became homes for statues of such as Mary Magdalene, Stephen and Barnabas. Cart loads of bones from the catacombs were brought as relics to be re-buried at the site, thoroughly Christianizing and sanctifying it. The glorious interior of the dome and the walls were stripped bare over the centuries to use as ornament in new churches and papal palaces. The Romans for centuries were notorious for re-cycling their classical monuments to erect new monuments; look at the Coliseum -- it has been positively looted.

Finally, today, the Pantheon is a parish church of the Diocese of Rome: St. Mary of the Rotunda. The magnificent dome is still the largest free-standing dome on earth, leaving the sports arenas out of it; three and one-half feet greater in diameter than St. Peter's. The angle of the dome as it reaches toward the ground is so subtle as to be virtually undetectable; the walls do not appear to curve. The natural lighting of the first century architect remains intact -- the hole at the top of the dome is twenty-seven feet in diameter. This opening is not covered even today with glass: the stone floor below contains small, almost unnoticeable, mathematically spaced holes which drain the Pantheon, when it rains.

Researching the Pantheon for my paper had made me hungry to see it. It had been closed when Uncle Jim tried to take us inside in 1989; today, at last, I would see it.

We got to it, and it was closed.

I was truly disappointed. This was the only chance we would get to see the Pantheon, as we were leaving Rome early the next morning. The kids could see how vexed and sorry I was and tried to cheer me up, as we turned out of Pantheon Square, but I was really feeling bad. I did not know when I would get back to Italy, let alone with my kids. Paul and Brigitta, focusing on the needs of the kids in a way I was not, found a gelato place, just outside Pantheon Square, and we stopped there. The kids tried to cheer me up, by pointing out all the wonderful flavors available -- tangerine and coconut and so on. I don't like ice cream, I said, nearing a full sulk, at that point, and intending to enjoy it. Paul got me an iced tea, regardless, which I did, in fact, appreciate.

We shortly came upon a little church that was open. Brigitta saw it there on the corner: King St. Louis Somebody of France. I don't remember now, which king of France he was -- they have had a lot of Louises. "We stop und we make oblations und thanksgiving to Our Blessed Mother for the safe und vunderful pilgrimage vhich now is ending," Brigitta exclaimed. She was simply jubilant. I looked at the little church and bitched to myself about going inside. To have missed the Pantheon a second time!

"Isn't it vunderful?" Brigitta was saying. "An open church for us to pray in on the Feast of the Assumption. We go inside und we give thanks und praise to the Mother of God!" Paul was game, and the kids were up for anything. Sighing and inconsolable, I followed my crowd of happy pilgrims in.

It *was* a pretty church; I guess most Roman churches are. It had high domes and high stained glass and impressive pillars and --

I stopped in my tracks and stared. The others did too. We looked one to another, shaking our heads, at first as if in disbelief, but a moment later, smiling, smiling deeply and radiantly. For there above the altar was a painting, a magnificent painting, not just of the Blessed Mother, but a painting of her Assumption, and here we were, her "special group" of pilgrims, as Slaviska had put it, on our last full day in Europe, come to say a prayer of thanksgiving to her on this, the Feast of the Assumption.

Every trace of sorrow and vexation over the Pantheon left my heart as if by decree. I walked slowly, deliberately up the main aisle toward the sanctuary, just staring at the painting, at this beautiful image of Our Lady, whom, I knew, had indeed brought us all the way from the Sacramento Valley in California, to visit Medjugorje and Italy. A journey of faith and prayer and joy, and also, at times, a journey of such doubt, confusion and challenges; challenges to my ability to let go and trust. She was arranging everything and she had arranged this moment, and dang! her timing was impeccable. We did pray before the altar, there at King St. Louis the Whatever of France. We took pictures in front of the painting. It was an unmistakable moment: if we had gone to the Pantheon, we would never have stopped in here. It was uncanny. The Blessed Virgin Mary herself wanted to make sure that we

168

understood: she was on this pilgrimage with us, and had been all the way.

We came out and trekked on through the Piazza Navona; it was late afternoon and a great national holiday to boot; the Piazza showed little hint of its boisterous life at night. We continued on to one of the bridges over the Tiber, getting a great view of St. Peter's above the river. Then we crossed along the tree-lined promenade above the river, cool in its deep and breezy shade, coming finally into the Via della Conciliazione, and the precincts of the Vatican.

We arrived at St. Peter's about twenty to five: we had wanted to be back in time for the late afternoon Mass. The kids took photos and I looked around for, and found, some of the rest of our group, including Mom and Trudi, already seated in the Holy Spirit Chapel, where the Mass was to take place. We rounded the kids up and got seated just before a long, long procession, starting with acolytes and ending with cardinals, crossed into the chapel. A gorgeously sung set of Vespers followed. It took long enough so that when it was over, some of the guys thought that was surely all there was going to be, in terms of a liturgical service.

"We're gonna go now, right?" some of the boys asked me.

"No," I answered, "now comes Mass."

"What the hell was that?" they asked, of the Evening Prayer service.

"Shhhh," I recommended. "You are in Rome. You are in the Vatican. Be cool with spending another thirty or forty minutes in Catholic worship, okay? I guarantee you, it will not do you any harm."

Mass started a few minutes later. It was in Italian, and reminded me of my early childhood at St. Joseph's, attending the Latin Mass. This was a great Roman finish to great day in Rome.

***

When we got in at the hotel, early that evening, some of the guys took showers, as they had been out in the hot Roman sun, all day. Jorge and Fonz, at some point, somehow found themselves out in the hall, completely nude, snapping towels at each other's bare butts. Brigitta stepped out of her room, saw the two naked boys and, clapping a hand to her mouth, laughed out loud. Fonz and Jorge, if inclined at all toward embarrassment, quickly overcame the inclination. They laughed, too.

The tendency of the boys to act as if all their rooms belonged to all of them continued at the Marco Aurelio. I went to one room that evening, looking for one of the guys, and found seven of them in the bathroom, where Oscar, busy with electric clippers, was giving haircuts. "Want me to cut your hair, Jim?" I thanked Oscar, but declined. "We want to look good, our last night in Europe," one of the guys said to me.

This comment brought once again to mind the fact that a hope I'd had for the kids, in Rome, would simply have to go unrealized, given our remote location and our almost-broke finances. Oscar had turned twenty the day before, and I would have liked to have been able to take him (and all the kids) to one of the city's great nightlife areas -- the Piazza Navona or Trastevere, or maybe, just so that they could say they'd seen it, the Via Veneto. If we could have done no more than sit at a sidewalk café with drinks and appetizers, it would have been very much worth doing. But it just was not possible. Everything was too far away.

Anyway, we were broke. We'd spent as much as we dared, that morning, on the cabs down to the monuments. I still had several hundred dollars from the group kitty, but I needed most of it to pay for our hotel, the next night, in Toronto. What's more, I had to settle up at the desk, that night, with regard to phone calls made by some of the kids to the States. The kids had had no idea how expensive phone calls home would be; I remember that Claudia and Mikey alone had bills close to fifty dollars. That was the moment that Mike Czernecki's two hundred fulfilled his prophecy, from our first night in Medjugorje. I remember watching the cash go out, covering those phone bills, and doing a quick mental calculation. Breakfast tomorrow would be on the plane. Lunch, in London, was on us. Dinner on the flight to Toronto; breakfast the next day was on the Toronto hotel. Lunch on the plane to California. Actually, we were probably just going to make it.

Our last night in Rome, though quite joyful, was a modest and tame one. We spent it, as we had the two before, between the hotel bar and the little café across the street, where they served Corona. It was very near the end of the trip, but it still WAS the trip, and we all enjoyed that evening. Maybe because it was so near the end, maybe because we knew now that we were safely past all the journey's difficulties, that Saturday night in Rome was a wonderfully relaxed

171

and breezy one. I remember watching the kids in bright conversation in the bar, with Mom and Trudi, with LaDonna and Michelle, with Loyd and Marge, with Vicky and Jane. I remember, too, being out at the sidewalk tables across the street, having a Corona with some of the male pilgrims. I think almost all of us were in bed by midnight.

We had to get up super-early the next morning – five, I think, for the London plane. I heard the next day that Mikey and Ada had stayed up all night, running around the hotel – they'd evidently knocked quietly on my door a couple times, at two or three. Lucky for them, they did not wake me.

We gathered in the lobby downstairs at five, or whatever the time was. I counted heads. It was still dark, as we climbed onto the bus, where Gino was waiting for us. I think most of us caught another half hour of sleep, on the way to the airport.

At the airport, Gino told Mom what a team she and I were; said we ought to run pilgrimages on our own, we were so relaxed and go-with-the-flow. We had just the right temperaments, he said, for this kind of work. I guess we had not told Gino that I was studying to be a priest. When he heard it that morning, he said, "You'll be a bishop!" Mom beamed; I prayed a prayer of exorcism over Gino.

The kids bounded ahead of us, toward the ticket line. It was five-thirty in the morning and even the airport looked sleepy, but the kids weren't. Mom or I must've said something about them, as Gino said, "They are young. They have to feel their strength. Now is the time." Mom and I smiled.

We got our tickets and waved good-bye to Gino. He had endeared himself to us, in his own way, which way was very different from Slaviska's, but that was okay. Gino was Gino, and I had enjoyed our time with him. I have thought of Gino many times, since. Though I have led several pilgrimages to Italy, in the years since, I have never run into Gino. I imagine he's retired by now, and in any event, I never again led a pilgrimage for Ave Maria Azurra Tours. I've never seen Sergio since, either – nor, for that matter, though she lives in the Bay Area, Maria Uribe. But I remember all of them fondly. They put this trip into place for us. I am grateful to them.

***

At London, we had a seven-hour layover, and so I had asked Sergio, in a phone call from Medjugorje, if he could arrange a bus to meet us at the airport, and take us into town for three or four hours. He'd said it was no problem, and what is more, we got the bus for free. Sergio told me he felt badly about the business with the "bridge accommodations" on the Sansovino. The free bus into central London was a way for him to say he was sorry in concrete terms. My last bit of anxiety about the trip evaporated, when, as we cleared customs, I saw a smiling, middle-aged man, our bus driver, with a sign, "Sullivan Group." We loaded all our bags onto the bus and went into town, the West End.

It was a beautiful Sunday morning in London. Our driver let us out at Pall Mall, and we walked the long red road toward Buckingham Palace, beneath the trees, in and out of the dappled late-morning sunlight. The kids and I lined up in front of the palace, and LaDonna took one of my favorite photos from the trip. We continued toward Hyde Park and the Serpentine; some of the group wanted to see

Westminster Abbey, or maybe it was Westminster Cathedral – I no longer remember which. I know that as it got to be time for lunch, the older pilgrims wanted a real English pub, and found one, a place near Whitehall called the Red Lion. I was not sure where the kids and I would go, but after checking the prices on the menu posted out front, I knew it was not going to be the Red Lion.

Coming up toward Trafalgar Square, I heard an excited cry from JD. "Jim! There's a McDonald's!"

Glory hallelujah, so there was. A McDonald's at Trafalgar Square. The only thing special about this McDonald's was that it was in London – no exotic interior design or architectural flourishes, such as we had encountered in the McDonald's at the Spanish Steps. Some of the kids still had a little money of their own – enough, anyway, for lunch at McDonald's. Some of them had to rely on the group kitty, which had been steadily depleted to the point where I did not know if we would come home with anything but some European coins. In any event, we had what we needed for lunch at the Trafalgar McDonald's, and the kids were in hog heaven about it. Two lunches in a row, at McDonald's! It just didn't get any better than that.

After lunch, I tried to interest a few of the kids in walking toward the Thames, with me. I wanted them to see the Houses of Parliament. But they saw all the Sunday crowds in Trafalgar, saw how the square was set up with musicians and artists and street vendors, and that was where they wanted to go. The square was on the way back to the bus, and we'd connected up with some of the adults in the group, at that point, so I let go of the kids and went to the Thames on my own. I went out on one of the bridges, to get a better look at Big Ben and Parliament. It is one of my favorite London views, and as I say, this was a perfect London summer Sunday. Temps just right, sunny and breezy.

As I got back to the bus, the kids – Nelson and Wally, I think, and maybe Pancho -- showed me the caricatures they had had done, in the square. They were very pleased with their few hours in the West End, as in fact, were we all.

The long flight to Toronto was a good chance for us all to catch up on sleep. I sat with members of the group, but have little memory of the flight, as I think almost all of us slept through most of it. At the Toronto airport we were at the Comfort Inn, and given our recent experiences, this was a well-named hotel. It had big rooms with king-sized beds and lots of pillows; lots of "extra" furniture in the rooms, and all of it comfortable; large bathrooms, big closets, heavy drapes at the windows, for privacy and quiet. Downstairs, there was a coffee shop and a restaurant, as well as a gym, a sauna and an indoor pool. The kids were in the pool before I was in my room.

We got into Toronto while it was still light. It felt great to be in North America, that evening; it felt almost as if we were already home. Prices even in the coffee shop being more than I could handle, for me and any number of the kids, I sent out for pizza, and several of the guys and I had a pizza party, in my room, just like youth group days. We got Cokes from the machine near the elevator. The kids were thrilled with this North American hotel and its amenities; after the pool, they were in the hot tub and the sauna. I understand that after that, Oscar and Pancho, coming back to their room to shower, streaked the length of the hall. I would find out about this sort of thing days, weeks, even months after we got back…

Thank goodness for breakfast-included packages at hotels such as the
Comfort Inn, because none of the kids nor I would have eaten,
otherwise, the next morning. The hotel had an excellent breakfast,
and the kids feasted. It was a bright, sunny Canadian morning, and
we had to be out of the hotel by some reasonable hour, nine-thirty,
maybe even ten. The overnight in Toronto had never been a part of
the original plan for the trip; it was just the way the flights landed.
But I look back on it as a Godsend. It gave us a real rest, and on the
flight to California, we were all wide awake and talking, laughing,
trading war stories about all that we had just done.

I remember that Mikey, Ada and I were seated in the very last row of
the plane, and when they ran out of the lunch options, except for fish,
which I won't eat, and the cabin attendant simply shrugged and said
she was sorry, I shrugged and said it didn't matter: after all, airline
food. But Mikey took it upon himself to right the injustice. He got
up and went to the attendants' station, immediately behind us, so that
I could hear his request: "Excuse me. My friend cannot eat fish.
Would you please provide him with something for lunch? He's paid
as much as anyone else, to be on this flight."

The stewardess returned a moment later, offering me a plate of sliced
apple, deli ham, a couple of cheeses, and peanuts, almonds and
cashews, and apologizing that this (in my view, excellent) lunch was
all they could offer. I wanted to apologize to her, for Mikey, but
Mikey was sitting right next to me, looking satisfied with the justice
he had brought about, and in any event, the young lady did not seem
offended. And in fact, knowing my boys, she was probably charmed
by him. I thanked her, and enjoyed one of the better airline meals I
have ever had.

176

Our bus driver was waiting for us, at SFO. He really had liked us, on the drive down the Valley, two full weeks earlier, and he had wanted to do something nice for us. So, he brought along a video of one of his favorite films, for us to watch, on the drive to Marysville. As I love staring out windows and watching the countryside roll by, I would not have been pleased with the plan, even if the dear fellow had supplied a Michelle Pfeiffer film. As it happened, he brought a film I can't stand: FORREST GUMP. Everyone else was pleased, and after all, our driver was showing us he valued us. I stared out the big windows, watching San Francisco Bay, blue in the early afternoon light, watching Oakland and Berkeley slip by, watching the golden hills of Solano County. I did my best not to hear a word of dialogue from the film. I did pretty well with it: California's beauty can absorb me. More to the point, my kids and I had just been to Europe. In a very, very good way, nothing would ever quite be the same in our lives again. I knew a serene satisfaction, that bright and sunny afternoon, a profound sense of accomplishment and peace. Even Tom Hanks could not intrude upon it.

FIVE

I had ten days, from when we got back, to when I was leaving for seminary. I remember those ten days with a special love. I got $128 worth of photos developed, getting double prints so the kids could take copies. I did not yet have them all developed, when we held the first of our two post-trip barbecues at Mom's, on Wednesday, August 19. Not all the kids made it to that bbq, but most of them did. As I am typing this up, I am looking at a photo from that evening of a group of them sitting around one of the patio tables at Mom's, steaks on the bbq, guacamole and chips on the table, and passing the photos among themselves. The way I framed the shot the kids seem surrounded by Mom's lush subtropical garden, palms and ferns and brightly blooming flowers forming not just the backdrop, but also the sides and even part of the foreground of the picture. Most people who see this photo love it. Ro thought I had taken it on Kauai, and wanted to know when the kids and I had visited the Islands.

The second of the post-trip bbqs was on the following Saturday, and this one was well-attended not just by the kids who'd been on the pilgrimage, but by many who had not gone, as well. This bbq went late and was, I suppose, the last of the activities of St. Joseph's Youth Group, under my supervision. A friend of mine, Dale Walker, took over the group in September, and, as had happened with me, three years earlier, Dale attracted her own group of young people and developed her own program. My kids no longer attended.

Though the post-trip bbqs brought to a close my work with the kids as Marysville's youth minister, they foreshadowed the ministry that was about to begin. I did not know just how I would keep a regular hand in with the kids, from St. Patrick's. I just knew that I was going to. I figured that at the worst, it might be a matter of getting up to Marysville a couple Friday nights a month, maybe being able occasionally to spend a Saturday there. I did not know what shape the ongoing association with the kids would take, whether it would continue a heavy faith-formation focus, be more relaxed and social, have a fundraising component, or what. I just didn't know what would be possible from the seminary, and would have to get there first to see. What I did know was that the kids and I were not saying good-bye.

I left for St. Patrick's on Thursday, August 27. I remember meeting Mikey for lunch at Casa Carlos, one of Marysville's most popular Mexican restaurants, my car already packed for the move. As I was dropping him off at his house, afterward, he stopped at the mail box, which was out on the curb, and pulled out, among other pieces of mail, an envelope addressed to him, with a European postmark. "Oh yeah!" he said, and waved the envelope in the air. I grinned. Then I turned into the street, on my way to St. Patrick's, on my way to the future.

***

I can honestly say that I have never in my life made such an easy major adjustment as I did, at St. Patrick's. The grounds, as noted before, were spacious and beautiful. I particularly loved the great oval of lawn in front of the main building, with its many Canary Island date palms. The seminary itself was magnificent – three stories in brick, with a breath-taking chapel, numerous classrooms, several elegant meeting rooms, a good library, and a grand central staircase that suggested the antebellum South. I remember telling

179

friends in letters, which I still had time to write in those days, that it was like a nineteenth-century Hilton.

The seminary faculty impressed me from the start for their dedication and enthusiasm. I sometimes hear of seminarians, across the country, who experience their faculty as adversarial, and I have to shake my head. This certainly was never my experience at St. Pat's; the faculty was supportive and encouraging. I had two important decisions to make, my first few weeks at the seminary, with regard to the faculty. I had to choose from them a spiritual director and an academic advisor. I asked Father Martin Tran to be my spiritual director. He was a young Vietnamese priest whose personal story – he was one of the "boat people" out of Vietnam, after the fall of Saigon – struck me deeply for its quiet heroism. I felt that a man who had been through what Father Martin had been through would be a great spiritual mentor. I asked Father Milt Walsh to be my advisor. I asked him both because I liked him, and because I realized that he would be a persuasive advocate for me, in faculty discussions, an important consideration, as the faculty is charged with voting on a seminarian's readiness, each year, to continue in the program. Milt and I were very close in age, but he had been a priest almost twenty years. He was a professor of theology at St. Pat's, and from my first morning in class with him, I was drawn by his sharp intelligence, his deep faith and his wonderful wit. Milt also had (and has) a smile that lights up the room. He was "my kind of priest," and I wanted him to be my advisor.

The staff, too, was gracious and supportive. Their offices were on the ground floor, and all of them made an effort to get to know us by name, and early in the semester. Various staff members would take up with particular seminarians and become sort of ex-officio mentors. The staff clearly saw their work as ministry – ministry to future priests.

There was a convent on the grounds – the home of the Oblate Sisters of Jesus the Priest. Take a minute to think about that title, about the name of this particular congregation of women consecrated to the service of the Church. The Oblates of Jesus the Priest. How often do we think of Jesus the Priest? Not often enough, I would argue. The Oblate Sisters were and are, in any event, simply beloved, by the seminarians. They cooked for us. They helped us with our Spanish (it is a Mexican order). They set an example for us, of what the consecrated life is all about. At any given time, there are eight to ten sisters at the seminary. It would be difficult to overstate their influence on life at St. Pat's.

I arrived at the seminary maybe around four, the afternoon of August 27, and was greeted at the main entrance by Clarence Zamora, a second-year theology student for the Diocese of Honolulu. Clarence got my room key and a packet of orientation materials together and showed me up to the third floor. Clarence had a gentle and ironic humor, and he made me laugh, several times, in those first few minutes of our friendship. And friendship it was to become. That bright August afternoon, Clarence was studying for Honolulu and I, for Sacramento. Today we are both priests for the Diocese of Oakland: we had some surprising turns ahead in our discernment! Clarence is today my principle confessor, and one of my best friends.

I had a long, narrow room on C Wing, third floor. The entire four years that I would live at St. Pat's, I would be on C Wing, third floor. I told other seminarians that it was the seminary's best real estate. No one above us, making noise; and great views, whether out toward the gardens and playing fields, or looking inward, toward the cloister. This room faced out. The windows in the student bedrooms at the seminary are nine or ten feet high, and four wide, and this was an eastern exposure: the room was filled with light in the mornings.

As I say, the room was long and narrow, but I liked that. I set it up as three distinct areas – sleeping (bed; next to the sink and closet); work (desk, chair and a couple of bookcases) and "sitting room," a couple of comfortable chairs and a couple of end tables, down near the big window. I hung the wall with pictures of the kids, and felt at home in no time.

My very first afternoon at St. Pat's, as I was moving in, I heard a bright "Hello!" from my open door, turned to look and saw a handsome Vietnamese kid with a Hollywood smile, in t-shirt and jeans, standing in my doorway.

"Hi," I said.

"I'm Van!" he said. "I'm for Oakland!"

(Everything Van was to say in this conversation, it seemed to me, needed to be followed with an exclamation mark.)

"I'm Jim," I said, moving away from my boxes and toward him. "I'm for Sacramento."

Van's bright brown eyes lit up. "Sacramento!" he said, extending his hand. "We're neighbors!"

I took his hand. "So we are," I said. "I might have been for Oakland. I lived there for twenty years."

"Really! How come you are for Sacramento?"

"Cuz I lived there for twenty years, too," I said.

"You're FORTY?!" Van said.

"I'm forty-two," I said. I looked at him a moment. When I called him a kid, above, I was not joking. I smiled at him. "How old are you?" I asked.

Van just laughed. "I'm younger than you!" he said.

I think he was twenty-four, that fall. His birthday is at the end of November, which would have made him twenty-three at the time of this meeting. Twenty-three, and a second year theology student at St. Patrick's. A year ahead of me in the program, at about half my age. I remembered myself at twenty-three, writing my first novel, and hanging out at the San Francisco rock clubs with my musician siblings. That had been 1979, and it was beginning to feel like a long time ago.

Van and I became friends quickly. I mean, everyone becomes friends quickly with Van. I don't know anyone who doesn't love him, and we all wish he had more time for us. When you are as popular as he is, everyone has to be satisfied with their ten-minutes-a-month, or two hours a year, or however it works out. Van and Clarence were among several seminarians who sort of took me under wing, my first few weeks at St. Pat's, helped me get to know the routine, showed me where the bathrooms were, told me where to find the Bank of America, the Safeway and so on, in downtown Menlo Park.

There was a moment, during the orientation weekend, when an elderly priest in a motorized wheelchair stopped in front of me and said, "Jim Sullivan?" I said, "Guilty." The old man smiled with a joy that I can feel today, more than ten years later. "So you're the nephew of Jim Poole!" I know I looked astonished. "Oh," the old priest said, taking my hands in his, "you don't know who your uncle was to us, in our student days. I'm Frank Norris, Jim. I was behind your uncle a good few years, but I can still see him on the playing field, like a young Olympian. And he had such a mind! Do you know what we called him, here?" I asked Father Frank what they had called my uncle. "God-Almighty Poole!" Father Frank beamed. "The Fourth Person of the Holy Trinity!" I laughed. Then I added, "I hope no one is expecting me to live up to that!" I was amazed at running into an old schoolmate of Uncle Jim's, there on the seminary faculty. This was 1998; Uncle Jim had been ordained in 1943. It was just one more reason why, I suppose, my transition to St. Pat's was so easy.

Sister Maureen McInerney, who along with Father Jim Murphy directed the Vocations Office for Sacramento, came to visit us Sacramento seminarians a couple of times, that fall. I remember

184

sitting with her in our private conference and telling her how easily I had adjusted to the seminary routine, how much I was already enjoying my life as a seminarian. Sr. Maureen smiled, commenting that, at my age, I could appreciate the greatness of this opportunity. At forty-two, I was the oldest of the Sacramento guys at St. Pat's, though there were a number guys there, studying for other dioceses, who were older than I.

In general, native-born American seminarians tend to be older, anywhere from mid-thirties to early fifties. The kids at St. Pat's, those under thirty, were mostly from Vietnam, the Philippines and Latin America. I think the gravitational pull of American culture is largely responsible for this. Young men have so many opportunities here; there are so many diversions and attractions. I believe that where a vocation is truly present, and where there is any openness on the part of the man, the vocation will finally assert itself, and the man will find his way to the seminary, and to priesthood. But he may have found his way to a lot else, before that. Nor do I think this a bad thing, not at all. My middle-aged friends and I at St. Pat's all knew very well what we were saying good-bye to. I think all of us were in the same joyous and grateful place, with regard to the change God was working in our lives, in calling us, at forty, forty-five and fifty, to priesthood. I remember joking with friends and parishioners during my years at the seminary that some men handled their midlife crises by buying a red Ferrari or marrying a trophy wife. I was handling mine by studying theology at St. Pat's.

Sister Maureen asked me about my kids in that meeting, and I told her I missed them every day. She clearly "got" it, but then, Sister Maureen got me. I was fortunate in having superiors of her and Father Murphy's caliber. A number of seminarians from other dioceses were unhappy with their Vocations Directors, but not us

Sacramentans. We were blessed, and we knew it, in Maureen McInerney and Jim Murphy.

***

In terms of keeping up with the kids, the first thing that had to be determined was when and how often we would be able to meet. This was settled my first few days at St. Pat's, as I went through the long-weekend orientation for new seminarians. There was a lot, a lot, of information given us during those three or four days, basically a crash course on seminary life, which is something of a cross between regular student life and life in a monastery.

One of the things I loved about the seminary routine was the "free Wednesday." Since seminarians frequently work weekends, either on their studies or in parish assignments, St. Patrick's offered us a weekly schedule that left Wednesdays open after noon – no afternoon classes, no afternoon or evening meetings. It was a block of time meant to be set aside for personal use. I heard this and I smiled deeply. Wednesday had, of course, been the regular meeting night with the kids – every first and third Wednesday. Marysville was a little over two hours away: leaving the seminary at noon, I would be in town in plenty of time for a meeting with the kids.

The next question, of course, was where we would meet. The Youth Hall was no longer ours. I don't think any other venue up at St. Joseph's was available, anyway, but beyond that, there really was not another meeting room there that was suitable for us. The Youth Hall had been ours, and we had made it even more ours, and it had been ideal. The question of when to meet was settled. The question of

186

where to meet would have to be decided, in part, through our meeting to talk about it.

I called Mom and explained the situation. Mom said that she had RCIA on Wednesdays, and Trudi choir practice, so the house was empty a couple hours each Wednesday evening anyway, and that we should meet there til we had another venue. I think she really did think we would eventually find one…

We didn't. I remember checking out possibilities up at St. Joseph's, and also next door, at St. Isidore's in Yuba City. I remember considering holding meetings in pizza parlors and restaurants, and checking out possibilities at Notre Dame Elementary, the Marysville parish school. My sister Liz compared the situation to John Bosco's attempts to find a place for his boys to meet, and I considered how grateful I was, to have only thirty or forty kids to deal with, rather than four hundred.

In the end, we stayed where we started. We were to meet at Mom's every other Wednesday evening for the next three years. People hear this and they say, "Your mom is a saint." Mom would tell them something surprising: when the group was to stop meeting on Wednesday evenings, three years later, and she would come in from RCIA to an empty house, she would say right out loud, "It's just not the same without the kids here." The bottom line is that I could not have managed, those three years, but for Mom's support and commitment, to "our kids."

I'd hoped to start meeting with the kids September 16, but something at the seminary that night prevented me from doing so. I think it may have been the evening social at the Dominican convent just a couple blocks from St. Pat's. The Dominican Sisters at Corpus Christi Monastery on Oak Grove Avenue have a sort-of open house for the seminarians, at the start of each year. I say sort-of because the sisters are cloistered, and most of the convent is off-limits. The social happens in the main public reception room, nicely set with hors d'ouvres and drinks, and the sisters stand on the other side of the counter and talk with the seminarians. It is a very nice evening for everyone. It may have been that event, the night of September 16, or it may have been something else. The seminary was celebrating its one hundredth anniversary, that year, and we went to a lot, a lot of special (and to me, anyway, surprisingly fancy) events that fall, that winter: champagne receptions and black-tie (or Roman collar) dinners. It was a great (though atypical) introduction to seminary life!

Anyway, the kids and I got together the following Wednesday, instead, September 23. This was the kick-off meeting of the new ministry, whatever it was to become and whatever we were to call it. I barbecued lemon chicken that evening. That was a first for the kids, and years later Elva told me she wished I would have done it more often, as it was pollo sabroso. It was only our third bbq, but already I had the drill down: a vat of guacamole, a couple bags of Santitas or Tostitos, and a lot, a lot of fresh veggies – carrots, celery, jicima, cherry tomatoes, olives and especially cucumbers. The kids loved cucumbers, which surprised me. They were not big on bell peppers, and I would typically cut up one, and end up eating it all myself, which was fine, as I was (and am) big on them. They liked the vegetables with Ranch dressing – another point of divergence among us: I like my vegetables raw and naked. They do not need anything on them; they are delicious just as God made them.

In any event, that first meeting was attended by about twenty-five of the kids. Over the coming year, we would have some meetings with as many as thirty-five former youth groupers: clearly, the kids wanted the ministry to continue, and it barreled ahead over the next few months. Heather Higgins, who had helped me with the group the previous two years, went to Cal Poly that fall. I hired both Oscar and Alejandra as my "of-age" assistants; again, I could not pay them much, but they were both thrilled with the opportunity to help direct the group, and they were very reliable.

We needed a name, and I told the kids at that first meeting to be thinking about what they wanted to call the group. I had spoken meanwhile with Father Leon about continuing with the group in my spare time from St. Pat's, and he was all for it. I think both he and I were thinking of a name for them that would somehow include the word pilgrimage, as we were all agreed on that much: another pilgrimage was something everyone wanted to see happen. But I remember Oscar saying that the kids didn't want to call themselves pilgrims because it made them think of clunky black shoes and those guys in weird black hats with buckles who shoot turkeys at Thanksgiving…

While we debated a name, there was also the question of what we were going to do. Clearly, if we were serious about a second pilgrimage, we were going to need to fundraise. Would the group do any more than that? Would we have day trips and dances and go to Kings and A's games, as we had done, when we were the youth group? Would we play "Catholic Jeopardy" as we used to do, competing for prizes like trips to Great America? How would our meetings be structured, who would run them, and so on?

As it happens, that first meeting set the pace for the next three years. The kids arrived and spread out around the patio with their sodas and appetizers. The talk was still overwhelmingly Europe, and those who hadn't gone were now hungry to go. The whole group energy and purpose seemed turned to the idea of making another pilgrimage. This fact pretty much implied what our main activities would be. Obviously, there would have to be fundraising. But just as obviously, there would have to be prayer.

The chicken was on the bbq when I suggested we say a decade of the Rosary. Ever the undershooter, I guess, when it came to the kids' capacity for prayer. We said one decade, with me leading, and Nelson said, as we concluded, "Why don't we just finish it, Jim? We always said all five decades in Europe." I smiled, and asked Nelson if he would like to lead the second decade. Claudia led the third. I forget who led the fourth and fifth.

We then talked business – that is, dreams. "Jim, I don't care what it takes, or how long, I am going back to Medjugorje," Wally said, at one point. Ten voices chimed in when Claudia said, "Me too!"

That, in a nutshell, was to be the format, for our meetings, over the coming three years. The kids would arrive somewhere between six-thirty and seven and have a long social hour over the guacamole and chips, over the vegetables and Ranch. Then we would say a five decade Rosary, sometimes saying the Chaplet of Divine Mercy, as well. Then we would have a short business meeting – virtually all of our business over the next several years would be fundraising activities. Finally, a throwback to the days in the Youth Hall, the pizza would arrive and the kids would have another hour or so of social time, the meeting breaking up, typically, about ten PM. Trudi was usually home from choir practice by eight, and Mom from RCIA by nine, and pizza became their standard Wednesday night fare. Mom and Trudi would visit with the kids 'til LAW AND ORDER came on at ten, at which point, their attention was on the Manhattan DA's office.

There was a teaching element in these meetings. I wanted the kids to have a deeper grasp of the mysteries of the Rosary, so I started, early on, maybe already at that first meeting, giving brief synopses of each mystery, maybe pulling in some Scripture, or quoting some saint, or simply re-telling the story of the mystery in everyday terms. This was, in fact, the beginning of an entirely new catechetical ministry for me: I have never once since led a public Rosary without giving short reflections at the start of each mystery.

Sometime that autumn of 1998, the kids agreed on the name they wanted for the new group. They wanted to be called the Teen Rosary Group. The name surprised me. I had expected something more – dynamic. After all, we were about pilgrimage, about travel and adventure, weren't we? There was nothing wrong with the Teen Rosary Group; it just sounded sort of...prosaic.

Mom did not agree. "I think that is a very appropriate name for them," she told me. "I think Our Lady herself suggested it. Nothing you are doing with them is more important, Jimmy, than praying the Rosary."

I could hardly argue with that.

SIX

By mid-autumn, I had a new routine with the kids. I was up every other Wednesday for the meeting, and then almost every weekend. In other words, I was seeing them five or six times a month. Leaving the seminary Wednesdays at noon was a breeze. Friday afternoon was a little trickier: if you time it right, you can enjoy four separate traffic jams between Menlo Park and Marysville, on a Friday afternoon. I usually got away ahead of the traffic, but occasionally, when I didn't, I would just wait 'til seven-thirty Friday evening, to drive up.

I remember attending several of the Lindhurst football games that fall, and on Fridays when there wasn't a game, as often as not, I was doing something with several of the kids. Dinner and a movie, maybe, or just hanging out at Mom's, maybe, but in general, Friday evenings during this period belonged to the kids. Of course, it could not be like the previous year, when I had been living in Marysville. But the time we had together was substantial, and we were all satisfied with it.

That winter's biggest news story was the Clinton-Lewinsky affair. I remember how completely the kids bought into Bill Clinton's definition of what constituted sex, and I was…appalled. In only a generation, we had gone from one ridiculous extreme to the other. I am old enough to remember the nuns telling girls not to wear patent leather shoes, because the boys would be able to see up their skirts, in the reflections. Thirty years later, here was our President with a definition of what constitutes a sex act that eliminated from the category most sex acts! And the kids were buying it. I remember some lively discussions on the subject. I'm not sure I convinced the kids, but I am sure I got them thinking.

We had plans for fundraising, but at that point, organizing fundraisers was a bridge too far for me. We had let go of the monthly parish breakfast, assuming that Dale Walker and the new youth group would want it. In fact, Dale was not interested in fundraising: her forte was service, and she was channeling her energies with her kids in directions very different from those I had taken. She had a successful group, and ran youth ministry in the Marysville parish for four years, but fundraising was a bare minimal part of her program. This fact eventually opened up a lot of opportunities for us, but as I say, over the winter of 1998-99, it was all I could do just to get our new bearings as a group, and to maintain regular contact.

On a Friday night in January, while I was on Christmas break, I had a dinner-movie date in Sacramento with several of the guys. Fonz asked if his cousin Tico could go with us. Tico lived in Woodland, about forty minutes southwest of Marysville. He was the same age as most of the kids in the group, born in 1982. I said he was welcome to join us, not really thinking anything about it, one way or the other.

Ten years later I can see Tico in my rearview mirror, a good-looking young athlete, intense and focused under his ball cap, asking me why the Church had sold indulgences at the time of the Reformation, and quoting a history teacher at Woodland High whom he clearly admired, to the effect that the Church invented the doctrine of Purgatory, precisely to sell indulgences. Here, I thought, was one rare teen ager! I don't remember what the other guys – Fonz and

Mikey – talked about on the way to dinner, but I remember me and Tico talking at some length about the underlying causes of the Protestant Reformation. Imagine! Questions about Johann Tetzel and Martin Luther and magisterial teaching, rather than the standard joshing and joking that transpired on our drives to Sacramento. I am fairly certain we said the Rosary on the way down as well, as that was something we had started to do, since returning from Europe.

Tico transferred to Lindhurst High that semester, living at Fonz's house. As a result, Tico became a member of the Teen Rosary Group, and he was, over the years, to very substantially influence the group's direction and purpose.

In April, Trudi and I arranged a big parishwide field trip to the seminary. We arranged it via the Parish Vocations Committee at St. Joseph's, of which Trudi was chair. We called the event Seminary Saturday. This was to become the signature note of my sister's chairmanship of the committee: we would do it every year for the next five years.

So many people from the parish were interested in visiting the seminary that we ended up chartering a bus. (I have only this spring of 2009, while preparing this narrative for print, discovered that that bus was paid for by an anonymous donor: who else but... Mama Warbucks.) The day consisted of a tour of the house and grounds, a short prayer service in the chapel, lunch, meeting with the Oblate Sisters and visiting the convent, and then rec time. Mikey, Jorge and Matt skipped lunch to play Frisbee out on the lawns, somewhere. They came in toward the end of the visit hungry and I took them to the little "night kitchen" off the dining commons, where there was always food available for the seminarians. I remember how the guys made themselves *right* at home, helping themselves to the sandwich makings, cookies, chips, sodas, etc. It made me happy to see them making my new home so easily theirs.

The bus and most of the Marysville visitors left late in the afternoon. Mikey, Jorge and Matt stayed behind, and after some more rec time (it was a beautiful April afternoon) we went to dinner at Su Hong, a good Chinese restaurant on El Camino Real. Our conversation included pilgrimage possibilities for the fast-approaching summer of 1999.

At the request of a number of the folks on the previous pilgrimage, I had agreed to run a Holy Land trip in August. Thinking it over, I had decided as well to set up a Fatima-Lourdes trip. I had arranged these pilgrimages in October. Given all that had happened on the 1998 trip, I decided not to go with Maria, Sergio, Neno et al. It wasn't that I didn't think Sergio could give us really professional service: I am sure he could have, given adequate lead time. For that matter, I didn't doubt that Maria could get a tour organized in an efficient and timely manner. She had done it dozens of times: we were maybe the exception that proved her generally excellent rule. It was just that, this time, if there were to be a lot of last-minute questions and hassles, I wanted at least for the tour company to be located on the same continent as me.

I wrote Milanka Lachman, the president of 206 Tours, a pilgrimage operator located on Long Island. I told Milanka what I hoped to do, and asked if she could set up both a June trip to Fatima and Lourdes and an August trip to the Holy Land. I assumed I would hear back in writing, from an assistant. Two days after I mailed the letter to New York, Milanka was on the phone to me. I liked that about her. She asked for "Father Sullivan," which made me like her even more. She explained how 206 worked with tour leaders (such as myself), explained how commissions and free trips worked, offered to get sample itineraries to me, for both trips, and I forget what-all else. Suffice it to say that I was sold, on Milanka and on 206, from that first phone call. I have led over a dozen pilgrimages in the ten years since that phone call, all of them with 206.

206, incidentally, means "twenty to six," the time of Our Lady's first apparition, at Medjugorje. I found this out from a guide in Israel who works regularly with Milanka. That guide, like every other one I have ever spoken with, has the highest opinion of Milanka and 206. I was in for something new, in aligning myself with Milanka: I was in for smooth professional service, careful attention to detail, four-star accomodations and a guarantee of the most convenient flights and travel arrangements available. It would not take three days, with Milanka, to get from California to Croatia.

Anyway, the boys and I were having dinner at Su Hong and talking about that summer's pilgrimages. The idea had been to use the Fatima-Lourdes trip as a fundraiser – if I broke into commissions, with the trip, I would have potentially several thousand dollars to put toward getting the kids to the Holy Land. We hoped to be able to add four nights in Medjugorje, as well, coming back from Israel.

Now, in fact, I had never had much faith in the possibility of travelling with the kids in the summer of 1999. It was a possibility, though, and after all, I had not, initially, had much faith in the likelihood of the first trip. But all along, given that I was no longer in Marysville, and could not make the concentrated effort that I had made the previous year, I was doubtful of getting the kids on the

196

Holy Land trip. I was looking with hope and confidence to 2000, and the Jubilee. My plan was Rome and Medjugorje, in 2000. I figured my tours in the Jubilee Year would book well, we would get lots of free tickets, I would earn commissions, and also, the kids and I had more than a year to fundraise. But the kids wanted to go again as soon as they could, and I had been willing to put 1999 in play, and see what came of it.

But I never really expected much to come of it, and that evening, at Su Hong, I had to start preparing the guys for the likelihood that we would not travel in 1999. The Fatima-Lourdes trip was booking *very* slowly. With just two months to go, it was a question of whether the trip would make at all, let alone make money. And as the kids and I were not yet doing fundraisers, everything really depended on commissions and free tickets from the pilgrimages themselves. I'd run ads in several diocesan newspapers, and had had a number of calls, but sign-ups for the Fatima trip were few and far between. What a difference from the previous year's experience! I have long since learned, of course, that what happened in Marysville with the first trip was very unusual: to have, basically, forty people all sign up at once for a tour is a feat I have yet to repeat, and obviously, is one I can take no credit for. Our first pilgrimage had truly been from the Spirit and through Our Lady.

Never wanting to get in the way of the Spirit, I told Jorge, Mikey and Matt that evening that we might yet make it to the Holy Land and Medjugorje, in August, but that if we didn't, we needed to really focus on Rome, in 2000. I talked to them about the Jubilee Year, its significance, and what a phenomenal trip that would be. Their eyes shone, and they had a goal, if 1999 turned out a disappointment.

197

***

Regardless of the kids, I wanted the Fatima-Lourdes trip to book. I wanted it to book for the sake of the eight, then twelve, then fourteen, then seventeen pilgrims who were signing up for it. The thought of raising a joyful expectation in the hearts of these faith-filled folks, and then having to disappoint them, was a cause of real anxiety for me. I also felt a responsibility to Milanka, and 206, who trusted me to book the tour. I learned a new way to handle worry, that spring of 1999, sweating out the numbers on the Fatima-Lourdes trip—three Hail Marys every time doubt assailed me. I sometimes had to say those three Hail Marys ten times a day. Well, there is nothing wrong with an extra thirty Hail Marys, on a given day.

The Fatima-Lourdes bookings were hampered by the fact that it had originally been advertised as Fatima-Lourdes-Medjugorje, and this was spring, 1999, the time of the Kosovo war. In fact, when the full-fledged war (with us and the Brits getting involved) broke out, the trip nearly fell apart. I had to change the itinerary, dropping the four-day stay in Medjugorje at the end, and adding instead a three-day stay in Paris. This decision saved the trip, which did, finally, make.

It was a small number of pilgrims – not quite twenty – but that may have been a blessing, given that most of them were folks I did not know. Rose and Brigitta, from the previous trip, were on this one, as was my sister Anne. Otherwise, I was meeting pilgrims for the first time, at the airport. I remain in touch with a few of these folks today.

It was a great trip, and I have fond memories of my first impressions of Fatima, of Burgos and its magnificent Gothic cathedral (burial place of El Cid) and, of course, of Lourdes. It was also my first time in Paris, and I remember joking with friends later that though I had been three nights in Paris, I never saw it. 206 is serious about Catholic sites on pilgrimage, about making sure that pilgrims get their money's worth, in terms of visiting sacred places: no "afternoon on your own to explore or shop" with this outfit! I appreciated the 206 approach, and loved our excursions to Nevers (where Bernadette lies incorrupt, looking as if she is asleep) and to Lisieux. And we did, of course, visit Notre Dame and Rue de Bac, in Paris. My sister Anne, however, an artist, could not be in Paris and not see the Louvre. She bailed on the Lisieux excursion, and spent the day at the museum. She later told me, "Jim, tell Milanka to put the Louvre on the itinerary. It is as much a place of pilgrimage as anywhere else in France. The Blessed Mother is the star of the place – there's hardly a gallery without a painting of her."

Anne and the rest of the pilgrims went home after Paris, but Rose, Brigitta and I went on to Medjugorje. The conflict in Kosovo had ended several weeks before. There were almost no Americans in Medjugorje that June, but there were plenty of Europeans, who of course, could get there by rail, bus or car. It was mid-June and the weather was perfect: sunny, breezy, low eighties in the afternoon; almost cool at night.

This was the trip on which I met Slavenka Jelavic, who had translated the previous summer, for Vicka, and who has been my guide on every trip to Medjugorje since. As Brigitta, Rose and I had been to Medjugorje before, Slavenka largely just made sure we knew what was happening each day, and let us do as we pleased. Doing as we pleased consisted of attending both the German Mass at eight

AM and the Croatian Mass in the evening, and climbing both Apparition Hill and Krizevac twice. Though we wound up at the Dubrovnik Club with our Kaltenbergs at the end of the evening, Rose and Brigitta had not come to Medjugorje to pussyfoot around. They meant to win grace for souls, and they put themselves, and me, through the paces.

I had, in fact, a very special kid "with" me on the trip—Chris Saavedra. Chris had been an eighteen year old senior at Wheatland High School (Wheatland is a town ten miles southeast of Marysville). He had been a sports star and student body president. He came from a big and active Catholic family, and I remember seeing him, at Sunday Masses, helping his grandmother into church, at St. Joseph's. Though Chris was not a member of the youth group, my kids all knew and liked him.

The evening he was to graduate from high school, Chris left the house for the ceremony, driving himself, his parents following him a few minutes behind. At the intersection of two county roads, rural roads lined by peach orchards, Chris was hit broadside by a truck and killed instantly. His parents arrived at the intersection just minutes later, before the police, and saw the wreck, saw their son. Ten years later the image of this tragedy haunts my mind. Father Leon, called to the hospital, could scarcely describe the scene, the depth of shock and grief.

This had happened just the week before we left on our pilgrimage, and I had made up my mind to go up Krizevac barefoot for Chris. The boys had dissuaded me from climbing Krizevac barefoot the previous summer. This summer, I was determined to do it, and to offer it up for this wonderful teen ager whom everyone had loved, and who had been taken from us on what would have been the happiest night of his life.

It was a bright, breezy late morning as Brigitta, Rose and I arrived at the base of Krizevac. The path up the slope was deserted. Brigitta said, "We offer zis up for the salvation of sinners and for the poor souls in Purgatory, especially those who have no one to pray for them!"

"Let's do this, Chris," I said, and took off my shoes and socks.

Brigitta took off like a shot from a howitzer, leaving me and Rose to stumble on as best we might.

There's a right way and a wrong way up Krizevac—we took the wrong way. It seemed much steeper and more difficult than I'd remembered; I imagined it was just because I was barefoot. After a long while, maybe close to an hour, when all it normally takes to get to the top is 45-50 minutes, with shoes on, I realized we hadn't seen any of the stations since Station Three, way, way, way back down the slope somewhere. We struggled on, and I began to realize that we were on the steep climb which Slaviska had taken down with Oscar and Jorge the previous summer. "I know a fast way down," she'd said. Of course, that fast way down was a long way up, because it was so steep.

Brigitta was undaunted. Well ahead of us, "Hurry up!" she said. "Zere's lots of rocks! Oh be careful—vorsicht!" Rose, practically on all fours, turned back and caught my eye, as if to say, "Are you going to slap Brigitta, or will I?"

Finally, we reconnected with the main trail. I think it was at the eighth station—just over half way up, in other words. I looked for cool dirt on which to put my feet; there had been none on the previous path, just jagged rocks and lots and lots of pebbles. At this point, I wasn't thinking about Brigitta, Rose or even Chris—I was only thinking, "How much more to the top?" I longed to put on my shoes and socks, and give my by-now aching feet a rest.

The climb up Krizevac is well marked, in terms of the placement of the Stations, for the steepest part of the climb occurs between the eleventh and twelfth Stations, that is, between the crucifixion and the death of the Lord. This part of the climb was a real struggle for me; I was hot, tired and drenched in sweat. I was tired of carrying my shoes and would have liked to put them on just for that reason. But there was more to it, in that, carrying my shoes in one hand, I only had the other to balance, steady and catch myself. This was twice and more the climb up Krizevac, in terms of energy and exhaustion, as the climb I had done with the kids the previous summer.

We came out above the twelfth Station and I saw the path leveling out ahead, saw the last turn before reaching the top. I breathed a heavy and grateful sigh of relief. The last part of the climb is a cakewalk, compared to what we had just done.

I cannot tell you how good it feels, to put your shoes back on, at the top of Mt. Krizevac. It was sheer luxury, sensual bliss. My shoes and socks -- just a pair of black sneakers and ordinary white gym socks -- had never felt so comfortable, so accommodating, so supportive and well-cushioned. I was soaked in sweat, but that didn't matter. There was a nice breeze, and the air at the peak was cool and fresh, especially if you got into the shade, which all three of us quickly enough did.

We had been the better part of two hours, getting up Krizevac. After such a climb, everything seems gift and grace: the view from the peak was beautiful, the light breeze through the overhead branches was soothing, the cold drinks we bought from the two or three vendors (who somehow haul their wares up the mountain each morning and down each evening) were ambrosial.

"We offer now to God our prayers of thanksgiving!" Brigitta said, and I slid a sly smile in Rose's direction. We were thankful all right.

As Brigitta was saying some prayers aloud for us, it hit me: Chris. I had said I wanted to come up Krizevac barefoot, for Chris. I had wanted to give that fine young man something, had wanted to do something for him, had wanted to tell him, "Chris, I am with you. If any grace comes from this climb, it is yours."

No wonder the climb had been so hard! It had been an offering for Chris, for his peace and joy in eternity. Suddenly, I was immensely grateful for its difficulty: I had done it for Chris. And in fact, a couple days later, I climbed Krizevac a second time, barefoot, although this time staying on the right path. I offered the second climb for all my kids.

***

I came back to Marysville with fundraising on my mind. I had failed
to get the kids on the Holy Land trip that summer, but I had never
been convinced that was a realistic plan, anyway. I firmly believed
that, with a full year's planning and work, we could get back to
Medjugorje and Rome, in the summer of 2000, for the great Jubilee
Year celebrations. We had a slate of fundraisers ready to go that
summer, including another rummage sale, a money raffle, car washes
(at commercial venues, now, not at the church) and, in the fall, we
were going to re-start the monthly parish breakfast.

I remember that the money raffle did not go over well: if Elva had
not sold almost $800 in tickets, we would actually have lost money (I
think we were giving a thousand away).

I remember making big signs for the breakfast one Sunday afternoon
in July, with the TV on. Watching television is, basically, something
I just don't do, and haven't, since Barbara Bain walked off the
MISSION IMPOSSIBLE set in 1969. Even when it comes to news,
I prefer written accounts. But this was a breaking story—one might
say a heart-breaking story. JFK, Jr.'s plane was missing off
Martha's Vineyard and he, Carolyn and Lauren were all feared dead.
It was like coming in that hot August night in 1997 and seeing the
live feed out of Paris—Princess Diana could NOT be dead. Nor
could JFK, Jr. I was not a particular fan of his on any score, and I
always felt his sister much the more serious of the two of them. But
the Kennedy story is so much our own American story: how could it
be, that this family was being asked to bear yet another tragedy?

I remember sitting there thinking how sometimes I'd envied John,
Jr.—"How JFK, Jr. made $22 million in six months" I'd seen only a
few months before, blared on the cover of THE NATIONAL

ENQUIRER. "Yeah, made twenty-two million and did WHAT with it?" I had said to myself. As if there were some sort of moral approbation to be bestowed for being rich in the first place, and then using your money to make more money.

I'll admit, while I am in a confessional mode, that for years while I was writing and trying to get published, I could give in, at times, to a mix of envy and contempt for successfully published writers my own age. Does anyone remember Mona Simpson? Tama Janowitz? Jay McInerney? Brett Easton Ellis? These, and others, were the Bright Young Things of the literary world in the eighties, when I was also writing: novel after novel, and working with agent after agent, in New York. My years as a struggling novelist were largely joyful, because I loved my talent, and loved what I could produce with it. But that joy was sometimes punctuated by resentment, when I would see what I judged to be inferior work reaping a harvest of success.

Well, anyway, the news, which Mom had given me, as I came in from church that afternoon, that John-John Kennedy's plane was missing, brought out all my best instincts, and by the light of those instincts, my occasional envy of, and even a mild contempt for him, were put to shame. He was thirty-eight. He'd grown up in the public eye and without a father. He'd seen his uncle assassinated on television. His mother had died young just a few years before. What was there in this young man's tragic life, to envy or resent?

Mom had the TV on. She was busy with something in the next room, but she had the TV on, just to hear the latest developments. I sat in the family room with my poster boards and my felt markers, making signs for our parish breakfasts, and I tried to imagine that John, his wife and his sister-in-law were going to be found alive.

205

But in my heart, I knew they had perished. When I thought what it must've been like for them as the plane spiraled toward the water, I felt for them as if I had known them, and I prayed for them, and for the entire Kennedy and Besette families.

And then I thought of my own life; my studies at the seminary, my pilgrimages, my writing and my hopes for the future, my own huge and loving family, my many friends, and, of course, my kids, and it was an a-ha moment; what the literary world in the eighties and nineties called "an epiphany." It was as if I had a short and direct personal catechism on the real evil of envy. The sin directly attacks the ninth and tenth commandments. It turns a whole set of proper relationships on its head. The envious are saddened or angered at the happiness and good fortune of others, and satisfied at the failure and grief of others. It should be clear to any right-thinking person that this is one twisted way to look at life. I am able to report that envy has never been one of my principle sins; but to the extent that I had ever indulged it, toward John F. Kennedy, Jr., or anyone else, I was, that July Sunday, ashamed of myself.

***

August came, and with it, my trip to the Holy Land. It was a small group, just nineteen of us, including Mom and Trudi. About half the group was from the Marysville and Yuba City parishes, people I knew well. I remember deplaning at Tel Aviv, and seeing the big "Welcome to Israel" sign, and thinking, "Wow. Israel. The land of the patriarchs. The land of the prophets. The land of the psalmists. Of David. Of Solomon. Of Jesus. The Holy Land." I also thought of this: 1948. The land itself, after all, is just that – the land itself. Until 51 years earlier, it had been known as Palestine. 1948 started something new. Something ancient. Something new. I mean, where are the Hittites today? The Midianites? The Jebusites? The Amalekites? The Amorites? The Edomites? The Canaanites? The existence of the nation of Israel, the Jewish state, re-established in the middle of the twentieth century, after a diaspora of nineteen hundred years, and the horror of the Holocaust, seems to me something huge, for our times. Something unmistakable.

We were met by our guide Amir, a bright and engaging young man who, over the course of the trip, we were to learn, held three masters' degrees (in archaeology, history and I forget the third). Amir was one of six Catholic tour guides in all Israel. Milanka guarantees Catholic guides on 206 pilgrimages; she will not settle for anything less. Catholic pilgrims must have Catholic guides. But the small Christian population in Israel has been squeezed by the tensions between the Jews and the Muslims. I do not know if Amir still leads groups in Israel.

In any event, our group loved him. We went up the Mediterranean coast a short distance, that first evening, to Netanya. Mom and Trudi and I had rooms next door to each other, with sea views. After getting my things squared away and taking a shower, I came to their room and we had drinks and appetizers sent up. By this time, it was dusk. We sat on the balcony watching the Mediterranean roll in. The color of the sea was a sort of steel-blue, in the twilight. "Mom," I said, at one point. "We're in Israel!" Trudi laughed. "How cool is that?" she said. Mom smiled and lifted her glass – red wine, of course.

The Holy Land. First time. Let me tell you about it.

Haifa above the sea, date palms and bougainvillea in brilliant summer sunlight; the Baha'i (of all things!) world headquarters. Carmel, where Elijah hid out, above the coast. Galilee, deeply subtropical with its royal poinsiannas, its jacaranda and its ancient ruins – Magdala and Capernaum among them. Galilee's churches – of the Annunciation, of the Beatitudes, there above the blue blue sea, of Peter's Primacy, of the multiplication of the loaves and fishes. Tiberias – which can give Chicago a run for the right to the title, "The Windy City" – with its luxury hotels on the Sea of Galilee, with its beachfront shopping promenade. The great lake that is the Sea of Galilee, and a wooden boat meant to replicate those of Jesus' time; our passage across the sea, the "dry" Galilean heat causing us Californians to cherish our truly dry summers, as we pulled our soaked shirts away from our backs. The gentle slopes above the sea, lined with orange and banana groves. The switchback road up Mount Tabor, where you have to leave the busses behind and take cabs to the top – was this in fact the mount of the Transfiguration? The desert. A veritable moonscape—it impressed all of us; California's lush green desert this was *not*. Jericho. THIS was more like it. Scripture's "city of palms" is very much that, and has as well lots of tropical flowers, fruit and vegetable-laden open-air markets, great restaurants, resort hotels and a casino. And, vastly amusing to Mom, a funicular up the Mount of Temptation. The Dead Sea in its salt waste. Probable location of Sodom and Gomorrah. Bleached and bare slopes rising above the palm-lined and flower-bedecked beaches, a couple of which boast high-rise hotels. Then, Jerusalem. A city thirty-five hundred feet above the desert floor, hence, "up to Jerusalem." A modern metropolis almost the size of San Francisco, with hotels, restaurants, clubs, bars, shops and shopping, a financial center and so on, and at the same time…Jerusalem, city of Melchizedek ("King of Salem"), city of David, city of Solomon, city of the prophets, city of the Babylonian conquest, city of Christ and His Passion. Our rooms were at the Notre Dame Center, just across the busy street from the walls of the old city, Vatican flag fluttering overhead as we sat with our drinks and hors d'ouvres on the terrace. Rode a camel, and all that. The old city, with its narrow cobblestone streets, its bazaar with tents and booths selling religious articles sacred to three great faiths. The Temple Mount with the Wailing Wall, the Mosque of Omar and (literally) above all, the Dome of the Rock – as absolutely holy a place as I have ever "felt" anywhere. The Via Dolorosa, that is, THE Via Dolorosa. St. Helena, mother of Constantine and Empress Augusta of the Roman Empire, first Christian pilgrim to the Holy Land, circa 330 AD. The churches on sites Helena herself selected, based on the testimony of the local Christian community. Holy Sepulchre, Nativity. Everybody's here – us Latin Catholics, the Armenians, the Melkites, the Coptics, the Greeks. We share jurisdiction in certain of the churches and it gets downright Byzantine, who's in charge of what altar, what chapel belongs to which Rite. The history—Canaanites, Jebusites, Hittites, before the Jews; Assyrians, Babylonians, Greeks, Romans, Arabs, Crusaders, Turks, Palestinians since. Jerusalem, sacred to half the world's population, perhaps the most significant city on earth.

Are you feeling a little overwhelmed, dear reader? Let me tell you, so was I. My first visit to Israel/Palestine is largely a rush of images, in my mind. I was to return to the Holy Land, the following summer, and I felt I "got" the place a little more deeply, then. But it would take, at the least, several more pilgrimages, for me to really deeply apprehend the Holy Land, to really begin to feel that I know it, that I have some understanding of how all that culture, religion, history, strife, glory, mysticism and experience of God comingle there, in that small and spectacular land. Israel is not a whole lot bigger than the Bay Area, yet it contains five distinct climates, from desert to alpine, is the crossroads of not just the three Abrahamic faiths, but of three continents, and in it, the ages themselves live and tell their distinct stories. I have never been anywhere like Israel. I suppose

the reason is that there is no place, like Israel. Palestine. The Holy
Land. God Himself chose it. The place overwhelms you.

***

As with the Fatima-Lourdes trip, I had added a four-day visit to
Medjugorje, at the end of the Holy Land pilgrimage. Only five of us
opted for the Medjugorje leg of the trip. The whole group flew to
Frankfurt where we spent the night. The next morning, after a huge,
very American breakfast that just *sold* Trudi on the Novotel at
Frankfurt Airport, the group split. Our planes were sitting right next
to each other and we watched as the San Francisco-bound passengers
boarded. Then we crossed to the Croatian air gate, and our two-hour
flight to Split.

Slavenka greeted us. She detailed events for the coming four days.
We opted for a day out to go to Dubrovnik, and Mom said we
needed, from now on, to plan to come to the city for a night or two at
the end of each trip. A few hours in Dubrovnik just was not enough.

Mom was a great hit with Slavenka. One morning, when Slavenka
came to the pansion, she knocked on the door to Mom and Trudi's
room, and Mom answered. They were still getting up, and Mom
assured Slavenka that she would be downstairs shortly, "I just have
to put on my face." Slavenka loved that line. She quotes it to this
day. She would not see Mom for another four years, but she always
asked me about her, whenever she spoke with me. When Slavenka
was visiting Milanka in New York, shortly after I had been ordained,
she asked if they could call out to California and talk "with Father

Jim and his mom." Mom was delighted with the call. The first thing Slavenka asked Mom was if she had put on her face.

It happened that our post-Israel visit to Medjugorje coincided with the Feast of the Assumption, August 15. It was a Sunday, that year. As Mom, Trudi, and I, and Annie and Judi, the Holy Land pilgrims who had come to Medjugorje with us, were walking toward St. James for the evening Mass, we noticed a stream of pilgrims headed in the direction of Krizevac. Looking toward the mountain, we saw why: the great concrete cross at the top of the mountain was illuminated. It shone a kind of pink-gold. It was not yet seven PM, so it was still daylight. I assumed we were looking at reflected sunlight, though how concrete could give back such colored light was beyond me. At this time, there was no electricity, on either Krizevac or Apparition Hill. Someone told Annie, from our group, that it was a miracle, a sign from Our Lady, to celebrate her feast day. "How charming," I thought, and headed into Mass.

When we emerged from the church at close to eight-thirty, it was getting dark – and the bright glow from the cross was steady as ever. It was clearly not a matter of reflected sunlight. What is more, there were now many, many lights flowing in a line, up the face of the slope – pilgrims with flashlights, going up to observe the miracle close-hand. We had caught up with Slavenka, somewhere in the street, and when Mom pointed to the lit-up cross and asked her about it, Slavenka simply smiled and said, "She does that, sometimes." Medjugorje is a place so deeply touched by grace that miracles have become part of the fabric of daily life.

Mom, Trudi and I were NOT up for a nighttime hike up Krizevac. Nor were Annie and Judi. We toasted the miracle from our table, at the Dubrovnik Club.

***

I returned to the seminary a couple of weeks after the Holy Land trip. I had arranged a great parish assignment for myself that year. It was at St. Anthony's, Liz's parish in Oakland. I had two responsibilities there. The first was with Oakland Community Organizations, a faith-based community organizing group for which my sister now worked fulltime. One of the participating Oakland parishes was St. Anthony's.

The second responsibility was to try to get a youth group going at St. Anthony's. Liz taught the Confirmation class there, and knew a lot, a lot of the teens, in that parish. She felt for them, in the lack of church responsiveness to their needs. St. Anthony's is a large inner-city parish with a diverse population, but the main group there was and is Hispanic. Given my success with Hispanic teens in Marysville, Liz hoped I would be able to develop a thriving youth program, as well, at St. Anthony's. She told the kids in her Confirmation class flat-out that she knew my Marysville kids and I would get to Europe for the Jubilee. She dreamed that maybe some of her St. Anthony's teens could join us.

Oakland is half an hour from the seminary, provided that you avoid traffic. Given my dual responsibilities in the parish, I was in Oakland two to three times per week, and had dinner with Liz and my Oakland nieces, Sara, Lupe and Marisol, at least once, and often twice a week. Because seminarians typically are at their parish assignments on Sundays, Liz, the girls and I also frequently had Sunday brunch together, and these dinners and brunches of course included my little great-nephews Anthony and Adrian, Sara's sons. They were so little then. Anthony had been born in 1996; Adrian just the previous spring – March 15, 1999.

Field education placements at the seminary are only supposed to involve five hours' work a week on the seminarian's part. But I was engaged by this assignment at St. Anthony's and was happy to put in the extra time on it. And I loved the fact that, by virtue of my placement, I now got to see my Oakland family every Sunday, and a couple times during the week as well.

My Oakland nieces and my Marysville kids were all the same age. They had already met, and though there was some joshing rivalry about who was really number one with me, in fact, they greatly enjoyed one another's company. There was a weekend in November when I brought several of the boys to Oakland, specifically to speak at the Masses at St. Anthony's, to try to drum up interest in the youth group that I was trying to get off the ground, there in the parish. I drove to Marysville after my classes on Friday, and spent the night. Saturday afternoon, I drove back down to Oakland, with Mikey, Ada, Fonz and Tico.

We put up at the Emeryville Sheraton and met with Liz, my nieces and some of the Oakland youth leaders for dinner at the Alameda Chevy's. This was one of the first Chevy's anywhere in California; it was right on the estuary, looking back at Oakland's night-lit skyline. The Oakland kids who made it to dinner that night were all girls. This was just fine with the guys. We went to a Bond movie afterward: THE WORLD IS NOT ENOUGH, and the only reason I remember that title is that Shirley Manson (and Garbage, her ironically titled rock group) sang the song of the same name, in the opening credits. Don't get me wrong, I love James Bond, but…does anyone remember any detail, the next day, from a Bond film? Garbage, on the other hand, was my favorite nineties group.

Anyway, the next day, Sunday, the boys spoke at all the Masses at St. Anthony's, and urged the local teens to check out the youth group which was meeting on Thursday evenings. Tico in particular spoke well, which I thought interesting, in that he had not been on the pilgrimage. The four of them made a strong and favorable impression, and I hoped for more St. Anthony's teens at our youth meetings, as a result.

St. Anthony's did not have a facility like Marysville's Youth Hall available, but Father Thuong, the pastor, had given us a good meeting space at the parish, and I was there two Thursday evenings a month, in the hope of getting a real youth ministry established in this very deserving parish.

I remember that, after we had done all the morning Masses that Sunday, the boys and I met up with Liz, my nieces and nephews, and a couple of the girls from the Oakland group, for brunch at a restaurant we liked, near Lake Merritt. Liz, my nieces and I had taken to calling this restaurant "Big Hat" because of the many, many Oakland churchwomen who arrived there for brunch on Sundays, wearing smartly tailored dresses and suits, and…big Sunday hats. The food was good, and the prices cheap. I have some very happy memories, from those Sundays, in 1999 and 2000, at "Big Hat."

After brunch, the boys and I drove over to the seminary, and spent the afternoon there; but for Mikey, none of them had seen it yet. We went to dinner at Chili's, and – somehow – I drove them home that evening, and then turned around, and drove back down to St. Patrick's. That would have been something between a four and five hour roundtrip, and this, at the tail-end of a very high-energy weekend. Heaven knows where my energy came from in those days. I remember that at the dinner at Chevy's, I said something to Liz about it being a free weekend for me, and so I was able to "take it off" and arrange this meeting of my Marysville and Oakland youth groups, and Liz just shook her head, sighing, and said, "Jim, you do NOT get the idea of a weekend off." This, though, from a woman to whom sixty- and seventy-hour work weeks were and are the norm.

***

On the pilgrimage front, I had gone all-out. This was, after all, to be the year we would return: the Jubilee Year. I scheduled several trips with Milanka – all Italy and the Holy Land, as I judged that those were the two venues that would be sure to book. My hope was to earn some strong commissions on the early summer trips, and be able to use them to help get the kids on an Italy-Medjugorje trip in August.

Toward this end, I had my brother Dan, who worked in print promotions and advertising in Los Angeles, create a gorgeous brochure for prospective pilgrims. In addition, I put together a substantial package of information, some provided by 206 Tours and some self-developed, so that, when I responded to a request for information about my tours, I could compete with the best. My presentation that winter and spring, 1999-2000, was very

215

professional; I knew it and was proud of it. I remember when the brochure my brother had done for me arrived via FedEx at the seminary. Some of the seminarians were with me when I opened the box up, and I can still hear their "ooohs" and "ahhhs" at the beautiful brochure Dan had done for me.

As to the seminary itself, well, second-year theology, which was my class, was reputed to be the toughest year in the program. I had some great classes that autumn, and the following spring, and I do remember working hard in them. I received the minor orders of acolyte and reader, and I served as an "altar boy" for the first time – at age 43! I was only nervous 'til Mass started. Once we got going, it all felt completely natural, and I have to say that it sometimes surprises me even today, three years after my ordination, how "at home" I feel, on the altar.

There were a few other things on my agenda that year, as well. At the top of the list, my long in-progress novel, GOLD COUNTRY. I look back on this now, and smile, but at the start of my second year at St. Pat's, I had a very deep hope of being able to finish the book there. There was also my thesis at the Dominican School, which I expected to complete first: the novel second. I really did expect to complete both, at the seminary, that year.

I remember writing my friend Lauren, who had been in classes with me at the Dominican School, about my ambitions for the year. I had seven or eight, and not one of them was minor. In fact, to achieve any three or four of them would constitute a substantial success. I, of course, was committed to accomplishing all seven or eight of them, and what can I say, ten years down the road, about that? I was what

I was, and I am what I am. I do not know, dear reader, that I am all that much more realistic about my limitations, today.

Anyway, I wrote Lauren, at the start of the fall semester, about my dreams and hopes for the coming year. She wrote back that it made her tired just reading the list. Lauren and I often went hiking with another friend, Mark, who was only my age, but who had been our professor, in Logic and Metaphysics, among other things, at the Dominican School. Mark and Lauren were really into hiking. I was NOT into hiking. But I was really into my friendship with Mark and Lauren. So, I got together with them, several times a year and…hiked. And…talked. Talked and talked and talked. I told Mark and Lauren everything, and so it is that I wrote Lauren in September, 1999, and outlined to her my ambitious plans for the coming academic year.

I smile now, thinking about it. Oh, in time, in time, I achieved all but one of those goals. But I was half a decade, managing it – nothing like nine or ten months. Nothing like.

SEVEN

I had started running ads for the Jubilee Year pilgrimages in November. I advertised in all the northern California dioceses, plus L. A. Right after Christmas, and straight through Lent, my phones, both at the seminary and in Marysville, rang off the hook. I sometimes got eight or ten requests for information on the tours in a single day. I had a substantial packet to send out, and to deal with the demand, I would take an afternoon or two each week, and simply assemble packets, so that I had them ready to go, as the requests came in. The trips were booking by the end of January, and I was confident that I had a successful summer ahead.

The kids came down to Oakland with me a couple of times, that winter, to help build the youth group at St. Anthony's. I had hoped for big things, after the boys had spoken at the Masses in November, but that had not happened. Liz talked the group up in her Confirmation class, and a few kids in the class started to attend the meetings, but we were very slow, getting the group to even fifteen kids attending on a regular basis. I had a core group of eight or ten Oakland teens, and to try to build excitement and interest, we decided to have a dance for Valentine's Day. The Marysville kids had held several dances in my time with them, and they were huge successes – way over a hundred teens every time. The group had been partly built through the dances, which served for many of the kids as an introduction to the youth ministry at St. Joseph's.

I put Maritza, the real leader of the Oakland group, in charge of dance preparations, and she organized her team to attend to every detail. They would take care of decorations, refreshments, getting the dj, and advertising the dance to local teens. Meanwhile, I told the Marysville gang about it, and they were very up for coming. I felt that if fifteen or twenty of the Marysville kids came, and if Maritza and her squad could get even thirty or forty Oakland teens to come, that would pretty much fill the Club Room at St. Anthony's, and as long as the space looked full, to the kids, the dance would be a success.

About a week before the dance was scheduled, we had to change the date, push it back from February 11 to February 18. I do not remember why. Nor do I remember how it was that this rather crucial piece of information never got to the Marysville kids. On Friday, February 11, Bishop Garcia, Sacramento's auxiliary, happened to be visiting the seminary, and he had issued a general invitation to all the Sacramento guys to join him for dinner, if we were available that evening. He took us to a pricey place in Palo Alto; I do not remember the name.

It was a very wet night. That was, in fact, a very wet winter: I remember waking up morning after morning that winter at the seminary, to the sound of heavy rain beyond my windows. Anyway, it was not a nice evening. I got home from dinner with the Bishop and the other guys, and was glad to be in for the night. I had nothing planned for the evening, and remember thinking that I could actually just sit down and read, for pleasure, if I wanted. Or I could write a letter to Ruthanne. Or I could…

The phone rang. It was my niece Lupe, in Oakland.

"Jim, did you forget to tell the Marysville group about the date change for the dance?"

"No. Why?"

"Just a minute," Lupe said, and handed the phone off.

"Jim, it's Wally. Where's the dance?"

"It's next week! What are you doing in Oakland?!"

"Next week! It's this week! We drove for two hours through a flood to get here, Jim!"

"'We?' Who else is in Oakland?"

"Pancho, Junior, Cruz, Alejandra –"

"Oh my God –"

"Ada, Leticia, JT, Lilin –"

"Okay, okay, I get it –"

"Angel, Talia –"

"I GET it, Wally. I will be right over. It's gonna take a while, in this weather."

"Drive safe."

"Is everybody there at Liz's?"

"Yeah, all of us. We're all okay. Your nieces are pretty cute, you know."

When I got to Liz's – it was maybe nine PM – I asked the kids if they had eaten; they had not. That was the first order of business. With my nieces, we went to the Lyons in Emeryville, out near the freeway. While the kids got settled and ordered, I went across the parking lot to the Four Points Sheraton, and got several rooms. Lupe had urged me not to do this, as the Sheraton was not cheap, and we could find a Motel 6 someplace for half the rate. I was not about to have any more uncertainty, tonight. The kids had driven two hours through one of the winter's strongest storms, to support my youth ministry in Oakland. Alejandra had told me that, at one point, the wind and rain were so bad they pulled off the freeway, and said a Rosary. I wanted this situation fixed as quickly, as conveniently, and as comfortably as possible, and I told Lupe that if the Sheraton had the rooms, we were taking them.

My kids were good-natured. They were disappointed about the dance, but they picked right up with the prospect of dinner out, and later, at the hotel, most of us gathered in one of the rooms, and laughed about the evening, and just shot the breeze. I went back to the seminary around midnight. I was back at the Lyons next morning, around eleven, to get the kids breakfast before seeing them off. The storm was clearing out by then, and though it was still windy, the rain was over. I waved the kids off, and drove back to St.

Pat's. The hotel had run me six hundred, and I don't know what dinner and breakfast had cost. This was turning out to be one pricey dance, for my Oakland youth group.

And, unfortunately, the Marysville kids could not return the following Friday (it was President's Day weekend, and I think a lot of them went up to the snow, which there would have been a LOT of that winter). The Oakland kids managed to get about thirty-five teens to the dance. My nieces helped out, too. The young people had a good time and stayed late, but the fact is, the dance just missed the critical mass that makes an event like this a success with teens: my fifteen kids from Marysville would have guaranteed that. And as it happened, after the dance, attendance at youth group meetings at St. Anthony's began to wane. People think of me as a can't-miss youth ministry kind of guy, but the fact is, I have had more failures, in youth ministry, than successes. It is just that my biggest success – the Marysville group – was so over-the-top that it is what my work with the young is judged by.

***

The idea of a year out had begun to appeal to me. Looking through my journal entries for the winter and spring of 2000, I can see why. My priority was getting my kids back to Europe. But though I could keep the Teen Rosary Group going with meetings, dinners out and some regular fundraisers, and at the same time fulfill all my obligations at the seminary, the kind of laser-focused concentration necessary to get the kids back to Europe – the sort I had exhibited in Marysville, in 1997-8 – was not possible. I was doing well, booking tours for the Jubilee, but I had no guarantee that I was going to be able to get the kids back, and if we missed, then I wanted to take a year out and focus solely on that goal.

There were other reasons, as well, for seriously considering a year out. Remember those seven or eight goals I had written Lauren about, in September? By late winter I was facing up to the reality that I am limited by physical space and time – an annoying fact which I every now and then need to be reminded of. If I took a year's leave from the seminary program, I could finish my thesis for the Dominican M.A., finish GOLD COUNTRY, start looking for an agent, and get back to work on one of my other in-progress novels. I would plan to finance the year away via commissions from pilgrimages, of which I would schedule several, throughout the year.

Add to this set of considerations the fact that my Grand Am, Robinson, at seven years, and approaching 200,000 miles, was beginning to act like an old car. (I always give my cars literary names. My first car, a 1978 Camaro, bought my last year in college, was named after my then-favorite novelist, Huxley. By the time, 1992, that I bought the Grand Am, Muriel Spark had long been my favorite novelist, and I named the car after her rollicking castaway adventure novel, ROBINSON. I did this because the car's beautiful color looked like tropical water, the kind that surrounded the island in Spark's novel.)

Anyway, the first real trouble with Robinson had come while we had been in Israel, the previous August. I had left the car with my niece Sara, and I guess it ran fine for a few days then suddenly would not start. The problem was not the battery. I no longer remember what the problem was. I do remember that when I came home from the trip I had the car towed from Oakland to Marysville so that my mechanic, Al, could work on it. I still remember Al's astonishment, as the flatbed tow truck let the car down at his shop. "Jim! All the way from Oakland? What did that cost?" I don't remember what it cost; it was worth it. I didn't want anyone but Al working on the Grand Am. To this day, no one but Al works on my cars.

Al fixed the trouble with the Grand Am – and he fixed more trouble with it, later that fall. One mercifully sunny and dry November afternoon, the car simply stopped dead on me, in rush hour traffic, on the skybridge in Emeryville. A couple of Good Samaritans stopped to help me, one of them fortunately equipped with a cell phone. I remember twice having rentals at the seminary that fall, because Robinson was with Al. There were also a couple days that autumn when I had Mom's red Mustang at the seminary, which drew a lot of admiring looks and comments. This was the beginning of three years of difficulty with my car; I remember calculating once that, in a 24-month period, the Grand Am had cost me just over $8,000 in repairs. Divide that figure by twenty-four, and you come out well above $300/month; that is, the payment on a new car. The difference of course is that, with a new car, you know that it is going to start in the morning.

I could not buy a new car, because I had no income. I had student financial aid, not an income. If I were to take a year out, organize and lead some successful tours, finish my novel and find an agent for it and who knows – maybe even sell it! – I would have an income. I could replace Robinson. I already knew the car I wanted, after the Grand Am: I wanted the long and sleek Monte Carlo. They were, at that time, running about $20,000. I would, of course, have the car on a five-year schedule of monthly payments.

All these factors were converging on my discernment regarding a year away from the seminary that winter and spring, and by March, I had made up my mind, to take it. I'd been given a push one sunny Friday afternoon at the start of the month, when I happened to be visiting at the chancery in Sacramento with a highly placed diocesan official, whom I will refer to as Father Montez. I had gone to see Father Montez because I wanted to talk to him about my pilgrimage plans for August. If it turned out that I was able to take the kids, I hoped as well to be able to take a couple of our young Filipino seminarians, as chaperones. These seminarians were only five or six years older than the kids themselves: I wanted my kids to meet YOUNG seminarians.

Of course, the seminarians would need help with their ticket costs, and I wanted to go into two or three of the Sacramento parishes where the seminarians were known, and make a pitch. The Catholic people LOVE seminarians (with good reason!) and tend to be very generous with them. I felt there was an excellent chance we could raise the money we needed to get two or three of the seminarians on the August trip, just by letting people know that we hoped to be able to do it. I had already cleared this plan with my superiors at the seminary, and with Father Murphy and Sister Maureen at the Vocations Office. As I wanted to go into parishes, though, I thought I should seek a green light from the top, hence my meeting with Father Montez.

I am not going to give many details, but a priest employed in a lofty position at chancery (a monsignor, of course) intruded himself into the meeting between Father Montez and myself and…made an ass of himself. This person (I will call him Monsignor Q) had seen one of my pilgrimage ads in the diocesan paper, and taken umbrage – at what, I to this day do not know. He had evidently demanded to know how "this seminarian" could be running pilgrimages in the summer, and when he was not satisfied with the answers he got from the Vocations Office, he went to the Bishop's Office. Informed (by whom I do not know) that Father Montez was meeting with me later that week, Monsignor Q invited himself to the meeting, and as I say, made a fool of himself. He was indignant, insulting, insinuating and intimidating. I amend that: he attempted to be intimidating. I recognized that that was his intent, but I was so astonished at his behavior that I didn't know what I felt – except that maybe the Diocese should get him into therapy, since he pretty clearly had some issues.

At one point, Monsignor Q indicated the 206 Tours logo in the newspaper ad and said, in a tone that implied grave lack of discretion, perhaps even something sinister, on my part, "Just what is your association with this organization?" (As Lauren was to put it, when she and I were on one of our hikes, the very next day, "Sheeesh! I'm glad it said 206 and not 666!")

I explained to Monsignor that I led pilgrimages for 206.

Q sat back in his chair, looking at me with eyes artificially, even comically, wide. "You lead pilgrimages for them." His tone implied that I had just inadvertantly admitted to a criminal offense. He looked to Father Montez, as if to say, "You have heard his blasphemy for yourself. What more evidence do we need?"

Father Montez sighed. (I should point out, perhaps, that Father Montez actually outranked Q, hierarchically. But Q was a VIP at chancery, and everyone had to take him seriously, hard as that must at times have been to do.)

Before the meeting was over, I had been accused of deceiving my superiors, of presuming on the good will of the people of the Diocese, of attempting tax fraud, of placing the Diocese at legal liability (should anyone fall, for instance, on one of my pilgrimages) and I can't remember what-all else. I do remember that Father Montez leapt into it, when the tax question was introduced, and defended me. I was told, by Monsignor, that if seminarians wanted summer work, the Diocese provided it. Just for your info, dear reader, the work Q was referring to is clipping the hedges and weeding the beds at the Catholic cemeteries in Sacramento, in the city's 100-degree summer heat. For minimum wage.

When Monsignor Q left, taking the odor of sulfur with him, Father Montez asked me if I were all right. I just shook my head. There are people like this everywhere, of course. The Church has no monopoly on bullies with fragile egos. The problem with people like this in the Church is the clerical culture which handles everything obliquely, rather than in a straight-forward fashion. I feel I should point out that there is such a thing as good clerical culture. But there is also a diseased clericalism which protects and even promotes people like Q. I could write a chapter (at least) on this diseased clericalism, but never mind. The problems of a dysfunctional corporate culture within the Church are beyond the scope and purpose of this narrative. (For a Biblical perspective, see Matthew 13:24-30.) Father Montez asked me if I were all right. I shook my head and said, "Don't worry. I'm cool." To this day I am not sure which would have been the more appropriate response to Monsignor Q: outrage, or laughter.

I was laughing about it, the next day, on the hike at Tomales Bay, with Lauren and Mark, but I was angry, too: Q had torpedoed any possibility of my going into the parishes where my young seminarian friends were known, and asking for help. A pastor at one of those parishes, hearing about it all months later, told me that I needed to draw a valuable lesson from the experience: "Never go to chancery for ANYthing, Jim, that you can take care of on the level of the parish. The only people whose approval you needed, to go into the parishes on this matter, were the pastors of those parishes. This is a basic tenet of Catholic social ethics: the principle of subsidiarity. Address and resolve problems at the level at which they arise."

Well, anyway, if I had had any lingering doubts about taking the year out, before the meeting at chancery, those doubts were extinguished, after it. In leaving the program, I would take myself out from under any malevolent influence, such as I had encountered in Monsignor Q, that might seek to derail my plans with the kids. If I were not a seminarian, Q could have no authority over me or my actions. He had no authority over me, in any event, but I was able to read the dynamic between him and good Father Montez, and I decided, as I was leaving the chancery that bright afternoon, that I was gone for the coming year – and glad of it.

I was glad of it above all for the kids; the year away would give me a safety net, if I failed to get them back to Europe this summer. But there were all those other factors converging on my decision as well: my thesis, my novel, my need to find an agent, my need to make some money, my need to replace Robinson. I felt a great sense of release, of freedom and opportunity, contemplating the coming year away from the seminary program. I felt as if it were the time-out I needed, to look to my own deepest priorities, to pull my plans and hopes together, and attend to them. Ultimately the plan for a year out would benefit my remaining years at the seminary: I would return to St. Pat's with my personal decks cleared.

***

One of the principles of Ignatian discernment is recognition of our desires and our feelings, is allowing ourselves to be led by what we are drawn to. That said, there has to be more to our discernment than simply lots of prayer and gut-level feeling. It is not always possible to hear the answer in prayer; and there are times when gut-level feeling must simply be set aside. I could not have known it, that day I left the chancery, but I was on the verge of making a serious mistake. I can only guess at the seriousness of the mistake by the deep improbability of the corrective action that was necessary to pull me back from making it.

I had made my decision the first week of March, and by March 23, a Thursday, I had not yet spoken of the plan to anyone, except Mom and Trudi, and of course, the kids, who were excited at the prospect of my being back in Marysville for a year. I wanted time just to sit with my decision, quietly, let it sink in, before talking to anyone about it. I knew I would need to let Fr. Murphy and Sr. Maureen know of the decision by May, because they would be busy, early in the summer, lining up parish residencies for me and my class, for the coming year. (The third year in the theology program at St. Pat's is spent in residence in a parish in the seminarian's diocese.) I did not want them to go to a lot of trouble finding a place in a parish for me when I was going to be in Marysville, on a year's leave.

229

I came in from St. Anthony's, where I'd been with the kids in the Oakland youth group, the evening of March 23, to a message from Sister Maureen to the effect that she had just set up my residency-year assignment: at St. Charles Borromeo in Sacramento. All I can say about this message is that I knew, in that instant, that my plans for a year out had just been cancelled. St. Charles Borromeo is the parish Uncle Jim founded in Sacramento in 1960, and over which he presided as pastor for thirty-four years. The rectory was a second home to me, and my family knew many people in the parish. Trust me, these facts would typically have ruled out St. Charles, as an assignment for me. The only parish in the Diocese less likely to be assigned as my pastoral year residence, would have been St. Joseph's, in Marysville.

Sometimes God writes His will in letters fifty feet high and blinking bright neon. There could be NO mistaking this assignment. God was telling me, through His reliable instrument, Sr. Maureen McInerney at Sacramento Vocations, "I want you in the program, next year." I was so stunned at Sr. Maureen's message that it took me some time, a day or two, to process the feelings it evoked. At once, sorrow for the loss of the freedom and opportunity I had glimpsed, via the prospect of the year out; and at the same time, a sense of astonished gratitude – to Sr. Maureen, and to God – for signaling to me so utterly, so unmistakably, His will. "You want me at St. Charles, Father? I'm there!" That was my response. I still have a copy of the letter I wrote from St. Pat's the next day, addressed to Msgr. Jim Church (a GOOD monsignor; the title itself neither implies nor conveys defect of character). Msgr. Church was an old friend of my uncle's, and was now pastor at St. Charles. Though my emotions were in flux over the news of the assignment, I knew that, in the circumstances, my emotions were not to be consulted. I had marching orders fifty feet high and blinking bright neon. I assured Msgr. Church that news of the assignment astonished me, that I could never have guessed I might come to my uncle's own parish, as a resident seminarian, that I was grateful to him for agreeing to have me, that I much looked forward to getting to know him, and the parish, in the coming year, and that I would be in touch over the summer, Sincerely Yours in Christ, Jim Sullivan.

That was that. I mailed the letter. Meanwhile I called Sr. Maureen, got her voice mail and I think I sounded genuinely joyful, in my message.

But…the kids…Europe?

By late March, I was getting nervous about the prospect of getting them on the August trip. The long rush over the winter of requests for information had begun to taper off, and though I continued to get bookings, the window of opportunity to get the kids onboard for August was beginning to close. I had, maybe, another six weeks, to bring it off, in part simply because I was talking about ten, twelve, fifteen young people, and this was the Jubilee Year. Spaces were at a premium, and Milanka would not be able to do a lot of last-minute bookings, as Sergio had had to do, in 1998. She would not be able to find seats on the flights, or rooms at the hotels. I had to know soon, just where I was going to come in on commissions and free trips. And I was prepared to find that we were going to come in short. I had been sanguine about that possibility, when I had planned next year off, next year given to one primary objective: getting the kids back to Europe. Now that year of opportunity, of laser-like focus and dedication, was gone. Gone, evidently, by God's own hand. St. Charles Borromeo! No, no, I could not regret next year's amazing placement. I just had to hope that the kids and I would, after all, make it to Italy, in August, for the Jubilee.

***

We did not make it. I was going to make several thousand dollars in commissions, on the June trip to Holy Land, which wound up with just over forty pilgrims. This was great, and if either of my Italian trips had booked as well, the kids and I would have pulled it off. But the first Italian trip, in late May, had just barely made: I had earned a free trip for our priest, Father Meka, a wonderful young Salesian from the Graduate Theological Union in Berkeley. Well, actually, he was from Fiji, but he was studying at the time at the GTU. I had gotten a free trip for Father Meka, but Milanka gave me my ticket on that trip; I had not earned it. And the August trip, the one I had wanted to get the kids on, though guaranteed to go, had not yet broken into significant commissions (and in fact, it would not do so: I remember getting a check from 206 for about one thousand dollars, for that trip; nothing close to the amount we would have needed, to bring the youth tour off).

I did not yet know, as the seminary's semester wrapped up, in mid-May, if the kids and I would make it, or not. I mean, remembering how the 1998 trip had still hung in the balance less than a month before we left, I could take hope in the possibilities that might yet develop. After all, this was the Jubilee Year. And I had knocked myself out, all semester, with the extra work involved, pulling these trips together, and doing the fundraisers with the kids. I had not complained of the eighty-plus hour weeks I had kept, since January: quite the opposite, the work had charged me up, had energized me. I was grateful for the opportunity to do it. I left the seminary that May determined in my hopes for the kids.

My first Italian trip left May 22; I remember that Matt and his mom, Lana, drove me to SFO. I remember too that, like the day we left for the 1998 trip, it was hot. Maybe the first real heat wave of that summer. Knowing me, I probably took some kind of precarious hope in that coincidence; probably took it as a sign. After all, God could do anything. But it was obvious, at that point, that if anything were going to happen, God would have to make it happen.

I had, meanwhile, a great Italian pilgrimage, small though it was (I think including Father Meka and myself we were seventeen). The weather in Rome, Florence and Assisi was perfect. Our guide was Priscilla, a beautiful young Italian who rode a motor bike, and I met several local guides on that trip whom I would become friendly with, over that summer, with my repeat visits to Rome. I bought a lot of rosaries and t-shirts for the kids. And Father Meka later told Marie Smith, who had introduced him to me, that the pilgrimage had given him the strength he needed to go back to Fiji, and take up a new assignment, an assignment he had been worried about, involving the formation of seminarians. I was very glad to hear that, consoled, even. Clearly, whatever might come of my own deepest dream, that Jubilee summer, these pilgrimages would prove fruitful for the folks who were on them. I was, by the summer of 2000, fully committed to pilgrimage as an apostolate, a form of ministry. I still see pilgrimages that way, and that is why I continue to book one or two each year.

Fonz and Lilin met my flight, when I returned to San Francisco. Fonz was playing a cd on the way back to Marysville, of a new rapper, someone I had never heard of before, and whom I am not going to name here: he has long since slithered out of the limelight, and gracias a Dios. I never listened to rap before I started working with the kids, and my general opinion of it was "put a 'c' in front of it." But this guy took it all to a new level; a level, in my view, of genuine depravity. The hatred he spewed in the name of "artistic license" was so vitriolic that I wondered if he might not be mentally ill. It actually made me angry, listening to him, angry to think that this sort of garbage was what the entertainment culture was prepared to reward. It astonished me, to think of record label executives, men and women with families, I supposed, with children of their own, sitting around a conference table and talking about this mental case as if he were an artist. An entertainment industry incapable of policing itself ultimately runs the risk of finding itself policed from the outside. I guess most people making decisions in popular music in twenty-first century America simply don't know enough history to realize as much.

Anyway, this cretinous rapper made me all the more determined to get my kids back to Medjugorje. The assault on our youth from the popular culture needs to be met with shock-force: our young people need powerful experiences of grace, tangible and profound, to be able to fight back. To even understand the need to fight back. They need to see that there is an alternative to the youth culture that is projected into their lives every day, by the media. In Medjugorje, they see that alternative. At World Youth Day, they see that alternative. At the National Catholic Youth Convention, they see that alternative. I knew I had an obligation to continue to provide my young people with that alternative, and our chosen venue was Medjugorje.

But…we were not going to Medjugorje, that Jubilee summer, nor to Rome. I do not remember any one moment when I let the kids know that our effort had fallen short. I do not remember, in fact, just when I myself knew. It was sometime between that May pilgrimage to Rome and the Holy Land-Rome pilgrimage that followed, in the second half of June. I felt bad for all the kids, but especially so for several of the girls – Alejandra and Elva at the top of the list – who had not gone two years before, and who had really worked hard, to try to make this trip happen.

This was the June that many of my kids were graduating from Lindhurst High: the single largest birth year for my kids is 1982. A number of their classmates were headed to Hawaii the week after graduation, for their senior trip. I remember that Ravi and Timmy were going, and had urged some of the guys – Jorge, Mikey, Nelson, Omar, Fonz – to join them. But the guys said no, because they needed to save their money for Rome.

This really made me feel bad: because I had put Europe in their plans for this summer, plans that had not worked out, my boys were missing their senior trip to Hawaii. I secretly resolved to someday make that up to them. I imagined that I would do it by taking them all to the Islands for a week, at some future point: some future point when I would have the money to get nine or ten young men to Honolulu. As it happens, I have in the years since taken most of them to a gorgeous tropical locale, either picking up their costs outright, or paying a large chunk of it. But the place we go for tropical water and coconut palms is not Hawaii; it is Venezuela. And what draws us there is not leisure but a group of young Venezuelans who might be brothers to my boys. That is another book.

In any event, the guys took the disappointment well. They took it very well. They showed what a classy set they are, in the way they handled it. We were all sitting out front one June evening, at Ada and Pancho's house, and the guys were excitedly talking about their new plans, given that Europe had fallen through. They had organized a California beaches road trip, and it included Baja California. I forget how many of them had decided to go, but it was most of the core group that had played and prayed for Rome: Jorge, Matt, Mikey, Fonz, Ada, Pancho, Lilin, Wally…I don't remember if Tico went, or Nelson, or Omar. But a good group of them did, and they had a blast. At one of the beaches in southern California, they were asked by a TV crew to join a crowd, and stand near the front, so that viewers could see them: no surprise there! Jorge came back from that trip a blonde, and Matt (who was already blonde) an uber-blonde. I have photos of bbqs at Mom's, that summer, showing Jorge with his yellow hair. I still smile, looking at them.

Meanwhile, I had a second pilgrimage, a big one, over forty people, to the Holy Land and Rome. This was the second half of June. It was a great trip – we were favored with beautiful weather in both Israel and Italy, and I made some lifelong friends, on this trip. One of our local guides in Rome, Esther, joked on the bus with the pilgrims that if they had any questions she could not answer, "Just ask Jim. He is practically a Roman. He is here every six weeks or so, and knows the city like the back of his hand." This was a bit of an exaggeration, but it is true that I spent a lot of time in Rome that summer, and I loved it.

Something at the very start of the June pilgrimage stays with me, perhaps because the feeling was so ungenerous of me, and I want to believe, so uncharacteristic. As our flight from San Francisco to Frankfurt was ascending over the bay, I found myself talking to my seatmate, a pretty blonde woman with bright eyes and an engaging manner, and found out that she was a chaperone for the large teen group that was spread out about our section of the cabin. She explained that they were from Menlo-Atherton High, and were going to Europe for two weeks, a trip that would include all the usual stops: London, Paris, Berlin, Vienna, Venice, Florence, Rome.

I smiled and related my own teen pilgrimage experience from two years before, and it was not too long before we were talking about my life as a seminarian, and St. Patrick's itself: the seminary is just down the street from Menlo-Atherton High. My seatmate had never visited the seminary, but now, having met me, wanted to. I was glad to steer the topic away from her teens, and mine, and for this reason: beneath my light and happy talk a mix of unhappy feelings had arisen, feelings that included almost a resentment of the young people from Menlo-Atherton High. The entire Peninsula south of San Francisco is upscale and comfortable, but Atherton is exceptional even by the Peninsula's standards. I assumed that the bright, laughing, excited and happy teens in our cabin had not had to wash any cars or work any parish breakfasts or rely on the tireless efforts of their youth minister, to make this trip happen, and as I say, I almost resented the fact that they were able to go to Europe, this Jubilee Year, and my kids were not. See my remarks on the ugliness of envy, in the previous chapter. I relate this set of feelings simply to underscore the depth of my disappointment, in having failed to get my kids back to Europe, that summer.

***

Something special that happened that summer was the dinner I finally gave, for the five guys who had been in the Sacraments class, in 1997-98. I had wanted to do this dinner for them for two years. It had gotten to be a joke among us: when something unlikely was being proposed, one of them would say, "That'll happen when Jim takes us out to celebrate our Sacraments!" If the guys came to learn nothing else about me, over the years, I think they came to learn this: I may be a very long time getting to everything that I say I am going to do, but by God, sooner or later, I do get to it.

We went to Black Angus, in Roseville, one of our favorite venues. It was Oscar, Nelson, Omar, Mikey and Jorge from the class, and Pancho. Pancho had not been in the class, but he came along because Pancho is Pancho. It was July and I had been twice to Rome already that summer, and once to the Holy Land, and I had lots and lots of little treasures for the guys: olive wood crosses, pricey crystal rosaries which I had held up against Christ's tomb and prayed over, six copies of a great little book on favorite Catholic prayers, 2001 calendars from Rome and Israel and I do not know how many t-shirts, including some that really grabbed the guys' imaginations, like the bright blue one that read HARD ROCK CAFÉ TEL AVIV.

The waitress, a willowy blonde girl, was in short order a great pal, and she not only took photos for us, but I took a number of shots with her and the guys. She really enjoyed our table, and, even though they thought she was great, the guys, as so often, objected that I way over-tipped her. We took some more photos in front of the restaurant, the boys showing off their loot, and every one of them wearing his new rosary, the crystal sparkling in the camera's flash. It was the same Black Angus that I had taken Wally, Fonz, Jorge and Mikey to, our first Boys' Night Out, in October, 1997, the night that Mikey had fallen out of the banquette, laughing. That night, too, we had stood out front and taken a few pictures. Already my history with these guys was so deep that a memory like that made me feel wistful. Already, maybe a little like a father missing the days when his children were toddlers, I was feeling…sentimental, about my earliest days with my kids.

238

Meanwhile, we had made some money: what were we going to do with it? There was no question in anyone's mind. We were going to make more. And we were going to re-calibrate, and aim at summer, 2001. Toward that end, we held our first-and-only mid-summer parish breakfasts. I remember putting an announcement in the parish bulletin to the effect that, though they had not realized their dream of getting to Europe for the Jubilee Year, the members of the Teen Rosary Group had picked themselves up, dusted themselves off, and were ready to get right back into it. To kick off their renewed efforts, they would be doing the parish breakfast that summer in both July and August, a first. The Marysville parish, as always, swung into line behind us: I remember making a record profit at one of the breakfasts, that summer, and doing very well at the other. The kids and I had taken a hit, but we were not even down, let alone out.

I was disappointed with the final numbers on the August trip, but my pilgrims (I think we were twenty-three in all) were delighted with such a small and manageable group. Mom, Trudi and Anne all were on this trip, along with some folks who'd been on previous pilgrimages with me, and also, Peggy Dempsey and Kathleen Stanton, from my office at Cal. Peggy, Kathleen and I had worked together over fifteen years, and Kathleen had retired that summer, and decided to celebrate by going to Rome for the Jubilee. I remember the three of us sitting on a café terrace overlooking the marina, at Capri, and just shaking our heads. "Who'd have ever guessed," I asked Peggy and Kathleen, "on November 19, 1980, the day I started at Career Planning and Placement, that twenty years later the three of us would be having lunch in Capri, the two of you happily retired, and me a seminarian?"

What was more, I wound up with youth on the August trip, after all. Tico had the money to go, and so did his younger cousin Nicole.

239

Nicole had evidently told her parents that she would rather go to Italy, than have a quinceanera. Her parents were rightly impressed, and so was I. I wished for Tico's sake that some of the other guys had made the trip, but he and Nicole were a good team, and the rest of the pilgrims loved them, and adopted them as "our kids," just as had been the case in 1998. The trip started in the north: I saw Venice, Padua and Verona for the first time. I was back in Florence for the first time since 1989, when I had been there with Uncle Jim. Assisi was just as we had remembered it, from two summers before: blessed with the spirit of serenity and quiet joy that Francis seems to have left as his legacy to the city. There were still a lot of scaffolds and construction cranes in Assisi, as the city continued to recover from the 1997 earthquake.

I loved watching Tico in Rome. Here was the teen who had queried me so intelligently about the root causes of the Protestant Reformation, the first evening we'd met. Well, unlike his mentor, Tico had NO problem with the Vatican; he loved St. Peter's, and went back more than once, on his own. (Our hotel that summer, each time I was in Rome, was the Michelangelo. It is about a block from the Vatican. Members of my pilgrimages that summer could walk over to the Vatican anytime they liked, and all of us had the pleasure of being there after four, when the great tour-related crowds are gone.)

We went to Pompeii one day, and I remember being struck, by the tragedy of the place. Mom loves Pompeii. She had been there before, with my dad, and wanted us to see it. It is certainly impressive, but as I say, I could not shake the sense of sadness that overcame me there. I remember that my sister Anne and I took some shots of Vesuvius from, I think, the Forum, or anyway an open, grassy space with some ruined columns and statuary.

"Four thousand feet," Anne said, of the volcano's height. "That's only as high as Diablo. Amazing the damage it can do." (Mount Diablo is the East Bay's highest peak. It is not, by California standards, a high mountain, and nothing near the heights of our own volcanoes. Vesuvius impressed both me and Anne for its lack of stature, given its destructive power.)

We finished the pilgrimage with the daytrip to Capri referred to above. Tico and Nicole and a few other pilgrims stayed in Rome – I think they wanted to visit Trevi Fountain, the Spanish Steps, and so on; maybe do some shopping. Having done it several times, now, I have to say that Capri is a great place to end an Italian tour. Just to see the Rock itself, rising from the sea and into the wispy summer clouds, is worth the trip. We took the ferry out to the Blue Grotto, and most of us went in, but the water was choppy and Mom decided against getting into the little boat, as did I. We sat on the deck and watched the pilgrims in the little boats, being rowed into the sea-cave. I know the water in the Grotto is very special – translucent somehow and aquamarine – but the fact is, the water in the Bay of Naples itself is a knock-out, and the views Mom and I had of the island in one direction, of Sorrento in another, and of Naples in still another, were magnificent.

We came home and the kids threw a bbq for us, at Mom's. It was a complete surprise to me, to Mom, to Anne and Trudi. I forget how many of them were there, but it was a lot of them, and it was a fun evening. Tico told the guys about his adventures in Italy, and everyone dreamed of being there the following summer. I never did get back to Italy, with the kids. I dream even today of being there with them again one day, and of ending the trip at Capri.

***

I'll leave my description of the summer of 2000 with this memory. When I returned from the Holy Land trip in early July, Jorge and Ravi met me at SFO. It was late afternoon, and we went to Fisherman's Wharf for an early dinner. Driving back to Marysville, I fell asleep. Because it was only seven or eight in the evening, the sky was still full of light, and maybe for that reason, I slept lightly, drifting in and out, occasionally catching glimpses of the summer orchards and fields stretching away from the freeway. At some point, while my eyes were closed and Jorge evidently guessed me to be asleep, he said to Ravi, "Yeah, I don't know where we would be, but for this guy. We were all headed in the wrong direction, 'til he came along, and got us all going to youth group. We were a bunch of little thugs, man, 'til we met this guy."

Ravi laughed. "I remember," he said.

"Jim came along and everything changed, man. Hard to say what would have happened, if he hadn't shown up. He changed our lives."

If I live to be one hundred-ten, I will not forget that moment, or those words, of Jorge's. And I have to say in return: it is hard to say what would have happened in my life, if my kids had not come into it. It is hard to imagine who I would be today, without them. Their lives changed forever, because of the youth group. So did mine.

EIGHT

St. Charles Borromeo in Sacramento is one of the Diocese's larger parishes, with well over three thousand registered families, three fulltime priests, nine weekend Masses (in a church that can seat 750) and a school. This was the parish my uncle built, and when I arrived there shortly after Labor Day, 2000, it was as close to coming home as I could get, not actually being at home. Msgr. Church and Uncle Jim had been great friends for decades. Father Church (as he preferred to be called) had known many of the deceased members of my family, and also many old family friends. What is more, his first assignment as a brand new priest in 1958 had been at St. Isidore's, in Yuba City, just over the Fifth Street Bridge from Marysville. Although this was the first time we'd met, Jim Church and I had something of a shared history, and talking with him over our first couple of lunches brought back a rush of cherished, and half-forgotten, childhood memories and sensations.

My uncle had died less than three years earlier, and his influence could be felt there at St. Charles in a manner somewhat analogous to that of Francis at Assisi: I remember the bright Sunday afternoon at the Fall Festival that Evelyn Maginnity described my uncle as "the patron saint of the city of Sacramento," and then amended herself, "Really," she said, "of the whole county." Evelyn and her husband Gerry were among the first parishioners to introduce themselves to me that September. But few in the parish were shy, coming forward to meet the nephew of Msgr. Poole. My coming to the parish had been announced in advance, and people were ready, anxious to meet me. I remember my first weekend in the parish, introducing myself at several of the Masses. I remember the thunderous applause at each introduction. I said the same thing, each time: "I know who that applause is for. I am not my uncle, but I am his nephew, in spite of being a Raiders fan." (Uncle Jim's allegiance to the 49ers was legendary.) "I hope that when I leave St. Charles, next summer, I will have earned the applause you have just given me."

It was a wonderful year. The best I had yet had, on my already lengthy journey to priesthood. I had invitations to assist in ministries across the parish – St. Vincent de Paul, the Knights of Columbus, RCIA, Adult Faith Formation, the Fall Festival Committee, Teen Sacramental Prep, Liturgy Committee, Youth Ministry, various devotional groups and of course, the school. I splashed in all over the place at once and was hip-deep in the hoopla before September was out. By mid-October, I had Msgr. Church convinced I was a workaholic. This is never a bad thing to convince a new supervisor of. I was in love with my uncle's parish, just weeks after arriving there, and it astonished me to think that I might have missed this experience, this huge set of opportunities, had I been truculent, had I resisted Sr. Maureen's phone message the previous March. There was even a financial blessing – the Diocese paid us something like a living wage, while we were on the pastoral year. If ever I needed proof that I would be happy as a priest, the year at St. Charles in Sacramento provided it, and abundantly.

I had arranged to take Wednesdays as my day off, precisely so that I could be in Marysville, for the Teen Rosary Group meetings. The kids and I continued throughout the 2000-01 academic year on our every-other-Wednesday schedule, at Mom's. We continued with our parish breakfasts – only now I could simply leave very early, about six-thirty, from the rectory in Sacramento on Sunday morning, to get to St. Joseph's for the breakfast, as opposed to needing to take the whole weekend. The proximity of St. Charles to Marysville (less than an hour, on the freeway) made my work with the kids that year just that much easier. It also made our ongoing get-togethers, both for fundraisers in Marysville, and for the many Boys' (and some Girls') Nights Out, in Sacramento and Roseville, that much easier. I was, at St. Charles, back in the neighborhood of Marysville, and that was just one more factor in the year's overall joy.

There was another factor in it, as well. I discovered, at St. Charles, that I could write on the rectory schedule. Life in a rectory is very different from life in the seminary. One of the jokes at St. Pat's was the alleged moroseness of the guys in third-year theology, their first few weeks back at the seminary, after their year in the parish. Though the life of a parish priest is demanding, and the scheduling challenges can be daunting, there is, nonetheless, a freedom, in the rectory to schedule yourself, that you do not have, at the seminary, where so much is perforce scheduled for you. Of course, I had other loves competing for my time and energy, my first two years at St. Pat's, but the fact is, I wrote more in two months at St. Charles than I had written in two years at the seminary. In fact, by mid-winter, it looked very possible that I might finish the novel, there at St. Charles.

By January, at St. Charles, I was writing 80-100 pages a week, on GOLD COUNTRY. This is about as good as it gets for a writer, in any set of circumstances. Here I was accomplishing this in the midst of the residency year in the seminary program, in one of the largest and busiest parishes in Sacramento. I was astonished – and deeply joyful. I told Mom about it, and she said it was no surprise to her at all: "You'll write as a priest," she said. She added that she thought her brother was behind some of my success with the book, which after all, was being completed in his guest suite. And I might add that Uncle Jim had always strongly encouraged me to write. "It's a God-given talent," Uncle Jim had said. "Use it."

I made a couple of my best friends in life, during the year at St. Charles: Will and Daria Young. Daria was director of the RCIA program in the parish, and also taught one of the Confirmation classes, and coordinated the overall Confirmation program at St. Charles. This strong parallel with my own ministerial experience made Daria and me fast allies and co-workers. I can still see Daria, the first time we met. It was after one of the school Masses on a Friday morning, maybe in September, maybe in early October. This beautiful woman who might have been one of my sisters (dark hair, hazel eyes, fair skin) came up to me and asked if I would be willing to come and speak at the RCIA class some Tuesday night, as she really appreciated my enthusiasm and energy. In fact, I had been planning to look Daria up and offer my help – Msgr. Church had thought we would work well together, and very much wanted us to meet. I had not done so yet, because I was on the Fall Festival Committee and our meetings (which sometimes lasted more than three hours) were on Tuesday evenings. As soon as the Festival was past, though, I was at RCIA. I do not think I missed a meeting the rest of the year, except for a couple times when I was out of town.

Anyway, Daria and Will invited me to dinner one Sunday late in October. I met several of their five children that evening, and after dinner, the three of us sat up talking til about midnight, when Will said, "I'm calling it a night," and went upstairs to bed. Daria and I, talking theology, ecclesiology and personal experience, called it a night about two hours later. I had spent eight hours with the Youngs. I knew I had seen the beginning, that night, of a lifelong friendship.

Go back up a couple paragraphs to where I was talking about how in a rectory, you really do have time to schedule yourself and your work, with a freedom that just cannot be there at the seminary, given what the seminary's mission is. The point I am (finally!) making here is this: I told Daria in maybe February that the reason I was getting so much writing done is that I was only working 35-40 hours a week here at St. Charles, as opposed to the eighty-plus hours I had been putting in, the previous year, at the seminary.

Daria scoffed at my estimate of my hours. "Thirty-five or forty?" she asked. "Think again. When I look at all you do around here, you have GOT to be putting in a minimum, MINIMUM, of fifty hours a week."

I laughed. "Daria, trust me. I am accustomed to long hours. I know a regular work week, when I have one. I have one here. And thank God. Because it is leaving me with lots of time to get the book done."

Daria challenged me to keep track of my hours for a couple of weeks. "Not just one," she said, "because it might be a fluke. Keep track of your hours over two consecutive weeks, and then…report back to me."

I did. And I was amazed. Amazed. I put in sixty-five hours one week, and sixty-three the next. When I duly reported this back to Daria and Will, they laughed. "You are one high-energy seminarian," they said.

I have ever since considered a sixty to sixty-five hour work week a perfectly reasonable week. I seem to have developed, in the years since, a certain barometric sensitivity to scheduling issues. Sixty-five hours a week in ministry is not too much. Seventy is too much. Eighty is way too much. I can handle (I do handle) the occasional eighty-hour week, as a priest. But the days when eighty-hour weeks were the norm are forever behind me. At sixty hours a week, I have an additional twenty or even thirty hours a week, for my own work: for writing, for reading, for research, for the development of special projects. At eighty hours, I have nothing.

And there really is a tipping point, a point after which too much time spent on parish ministry will negate any possibility of my getting anything else done. It's a little like my sensitivity to the Sacramento Valley's heat in the summer. I love the hot, dry valley summers; in fact, I made my initial decision to become a priest for Sacramento instead of Oakland, because I preferred Sacramento's summer weather. Accustomed as I am to Sacramento's summer heat, I assure you, I know the difference between a 102-degree day, which is not a problem, and a 106-degree day, which is just too damned hot. Somewhere between 102 or 103 degrees and 106 or 107, you reach a tipping point, and the day is no longer just a typically hot summer day in Sacramento; it is a helluva hot day.

It is much the same principle, where work is concerned. I have said I am cool with a sixty-five hour work week: it leaves me with twenty hours a week to get my own projects attended to. It is not as if you can say, well, I had a seventy-hour week, last week, so I only had ten or fifteen hours for my own work. No. A seventy-hour week in ministry in the parish means I had ZERO hours for my own work, for my writing, reading, research, special projects. Because between sixty-five hours and seventy is the tipping point, is the point of no return. I have come to realize that, if I am going to work seventy hours in a given week, I may as well work eighty, because while I can and will find the energy for parish ministry, in that situation, I will not find it for anything else. This was an awfully important thing to have learned about myself, and I learned it that winter of 2000-01, at St. Charles.

***

In January, 2001, I went to New Orleans for a week, at Msgr. Church's recommendation, to attend a training session for PICO, the Pacific Institute of Community Organizations. PICO partners with faith communities to address local issues such as crime, education, youth concerns, neighborhood development and so forth. My sister Liz works for a PICO affiliate, Oakland Community Organizations, and I had worked with her the previous year, in Oakland, as part of my field ed assignment from the seminary. On a tangential note, I thought it was too bad when Sarah Palin knocked Barack Obama's community organizing experience, at the 2008 Republican Convention: I know from personal experience the very good things that can come from organizing a local community.

In any event, I spent the second week of January at a Dominican retreat house just outside New Orleans, learning organizing techniques and hearing the wonderful stories of folks from across the country who do this work. We went in to New Orleans a couple times, of course – both times on a day that was bright, breezy and mild, and though I have no pictures from that week, its teachings and its joys are vibrant in my mind.

I mention the week in southern Louisiana because it was there, at the retreat house, praying in the chapel, the next to last night of our stay, that I discerned without a doubt that I was to take the coming year off. I had, of course, originally promised myself that I would take

249

2001-02 out, when I said yes to the assignment at St. Charles. But the fact is, the year at my uncle's parish was so good, so pleasing, so effortless, and the response of the people to my emerging priesthood so gratifying and affirming, that I had begun to seriously question whether I needed to take a year out, after all.

I mean, I was going to finish GOLD COUNTRY, there at St. Charles. The fact is, with a concentrated effort, I could get my thesis written over the summer. I could thus return to the seminary with two of my biggest ambitions accomplished – and as for the kids, well, I was hoping all that fall and winter at St. Charles, to get them back to Europe the summer of 2001. If that, too, happened, then what good reason did I have for a year out of the program, and why would I want to take it? Especially given the response of the people at St. Charles to me – couldn't I see that the sooner I was ordained, the better?

When I say that this had become a question, I mean it. I did not know the answer. The idea of a year out still appealed to me, and not least because I really could use any money I might make from pilgrimages scheduled during the year away. But I had a couple of trips planned for the summer; if I made even half of what I had made the previous summer from pilgrimage, I would be in good shape, to get through the coming year at the seminary. It really was an attractive possibility that began to occur to me, over Christmas, there at St. Charles: the possibility that maybe, after all, with the novel, the thesis and the trip with the kids behind me, I would be able to avoid a year out, and simply stay with the seminary program.

Maybe it was getting out of the parish routine that gave me clarity on this, there in Louisiana. I don't know. I know that I was wrestling all week with the question, in prayer, and out of it. I went to the beautiful chapel there at the retreat house every evening, after the last of our sessions on community organizing, and I prayed to know which way to go with this decision. I will point out that I was wrestling with the decision alone – well, just me and the Holy Spirit. Later, Milt Walsh at the seminary would express to me his perfectly justified disappointment that I had not consulted with him, before making the decision to take the year out. He was my advisor, after all. Milt had a right to input in the situation, and I did not give him the opportunity. It's funny now, thinking about it, that I took almost no one into confidence over the decision -- no one but Daria Young. Daria had made no effort to influence me one way or the other; she simply listened and helped me look at the possible ramifications of deciding one way or the other.

I made the decision, in any event, alone, there in the Dominican chapel, the next to last night of the PICO conference. It was Friday, January 12. Don't ask me how I remember such things: I just do. On the other hand, why shouldn't I remember the time, the date and the place of this decision? This decision changed the course of my life.

The decision to take the year out was followed by a flood of peace in my heart, a sense of release. This sort of feeling can in fact indicate accurate discernment. But as Msgr. Church would point out, months later, when I let him know of the decision, "You can't necessarily count on a sense of peace to be your guide. When you have been weighing options for a long time, and have been unable to make a decision, any decision is going to bring an immediate peace, but that does not guarantee you made the right decision."

I knew that Msgr. Church was right on this point, and I concede that he and Milt Walsh had a right to input into my discernment which I denied them. I didn't deny them that input because I was afraid of what they would say – I KNEW what they would say: they'd tell me to get back to the seminary and get ordained, ASAP. I suppose that, because I thought I already knew their input, I felt no need to seek it. But of course, I did not really know their input: I was just making a guess as to what it would have been. A solid and educated guess, but a guess, all the same. The seminary program is structured precisely to guarantee seminarians good counsel in such decision-making, and I had bypassed that counsel entirely.

Having conceded the above, I need to say that I firmly believed then and I firmly believe now that I made the right choice, that Friday night alone in the chapel in Louisiana. I remember writing my friend Mike about it, the following week. Mike and I had met fifteen years earlier, at the Squaw Valley Writers' Conference, at Lake Tahoe. He was and is a writer. We'd spent many long evenings, in bars, in restaurants and pool halls, in the Bay Area and L.A., talking books, talking agents and publishers, talking the dream each of us had for his life. I figured Mike would understand my decision and approve.

I told Mike that the decision, once it came, came as an absolute no-brainer. I wanted to return to St. Pat's, and I wanted to be ordained. I also wanted to finish GOLD COUNTRY, and find an agent for it; get back in business, so to speak, as a novelist. I wanted to finish my thesis at the Dominican School, and put that part of my education finally and successfully behind me. I wanted to run several pilgrimages – too many for a mere summer schedule, because, my comfortable circumstances at St. Charles aside, I needed money in the worst way. My car had been in the shop twice already at St. Charles: I remember watching with Msgr. Church one sunny autumn

Sunday as the tow truck hauled the Grand Am off to a local garage, and Monsignor commenting to me that the car LOOKED like a million bucks, and it did. The Grand Am was in beautiful exterior shape 'til the day it gave up the ghost. But in fact, if it gave up the ghost while I was at St. Pat's, I would not be able to replace it. And I was not going to be car-less at the seminary -- not at my age.

I know, though, that the main reason I gave Mike, writing him about my decision, was that I was as determined as ever to get my kids back to Europe, and in January, 2001, that goal was no more secure than it had been in 2000, or in 1999. If we made it back that summer, great. If we didn't, frankly, I just did not want anything getting in my way, where the kids and pilgrimage were concerned. Bottom line: the seminary was second on my list of priorities. Until it could be first, where it needed to be, I could not happily return.

I returned from Louisiana with clear discernment, with an absolute conviction that I understood God's will for the coming year. As with my previous decision about taking a year out, however, I mostly kept quiet about it for the rest of the winter, and way into the spring. I told Daria as soon as I saw her, and she backed the plan 100%. I am not sure if she had been hoping I would opt for the year out all along, or if it was simply that she trusted me to make the right decision, regardless, and was prepared as well, to have so backed a return to the seminary, had I decided on that.

I told Mom, of course, and the Oakland family. Mom was cool with it, but she probably would have been happier with a decision to stay the course with the seminary program. Liz and my Oakland nieces were very enthusiastic. I think Lupe took it to mean that I was going to junk this whole priesthood thing and get back to what I most loved, my writing, and get back to it big-time. Certain friends and some family had really begun to worry about what I seemed willing to sacrifice, to become a priest; above all, they were worried about what would become of me, if I were to deny my talent and my love for writing. That talent and that love, after all, had defined my youth and shaped my life.

***

And my talent had come roaring back, that year at St. Charles. By late March, I was so far toward done with the novel that I decided to start contacting New York about it. You do not have to have a book finished, to get agents and editors interested in it, indeed, even to sell it. I know my decision to start showing GOLD COUNTRY that spring was partly motivated by my ongoing deepest ambition: if the novel could be sold by the summer, I would have money to help the kids get back to Medjugorje.

By the spring of 2001, I had extensive experience dealing with literary New York. It was twenty years since my first agent had taken me on as a client, with my first novel; a satire about a rock band on the make in California called ALL THE ANGELS AND SAINTS. In the intervening two decades, I had completed several more novels and worked with three more agents. A couple of my agents were to prove to be among the best of the young, new agents in the city. I did not need anyone to tell me that I could write and write well; I did not need anyone to tell me that without an agent your chances of success in commercial New York publishing are (to borrow a phrase) less than zero. I also did not need anyone to tell me how to go about finding an agent. I had done it four times, over fifteen years.

The last agent I had worked with, Aleta Daley, had represented me with one of my later comedies -- a light fable about an international theft ring of exiled East European aristocrats, stealing back the valuables they had lost when their fictional Adriatic homeland had gone communist. The book, titled A RESTORATION COMEDY, was written purely to entertain. GOLD COUNTRY, by comparison, was close to three times the length of RESTORATION, and it was an unabashed epic love story: dramatic, realistic and tragic. I wondered whether Aleta, who had so delighted in the almost fairy-tale-like atmosphere of A RESTORATION COMEDY, would much cotton to the sprawling and deeply human GOLD COUNTRY. Another consideration was that Aleta had been showing A RESTORATION COMEDY in the mid-nineties: we worked together from 1993 to 1995. It had been six years, since she had shown the book, and we had had little contact in that time.

Still, we'd never broken up, never officially decided to quit working together, as had been the case with each of my three previous agents, and it almost seemed to me a matter of professional courtesy, to say nothing of the hope that Aleta would love GOLD COUNTRY, to offer her what in the business is called "the right of first refusal." I wrote her on March 29, frankly expecting her to at least want to have a look at the novel. Given this expectation, I hoped as well to be getting sample chapters and an outline off to New York in the first half of April. The prospect – showing my work again in Manhattan – made me very happy. Except that…

Aleta never wrote back. I followed up with a note, a couple weeks into April, which also went unanswered. Surprised, but very okay with it, because after all, I had had my doubts about whether Aleta would like this new novel, I turned my attention to my list of "agents-I-would-like-the-chance-to-work-with." This list had been compiled in the early nineties, while I was between agents, and showing various novels in New York, hoping to land a new representative. During this time, my work had been read by a number of agents who had refused the particular book in question, but who had all the same enjoyed my writing, and in several instances, urged me to keep them in mind, with future projects.

This "wish-list" of Manhattan agents contained ten or twelve names. It may sound like hubris, but after all, I believe (and always have believed) in the depth of my talent, and in any event, I had four times previously landed an agent – every time but one, in fact, when I went looking for an agent, I got one. I was energized and enthused at the prospect of showing the first couple hundred pages of GOLD COUNTRY to the agents on this list. I was strongly inclined to believe that my future agent was among them. I double-checked with LMP (Literary Market Place, the bible of the publishing industry) to make sure I still had current addresses for these agents, and set to work.

I had ranked the agents on this list according to my preference – this preference being largely a matter of intuition: they had all said very complimentary things about my work. But I decided to go with agents who had written me about my novel BURNING ALEXIS, a political satire about a book-banning effort in a small town in the Sacramento Valley, because I judged ALEXIS to be the most serious of my earlier novels, and I thought an agent who liked ALEXIS might not have to travel too far, to also like GOLD COUNTRY. The first agent on the list was Lisa Ross, who'd said BURNING ALEXIS would make a great movie. I wrote a carefully tailored letter to Ms. Ross, including a copy of her letter to me on BURNING ALEXIS, so that she could place me. It had, in fact, been a decade since she had written the letter, but LMP said she was still working in New York, and, after all, I was still writing in California, so, sometime in the second half of April I put the query to Ms. Ross into the mail, and…

She never wrote back. I sent a follow-up – not a note; a second letter about the book, and do understand, dear reader, that submissions to agents ALWAYS include stamped and self-addressed envelopes for their convenient reply. Ms. Ross never responded to the second letter, either. Surprised and – feeling kind of bad about it – I moved on to my next agent on the list, a guy whose name I am blanking on now, but I do remember that it was an Armenian name. He had thought BURNING ALEXIS "bold, original and damned funny," and had recommended I stay in touch. I followed the same careful protocol with him as I had with Ms. Ross and…

He didn't write back either.

I tried the next agent on my list. Same thing. I tried the next agent on the list – and this time I did get a response: the executor of the agent's estate wrote to tell me that the agent had died over the winter.

By this time it was late May, and I decided to hold off anymore special queries to special agents, 'til I had the novel done. It had been a surprising and somewhat demoralizing experience, writing five agents who had reason to take me seriously, and hearing back from no one but the executor of the one who had died. I wondered if the letters had ever arrived, it was so bizarre. I remember, too, deciding to see the hand of God in it: this was not the time to get an agent. Better to concentrate on finishing the book, and get back to marketing it later. It was too late, as well, at that point, to give anymore thought to a trip with the kids that summer: both the summer pilgrimages I had planned had failed to book, as can happen. I myself wasn't going to Europe, that summer, let alone my kids.

***

The peculiar business with the literary agents, and my failed tours aside, the second half of the pastoral year at St. Charles went as swimmingly as had the first. With seminary evaluations due in late April, I finally let everyone, Sr. Maureen and Msgr. Church, as well as Milt and the seminary, know that I had decided on taking a year out. I gave as my principle reason the need to finish my thesis, as I figured that would be a reason everyone could respect. I knew that my discernment would surprise everyone, but if there were to have been any real opposition to it, I imagined that it would come from Sacramento, not from the seminary. I was wrong; it was just the opposite. Both Sr. Maureen and Bishop Weigand, in Sacramento, were cool with, though quite surprised by, my decision. They thought getting my thesis done was a good thing to do. The plan drew serious fire from my superiors at the seminary, but Milt Walsh, setting his own doubts aside, evidently made well-reasoned arguments in the faculty discussions, on my behalf, and after a couple of weeks, everyone was, even if reluctantly, on board with my taking a year's leave.

Sometime near the end of that happy year at St. Charles, Msgr. Church and I were talking about the plan I had made. We were outside in the bright June sun, walking between the rectory and the church. Monsignor said something that sent a shiver through me, and I remember that I immediately discounted it as an extreme improbability, if not an outright impossibility. Yet what Msgr.

258

Church said was to prove prophetic. He said something very like this: "I would not plan on your plan, Jim. I have a feeling about all of this having come about as it has. I know you see a year out ahead and a straight shot back to the seminary, in 2002. I don't. I think you are in for three years of wandering in the desert." Monsignor smiled, as he said this; he was obviously confident of my capacity to handle such a development. "The Holy Spirit is full of surprises, you know," Monsignor continued. "I don't know what lies ahead, but I am sure that ultimately it will be for the good of your priesthood."

I do not remember how I responded to Msgr. Church's words. As I say, they sent a bolt of fear through me. But I do remember sitting in my suite in the rectory there at St. Charles one afternoon in June, after the year's leave had been accepted by everyone and was now an inevitability. I remember that it was a quiet afternoon, probably because it was June. The school had let out and many of the parish ministries had gone on their summer hiatus. I had time, that afternoon. I had time to sit and think about the great year I had just come through, at St. Charles: time to think about the year out I had arranged for myself, in Marysville; time to think about all I hoped to accomplish with that year out. I remember sitting there in my quiet suite, looking out the window at the sundrenched greenery of the parish grounds, and…

I remember being suddenly seized with fear about the year ahead. After all, the whole thing was a gamble. There was not one part of it that was guaranteed to happen, guaranteed to come through. I mean, I knew that nothing much short of death would prevent me from finishing both thesis and novel, but what then? Suppose I could not find an agent, for GOLD COUNTRY? The peculiar lack of response from New York in April and May, from agents who knew my work, may have triggered this sudden set of fears; I don't know. If I failed to get GOLD COUNTRY agented, it would not sell. If the novel did not sell, then I needed for my tours to succeed, but so far, bookings were sluggish. As mentioned above, the summer, 2001 trips had failed completely, and the trips to Italy in September and to Fatima and Lourdes in October were doing only moderate business. Although it looked as if both would go, neither that quiet afternoon in June, looked like much of a moneymaker.

If the autumn tours did not make money, then I would need to succeed with the trips I had planned for spring and summer, 2002. But why, beyond native optimism, would I expect my 2002 pilgrimages to do land-office business when it was fairly obvious already that my 2001 trips were not going to do so? If the 2002 trips failed, or more likely, if they made, but only just barely, if they booked just well enough to go, but not well enough for me to earn much in commissions…then what?

I would not get back to Europe with the kids, number one. There were other questions, too, including the question of whether I would return to the seminary financially exhausted. But my one overriding concern was the kids. There is no point analyzing this, or trying to explain it: I am telling you how it was. I HAD to get my kids back to Medjugorje. They had to know that 1998 had not been a lucky accident. They had to know that if they were willing to dream big enough and work hard enough, they could set their goals anywhere they wanted. They had to know that God is real, and that God has a plan for each one of them that no one else can achieve. They had to grasp the fact that God wanted to work through them, for the good, for the salvation, of others. Somehow, all of that was caught up with the second pilgrimage. Until the second pilgrimage came to pass, really, my life could have no other focus. The second pilgrimage was non-negotiable.

This was a pretty sobering realization, and I remember sitting there with it, that afternoon in the Sacramento rectory, for some time. It was unlike me to entertain such doubts, which I am sure is one reason why I remember the moment so clearly. Another reason, of course, is that these doubts and more were to come true, over the course of the coming year; it was as if in that quiet moment I had a premonitory flash of what really lay ahead: not the fulfillment of my dreams, but the death of them.

None of us is much inclined to contemplate the death of our dreams, and I shook myself out of my doubts and fears that afternoon with a conscious assertion of optimistic self-confidence. I would finish the thesis, and the Dominican M.A. GOLD COUNTRY might or might not sell, but I would surely find an agent with it. Once I had an agent, I would be back at bat, as a novelist. I had other novels well-developed, just waiting for GOLD COUNTRY to be done for me to get back to them. By this time next year, I would have another novel done, and be well along with the next. The September Italian trip, while not booking like gangbusters, was in fact, already in profit, and the October trip to Fatima and Lourdes was within striking range of becoming profitable. There could be as many as five pilgrimages, the first half of 2002 – if any one or two of them booked solidly, I would be able to get the kids back to Europe. And if I got the kids back to Europe, and if GOLD COUNTRY landed an agent, and if I had my M.A. from the Dominicans, then there was no way that the year ahead could be called anything but a success. I looked out the window there at St. Charles, looked at the bright June light shining through the varied greens of the hedges and shrubs, and I very deliberately put my fears out of my mind. I resolved to plunge into the coming year with all I had. No way was this year out going to be anything less than a good, maybe even a great, success.

***

Sometimes I think the reason we don't know the future is that, if we did, it wouldn't happen. We would be afraid to go there. We'd look at what it was going to require of us and figure, "I haven't got it." I'm convinced that there are times in our lives, times of deep trial, when the courage we need to face the situation, the strengths we need to deal with it, can only be brought forward in the situation itself. Prior to being forced to summon such strength, we would not believe ourselves to possess it.

And it is not just ourselves we would sell short, in this respect: it is also God. We get through tough times not just by calling forth strengths we didn't know we had. We get through them as well by the intervention of grace. People and possibilities we had not been looking for come into play. A way through the difficulty develops within the parameters of the situation itself; it is not something we could have charted out in advance. The dynamic seems to me to suggest that until the problem itself appears, its solution, too, will be invisible. The scary part is the lag time between the appearance of the difficulty and the development of its solution.

I could not have known, leaving St. Charles that summer, what lay ahead. It would have astonished me to realize it, that quiet afternoon, but less than a year later, I would describe my circumstances as those of a man adrift, a man who had lost sight of the shore, a man who no longer understood what God wanted of him, or indeed, why God had made him.

NINE

On the morning of September 11, 2001, I was pouring a cup of coffee in the dining room at Mom's, having just got out of the shower. It was not yet nine AM. Mom and Trudi came in from the morning Mass as I was setting the coffee carafe back in its place.

"There's been a terrorist attack in New York," Mom said. "The World Trade Center has been destroyed."

"WHAT?" I said.

"Ita told us," said Trudi, of the parish secretary, Ita Fuller. "We went into the office after Mass, and she told us two planes were flown into the Twin Towers, and they have both collapsed."

I crossed into the family room to put the TV on, switching the channel to CNN. I figured that whatever may have happened in New York, what Mom and Trudi had just reported could NOT have happened. Judy Woodruff's intelligent, restrained commentary was shortly filling the room; but the live feed did not immediately support Mom's account: it was street crowds, emergency vehicles, and smoke. Lots and lots of smoke. Then CNN replayed the scene from the crowd, the scene of the second airliner plowing into the second tower.

"Oh my God," I said, slowly, not quite able to take in what I had just seen. "My God. Mom, Trudi. Come in here. Look at this."

CNN showed the replay a second, maybe a third time. Mom and Trudi gasped.

In all my many trips to New York, I had only visited the World Trade Center once. It was in June, 1988. I was in town to meet with Deborah Schneider, my then-agent, to discuss marketing my latest novel, A COMEDY OF EROS. I was staying with my buddy Taizo. Taizo and I had met at Berkeley in the summer of 1976; I was an RA (Resident Assistant) in the dorms and he was a summer exchange student from Tokyo in a six-week program called CAL (Course in American Language). Over the years Taizo and I had become best friends, almost like brothers; I was best man at his Central Park wedding in 1994.

Anyway, one bright June morning in 1988, I went downtown to visit Taizo at his office, because he at that time worked at the World Trade Center, and I had never been there. Taizo worked on the 96th floor. I forget which tower it was. I remember changing elevators at the 78th floor and understanding for the first time that there were limits to elevator technology. I remember, too, being a little amused at the thought of how out of place I must have looked there, in my khakis, western boots, and a white dress shirt with the sleeves pushed up and the collar left open.

Taizo showed me around the firm's offices, introduced me to his colleagues as his novelist friend from California, and I think he was as proud of our friendship, in that moment, as I was – he looked very professional in his midnight-blue suit and rep tie. In his personal office, I took time to look out the huge windows. I remember telling my friend Joan that I could see her house (in Bermuda) from up there. Bermuda was not visible, but all of New York Bay was, and you could see way out into the Atlantic. There was a helicopter flying near the tower – it was BELOW us. By maybe twenty stories. The place was amazing. I've never forgotten the view.

By 2001, Taizo was long gone from the World Trade Center. He and Kay and their two children were living in Boston. Taizo told me he heard of the attacks that morning at a finance conference. As the full scale of the atrocity became known, the conference was cancelled, and he did what everyone else on the East Coast did, that day: he went home.

I don't know how many of us on the West Coast went home that day, but certainly most of us stopped whatever we were doing, and stayed close to the television. Actually, my friend Cat, who lives very near the seminary, in Atherton, told me that she turned her TV off, called Scott, her husband, at his office, just to hear his voice, then put on classical music, and spent the day attending to their garden, and to the needs of their infant son. I've never forgotten that. I think Cat's response to the horror in New York was one of the healthiest of anyone I know.

In any event, I got no work done the rest of the day. I had planned to spend it with the novel, but I could not concentrate. I e-mailed my sister Flo, then a graduate student at Columbia. She e-mailed the entire family an eye-witness account of that morning. I wrote post cards to Barney Karpfinger and Deborah Schneider, two of my former agents, telling them that they, and all New York, were in my thoughts and prayers. I wrote a letter to Father Milt Walsh, at the seminary. I was writing Milt on another matter, but the letter included my immediate reaction to the events on the East Coast. I remember telling Milt that I felt these attacks presaged what we could expect in this new century, and I told him as well that the images from the television seemed to me to have an apocalyptic air about them.

I do not remember if I talked with 206 Tours that same day, or later in the week – it may have been both. But I suddenly had travel business to attend to, as a result of 9/11. President Bush closed every airport in the country, as you probably remember, and they remained closed all week. I had a pilgrimage leaving for Italy the following Monday, September 17. Milanka was forced to cancel it, and in any event, it is very doubtful that any of the thirty or so pilgrims would have wanted to travel.

We had to scramble to get information out to folks about company policy in such a situation – insurance does not cover acts of war, which this was, and all we could do was guarantee people the same trip (or a comparable one) anytime they wanted to travel in the coming year. I was angrily told off over the phone by a gentleman who wanted his money back, and he made a particular dig about my honesty, "as a Catholic seminarian." I could understand his frustration, but there was nothing we could do: the airline and the vendors in Italy had all already been paid. We no longer had anyone's money, and we could not get it back. Nor, of course, could we guarantee when it would be safe to travel again. We could only do what everyone else was doing: deal with the fallout of 9/11 as best we could.

And there was fallout, of course, and not just in the financial, military and political worlds. The terrorist attacks sent a devastating shock wave throughout the travel industry: tours were postponed for months and bookings simply dried up. These facts hit my own plans hard. I no longer had any hope of making money from pilgrimages, with my year off.

But I was not yet worried about that. I had GOLD COUNTRY almost done. I would start looking for an agent for it, as soon as it was done, then move on to my thesis, which I expected to finish over the winter. By the spring of 2002, I would be at work on my next novel, THE BEST MAN, which was well-developed and needed maybe just six good weeks of concentrated effort. By the summer of 2002, I expected to be back at work at yet another long in-progress novel, LOVERS AND OTHER LIARS. The fact that I was writing as well as I was, and that I had an entire year to put something in place, in terms of positioning myself for literary success, gave me hope, and the hope gave me energy, and in October, GOLD COUNTRY was done. I started looking immediately for an agent, and meanwhile, turned my attention, at last, to getting my thesis done.

***

The kids and I had stopped meeting on Wednesday evenings. Our last regular meeting as the Teen Rosary Group had been August 22, a barbecue at Mom's, attended by about ten of the guys. This may sound odd – for three years while I was away, we met every other Wednesday; then I come back to Marysville for a year off, and we stop meeting. In fact, it was precisely because I was back in town that we figured we could let go of the Wednesday meetings. Attendance had waned, over the past year, to where, instead of having two or even three dozen kids at a meeting, we frequently had only ten or twelve. The principle reason for the decline in attendance was changes in the kids' lives. Alejandra had left for Cal State

Stanislaus; Elva was at Chico. Alma had moved to L.A. Oscar had moved to Lincoln, one of Sacramento's fastest-growing suburbs. Mikey – who about this time, began regularly to refer to himself as Miguel – had gone to Holy Names in Oakland on a basketball scholarship. The core group was still dedicated and determined. It in fact continued to include a few of the kids who had moved away: they were available on the weekends, and I had no problem, turning the kids out for fundraisers.

In any event, I wanted to help Mom with RCIA, which met Wednesdays, and for various reasons, Wednesday night was no longer easy for several of the kids who were still in town. It went without saying, among me and the kids, that we would be seeing each other all the time, with me back in town, so we decided to drop the Wednesday night meetings. But our fundraisers continued – we did the parish breakfast every month, we held raffles and t-shirt sales, and Fonz and some of the guys had a couple ongoing self-developed fundraisers as well. And we did, indeed, see each other all the time. Not only by design but by accident. We would run into each other downtown, at the mall, at the gym, or gee, even at church!

We had money in the bank, and until September 11, everyone had assumed it was for a return to Europe, in the summer of 2002. With 9/11, we were no longer so sure. I remember being at my health club one autumn afternoon with Nelson and Pancho, and they suggested we have a "final blow-out" with a three or four-day trip to southern California, to Disneyland and Magic Mountain. I was not going to rule out such a possibility. But despite the bleak outlook for international travel, I could not bring myself to relinquish the dream of returning with the kids to Europe. I said, "Let's see how things look next spring," and at the same time thought, "Who knows? Maybe I'll have GOLD COUNTRY sold, next spring."

Meanwhile, I was living on student loans and a couple scholarships. Mom charged me no rent. I bought virtually all the groceries, saving her the hassle of having to shop, for she was still teaching fulltime at Yuba College. I also did all the yard work, which was a pleasure to me. (It would also have been a pleasure to Mom, but she did not have the time.) My folks were always cool with having adult kids back at home for one reason or another, and for varied lengths of time. My siblings and I were fortunate in this, and we knew it.

I suppose I should not say that my income was solely student financial aid. I also earned fairly regular checks for speaking gigs or retreats, usually involving teens. I was, by this time, quite well known in the Sacramento Diocese – more as a youth minister with the golden touch, than as a seminarian. But the fact that I was a seminarian added to my cachet, so to speak, and I had opportunities to speak to groups and to give retreats, and I took them. I also began to pick up volunteer gigs in the Marysville parish, where we now had a new pastor, a young Tongan named Father Soane (pronounced Swanee, like the river; it means John). Father Soane thought it was great that he'd had, as he put it, "a seminarian tossed on his doorstep," and by the winter he had me working in several capacities involving teaching and evangelization. I liked him, loved the parish and enjoyed the work, and it did not take me away from my principle focus, which was by the winter, my thesis.

***

I have written many, many times for academic purposes, obviously, but the thesis for my MA at the Dominican School was more than just a "really big paper." It took me 'til late January to have it ready for my advisor, Father Steve Ernest, at the Dominican School. It did

269

not take that long because I was unengaged by it. On the contrary, I loved writing it, and could forget the whole world, while I was immersed in it. The topic was the social philosophy of Erich Fromm, the German psychologist and author, and the eventual title was GOOD GOVERNMENT WITHOUT GOD. I provided an Aristotelian critique of Fromm's philosophy, rather than looking at it from a Thomistic viewpoint: I felt that Aquinas would sink Fromm's brave little boat, and as that boat relied greatly on presuppositions from natural law, and I am a big fan of natural law, I did not want to sink Fromm. I wanted to discuss the possibilities of developing a realistic morality from atheist tenets. This was not the typical thesis at the Dominican School, which more often than not examined a particular question from a particular paragraph from a particular section of the SUMMA THEOLOGICA. But it was the thesis I wanted to write, and in the end, it not only passed, it passed with honors. I say this to point out that the year under discussion here, for all its setbacks and deep disappointments, was not without its successes.

Writing about the winter of 2001-02 in Marysville, from the vantage point of the spring of 2009, here at my parish in Fremont, I have to tell you that I am a little unsympathetic with the mood which overtook me that winter. I am not, on the whole, a moody guy, but as I have said before, I can indulge a mood when it comes over me. I like to think of myself as upbeat, can-do and resilient, and in general, I think this is a fair description. But it does not describe me, that winter. I suppose that, to be fair to myself, what came over me that winter in Marysville was no mere "mood." It was a head-on collision with what was, for me, a simply unbelievable reality; an unacceptable reality: the reality that I was being asked to give up, as a novelist.

Who was asking me to give up?

God.

How do I know? Well, all I can give you are analogies, and they are never perfect. Imagine a woman who six times brings a baby to term, only to have each infant stillborn. Except this analogy does not work, because my novels were not stillborn. They were alive and kicking: I had the testimony of the midwives, to prove it, the midwives being, in this analogy, my agents in Manhattan. Four of them in a row, including a couple of the best in the business. Agents work on commission: they don't take a writer on as a client, unless they are convinced they can sell his or her work. And you must understand, dear reader, that no author can hope for commercial success, without an agent. This is simply the business. Without an agent, you may as well dig ditches.

Well, by the day I was putting my thesis into the mail, I had been looking for an agent for three months, and not only had I not found one, I had thus far failed to get a single positive response on the query letter I was sending out, on GOLD COUNTRY. That is, not one agent in over one hundred queried had asked to see the novel. Typically, I would get four or five requests for a novel, in every twenty or twenty-five queries sent. The logical reaction here would be to imagine that there was something wrong with the query letter: that it was not advertising the book as it should.

On this one, dear reader, you are simply going to have to take my word. The letter was bang-up; it was probably the best query letter I have ever written. It would make sense if that were the case, as

271

GOLD COUNTRY was and remains my best novel. Writing queries is a minor art form in and of itself: you must in a single page convey the plot and the excitement of the novel you are describing, whether the novel is one-hundred or one-thousand pages long. GOLD COUNTRY was more than twice the length of any of my other books: had it seen print, it would have been a 700-page novel. I was not concerned about its length: over the summer and fall of 2001, three different novels, all between six and seven hundred pages, had been on the best sellers list. I wasn't trying to write a best seller, in any event. My concern was writing the best book I could write, was telling the story just as it needed to be told. I would have been satisfied -- much more than that, ebullient -- simply to break print with GOLD COUNTRY.

I knew that the query letter I was sending to New York was good: it did its job. It conveyed the drama, the intelligence and the passion, of GOLD COUNTRY. I followed the same routine I had always followed, in finding an agent: I would send the query to twenty agents at a time, and I confidently expected three or four or five agents, each time out, to ask to see part, or all, of the book.

One hundred-plus letters into it, I did not have a single request for the book. Most of the responses were pre-printed rejections. A very few showed that the agent had actually read the query. One of these agents, trying to be helpful, "strongly urged" me to associate myself "with a community of writers," the idea of course being that you get an agent because someone recommends you. That was not how I had ever gotten an agent. My writing is what recommended me to my agents.

I turned forty-six, January 25, 2002. I had written my first novel, ALL THE ANGELS AND SAINTS, over the summer of 1979, when I was twenty-three. Half my lifetime ago. I had spent some time, after finishing that novel, learning how to write a good query, and figuring out how to approach agents, and after a few months of effort, I had not one but two agents, offering to represent the book. I had been, in other words, farther along the path to publication, at twenty-three, with my first novel, and with no experience, than I was now, at forty-six, with my sixth novel and -- though this hardly seemed to count -- with twenty-three years' experience.

This was pretty mystifying. And damned demoralizing. And this is why, over the late autumn and through the winter, of 2001-02, I drifted into a genuine depression. I need to just say this and be done with it: my whole self-concept, my whole self-understanding, my whole idea of what I was supposed to be doing in the world, was caught up with my talent and my commitment to it. And I need to say this, too, because it is, so far as I am able to judge, the truth: there was, by the winter of 2001-02, nothing idolatrous, in my self-understanding. In my twenties, yes, I think I could have been fairly accused of putting literary success where God was supposed to be. But already by my early thirties, I was past that, and by my mid-forties, well, I was way past it. I wrote because it was true to the way God made me, for me to write. Flannery O'Connor said right up front that she wrote because she wrote well. Well, I also wrote well. I was in the world to write, and I knew it. The conviction was so strong that it had never once, in all those years of effort, entered my head that I ought to stop.

In the late winter of 2001-02, the thought that I ought to stop began to occur to me. I looked at the growing pile of meaningless replies from New York, and thought back to the previous spring, when I'd

273

ventured back out as a writer. I had contacted agents who had good reason to take me seriously, and the only one from whom I got a reply was the one who was dead. I took all of this into consideration, and then added to it the twenty-two years as a writer which had preceded this last year. Always so close, so close – but in this business a miss is as good as a mile. "ALL THE ANGELS AND SAINTS is laugh-out-loud funny, but rock music fans don't buy books...;" "RUNNING FOR ATALANTA is a fine novel, so take my opinion with a grain of salt...;" "I admire BURNING ALEXIS, it is witty and provocative, and I hope you will keep me in mind with future efforts...;" "A RESTORATION COMEDY will make a great movie...;" "A COMEDY OF EROS is an outright romp, and I know another editor will pick it up and give it (and Brawn) a good, and much-deserved, launch."

This last was a frequent prediction, editor to editor, in sending my books back unbought, to my agents. "Someone else" is going to take this up and give Brawn a much-deserved launch. For twenty-three years I had believed that that "someone else" was out there. For twenty-three years, I believed that God had created me with a specific editor in mind, and that that editor and I were bound to link up, given time, given talent joyfully and continually applied, given steady and intelligent marketing effort.

By the end of the winter being discussed here, I no longer believed this. Not only did I come to doubt the existence of an editor for my fiction; I was now coming face to face with the shocking possibility that there might no longer be an agent for me, either. After all, one hundred-ten, one hundred-twenty queries, and not a single positive response. Nothing like this had ever happened in twenty-three years, and its singularity, its immense improbability, began to say to me, "God Himself is asking you to lay it down. This is your Isaac. Isaac was everything to Abraham, and God wanted to test Abraham, to see whom he loved more: Isaac or God. God did not do this to Abraham because God needed to know: he did it because Abraham needed to know. Only a test would prove to Abraham where his priorities lay."

I already knew where my priorities lay. Much as I loved them, my characters did not have eternal destinies; my kids did. Central as my writing was to my life, there were things I valued more. I had not worshipped literary idols since my twenties. The Lord knew I was his, and I could not see my darkening prospects as a writer in terms of some kind of "test" from God. That just isn't me.

Yet as I say, I came to suspect that winter that God might just be inviting me to lay it down, as a writer. The suspicion left me baffled and disoriented. I had dealt with failure as a novelist for two decades: it was part of a process which also included success. I successfully wrote novel after novel and I successfully landed agent after agent; I had failed thus far to find a publisher. But I was not that winter looking at mere failure; I was looking at defeat. The very thought of it cast me into a sadness that I still cannot adequately articulate.

***

I remember articulating the practical aspects of it all, to Daria, in Sacramento. Daria and I saw each other a lot, during that year. I was still a member of her RCIA team at St. Charles, driving down every Tuesday evening, to help out. We'd often go to a late dinner, afterward.

"I've been aced out, on pilgrimages," I said to Daria, one evening, "and so cannot hope for any income there. I can't get an agent to look at GOLD COUNTRY, let alone get one to take the book on, still less hope for a sale with it, so there's that possibility lying dead in the road, as well. If something doesn't give, I will have two choices: go back to the seminary destitute, which given my temperament would be a reckless thing to do, or…take another year out, and…get a job…and…"

And generally I would stop processing the possibilities at this point, because they were so unacceptable. It was not just my writing career that seemed headed for oblivion, that winter. My progress through the seminary program was also imperiled. Take it or leave it, dear reader, I knew myself: I knew I could not go back to St. Pat's constantly holding my breath in case my car should break down, and I not have the three or six or eight hundred I'd need to get it running again. I could not live on the one hundred a month Sacramento sent its seminarians, and I had better sense than to try. There were a lot of hopes and ambitions colliding with an unhappy set of prospects, that winter, but there was also a common-sense, pragmatic bottom line: I needed a few thousand in the bank, if I was going back to St. Pat's, in the fall.

Daria was my best friend and first confidante throughout this difficult period of discernment. She listened not just carefully, but prayerfully; she was prudent in her judgments, and she was right where I needed a friend to be, emotionally. She "got" my growing dread, regarding my life as a writer. She got it. A number of well-intentioned people, over the years, people who did not "get" the whole writer thing, but who were very enthusiastic about me as a future priest, had told me that I needed to give up my writing. These folks apparently thought of it as an unhealthy love, a source of "competition" for my energies as a seminarian, as a priest. It never seemed to occur to them that they were recommending that I ignore the Parable of the Talents. It never seemed to occur to them that they were dismissing as wasted time and effort more than two decades of my life. Nor, apparently, did it occur to them that it was precisely my path as a novelist that had brought me to the seminary, to my future priesthood. How could they condemn such a path? Grace builds on nature; it does not destroy it.

I am always (well, almost always) smiling and diplomatic, and I never told these people to take a long walk off a short pier, but that is exactly what I would have told them, were I not smiling and diplomatic by nature. Daria, on the other hand, grasped the fact that I understood myself as a writer. My writing was not something I was doing "for myself." It was something I could stop doing only at the risk of no longer being myself, no longer being the man God had made; the man, as Daria would put, "God made a writer. God has called a novelist to priesthood," Daria more than once said to me. "Those are the facts and we have to respect them and deal with them."

It was hard to deal with the fact that neither the novelist nor the future priest could move, that winter. There was a moment when Daria said, "This is not your problem. This is God's problem. God saw these circumstances before they arose, and God sees the way through them, even though, right now, we don't. Give this all to God, and let him figure it out for you." This was sound advice; the best I could have been given, in those circumstances. Daria's words would resonate with me throughout the next four or five months, as God did, in fact, "figure it out" for me.

But back to the bottom line: I needed to make some money, or not only would I die as a novelist, but my hopes for the priesthood would also expire. And it is interesting, because just as I was coming to the conclusion that I was going to have to get a resume together and go out looking for a job -- something I had not had to do, in twenty-two years -- jobs started looking for me. Before I had told anyone that I was even thinking about looking for a job, job offers began to come my way.

Jorge told me to come sell cars with him, in Davis. He and Omar were making money hand-over-fist, and given my natural sales abilities, he was sure I could nail eight or ten grand a month, as well. All I had to do was show up at the lot. He had so primed the manager for me that the job was mine, if I wanted it. Daria, too, had a job for me, though it was only part-time and temporary. It would pay about $4500, if I wanted it, and it would not interfere with other goals, because of its part-time and temporary nature. Dale Walker, the youth minister in Marysville, who had succeeded me, four years earlier, called me from out of the blue one day in March and asked if I would be at all interested in taking the youth ministry back, just until I returned to the seminary in the fall, as she had a demanding new job, and in any event, she wanted to move from the youth group to young adult ministry. I got an invitation to apply for a youth ministry position in a large and wealthy parish in the foothills, east of Sacramento, and a friend from Cal called one day, in February or March, and asked if I might be interested in a six-month assignment back at my old office on campus.

I did not want a job. I wanted a publisher. And I wanted to return to the seminary. By February, though, I was beginning to grasp that I would need to take a job, that doing so would necessitate another year away from the seminary, that the repercussions at the seminary and in Sacramento could be serious, and the dawning realization just knocked me over. I was a novelist by God's hand; I was studying for the priesthood by God's hand – how did taking a job further either one of these hopes? My situation that spring just did not make sense, to me.

I remember sitting at a café on the north side of the Berkeley campus one afternoon with Lauren. This was not a hiking date; we were just getting together for lunch. It was a mild afternoon in late February or early March, my favorite time of year in California. The air was fresh and cool and the sunlight warm and we sat at an open window in the café, and talked, as Lauren and I invariably do, about our lives. I told Lauren that for the first time since before I had taken the job at Career Planning and Placement, in the autumn of 1980, I had no idea where my life was headed; I could not say where I would be or what I would be doing in six weeks, let alone six months, or six years. And for me, as self-directed and self-confident as I had always been, this was a profoundly disorienting experience.

***

In fact, I retained one deep (and in retrospect, desperate) hope, that February, that March, and into April. The hope was this: that Deborah Schneider, my third agent, and I would reunite with GOLD COUNTRY, and that I would yet succeed as a novelist, and in the process, rescue my future as a priest. Sometime late in February, it occurred to me that I ought to write Deborah about GOLD COUNTRY. I know, I know, dear reader: you are wondering why I did not think of this a year earlier. Here is why: once you have left an agent (and I left three) your chances of being able to work compatibly together in the future, are no better than fifty-fifty. Think about it. There were reasons why I left Barney, Julie (my second agent) and Deborah. Those reasons had to do with deeply held convictions about what constitutes good writing. In each case, I found a new agent who agreed with me: that was all I needed to tell me that I had done well to trust my own judgement. To return to a former agent is to invite a revival of the old disagreements, whatever they may have been about. Of course, other factors, such as maturity and development of talent, can come into play as well, and these may augur well for an author and an agent getting back together. But it is, really, a dicey proposition.

Having said that, I need to say this: Deborah Schneider was (and I am sure is) an exceptional literary agent. She is can-do and encouraging, strong-but-open-minded and she has tremendous energy. Maybe most importantly, Deborah knows how to inspire a writer to his/her own best work. No agent ever worked for me the way Deborah had, over five years in the late eighties, with several of my novels. I always imagined that Deborah would be the agent I would succeed with, and when I didn't, I was not only amazed, I was truly disheartened. I never wanted to leave Deborah, but "artistic differences" forced me to. Simply put, Deborah loved half my work. I loved all of it.

Well, I had the sense that, of all my former agents, Deborah might just cotton to GOLD COUNTRY. It would be – wonderful – to work with Deborah again. Unlike the one hundred-plus agents I had sent the GOLD COUNTRY query to, Deborah would not assume that I was someone from nowhere, a neophyte with no experience, who needed to be advised to "associate yourself with a community of writers." Deborah knew who Brawn Sullivan was. She might argue with him; she might disagree with him; she might tell him to his face (as she did, always with great good humor) that he was "preachy and didactic," even "bombastic." Deborah knew who Brawn Sullivan was, and I had a sense, that spring, that Deborah would give me and GOLD COUNTRY the time of day.

So, at the end of February, I wrote Deborah. I did not send her a query letter. I sent her a St. Patrick's Day card, and hand-wrote the note, in which I asked her if she would have any interest in seeing GOLD COUNTRY, and if not, then the two of us would just think of this as the time Brawn sent Deborah a St. Patrick's Day card, and wasn't that sweet?

Deborah responded immediately. "It's so weird," she said. "I was sitting in my office Friday afternoon thinking about you, wondering how you were, and what you were up to; whether you were still writing. And here on Monday, is your card. Of course I'll read your new novel."

Remember, faithful reader, my religious sensibilities. My belief that nothing is an accident. I was – electrified – at Deborah's response. "I was sitting in my office Friday afternoon thinking about you…" What were the odds?

I have to take full responsibility for all that followed. I allowed myself to hope. I allowed my hope to soar. Think about it. I was twenty-three when I wrote my first novel. That had been twenty-three years earlier. How unmistakable was that symmetry? I had been shut-out, with all other queries, on GOLD COUNTRY – over one hundred-twenty letters to New York, and a good dozen of them to agents who had reason to take me seriously. No one would even LOOK at the book, let alone offer to take it on. Nothing like this in twenty-three years of effort had ever happened before. Had God himself been clearing the path for Deborah? And think of the "Perils-of-Pauline" rescue aspect of it. Here I was, about to die as a novelist AND as a future priest. Would my novels at last, through Deborah, come to the rescue of my priesthood? Would my past pave the way for my future? Would Deborah fall in love with GOLD COUNTRY, and sell it, and so end the senselessness of my current situation?

Gentle reader, can you blame me, for entertaining such hopes? Even I do not blame myself, seven years after the fact. I was desperate. And to this day, I will argue, the situation was singular. Deborah's response, the ONLY response I got from New York, on GOLD COUNTRY, "I was sitting in my office thinking about you on Friday," all but told me God's will in this situation. The Lord willed that I return to Deborah. The Lord had prevented any other agent from getting in the way, until I realized that Deborah Schneider was, in fact, my once and future agent.

I sent Deborah just the first half of GOLD COUNTRY. To send the entire novel would have been another box and two more envelopes (since you have to send the agent a return envelope, with postage). I knew Deborah would know from the first half of the book, whether she wanted the rest. I was very prepared for Deborah to write back and say, "All right, Brawn, I love this, BUT…" and insist on a number of changes. I was very prepared to discuss the book, this way, with Deborah – we had collaborated in this way on a couple of earlier books, and in fact, Deborah's recommendations had helped make those books the best they could be.

I was not prepared for what happened. Just not at all. Before I say anything else, please believe me, long-suffering reader: agents do NOT call authors on the phone, to REJECT their work. Rejection letters are precisely that. Phone calls are to say, "I love it! I am going to sell it!" So, when on the morning of Tuesday, April 16, 2002, Trudi told me that Deborah Schneider was on the message machine, and asking me to call her back, my heart leapt. Twenty-three years' experience told me that no matter how much Deborah and I might have to haggle over specifics, she was on board with GOLD COUNTRY; she wanted the novel, and she wanted me back as a client. I returned Deborah's call in this frame of mind.

Think of all the air going out of the Hindenburg. That was a zeppelin that crashed into a radio tower in Lakehurst, New Jersey, in 1937, in case you are not familiar with that tragedy. And I know, I know, it was hydrogen or helium or something, not air, that the Hindenburg was filled with. What I am saying is, imagine hopes that had risen into the stratosphere, from a man who saw no other way out, suddenly crashing – and, like the Hindenburg, burning – to earth.

"It's three books!" Deborah said. "I can't sell something this long, this big. There's no market for a book like this." Deborah said other things, too, some of them quite complimentary, but that is beside the point. She did not say, "Let's make this book work;" she said, "I cannot sell this book." Deborah and I had known each other since 1984. I knew what she was saying to me.

I had just endured a ten thousand foot plunge through the atmosphere, and what is more, I was on fire, and crashing to the asphalt. In the circumstances, I thought it best to try to gracefully end the conversation that had ignited this inferno, and so, "Deborah, I cannot thank you enough, for your willingness to look at GOLD COUNTRY, and your willingness to think about working with me again."

"Brawn, I am ALWAYS here for you! I need you to know that. You know I believe in you. Write me anytime you have something new to show."

Deborah was always gracious; but this was not just graciousness. She meant it, and I knew it. And I appreciated it. And...I was burning on the asphalt, and I needed to hang up. And I did.

It was over. My twenty-three-year-six-novels-four-Manhattan-literary-agents-ever-waiting-to-begin career as a writer was over. I was in a state of shock, but I was still rational, and I grasped that much. This is your Isaac. There is no ram in the bushes for you. Plunge the knife into the beloved's heart; burn it all up, a whole-offering. It is over. You are dead, as writer. It is over. By God's own hand, it is over.

***

Two weeks and a day before the phone call with Deborah, I had a lunch date with Sandy Coffey, from the parish council, at St. Joseph's. Sandy was a family friend. She had been on the 1999 Holy Land trip with me; she had been on the first Seminary Saturday with me. When I came to Marysville, in the second half of the summer, 2001, Sandy saw opportunity and wasted no time, cashing in on it. She had me helping out with, and even directing, various

284

parish events, from September on. By April 1, a Monday, and the day after Easter, that year, Sandy was ready to make a bold pitch to me.

"Father Soane has been watching you the past few months," she told me, over lunch at Dragon Inn, one of Marysville's better Chinese restaurants. "He is convinced you are just what he needs for his plans for the parish for the coming year. He wants to create a one-year position, call it evangelization coordinator, a position in which you will oversee all catechetical and faith formation activities in the parish. He believes that, because of who you are in the parish, and because of your innate skills in this area, you can put into place the structure for evangelization that he wants to see here, in Marysville. He has asked me to offer you the position. We know you want to get back to the seminary, but this is only another year. Would you be willing to consider taking one more year away, to do this job? You can tell us your start date and name your price. We will guarantee both."

This was April 1. I was waiting to hear from Deborah, and as you know from the above, dear reader, I was NOT hoping to have to take the position of evangelization coordinator, at St. Joseph's.

But I did take it. Of the several jobs that came looking for me that spring, this one alone unquestionably had my name on it. It would play to some of my deepest strengths, while expanding my overall experience. It was in fact to prove the best job I would have in my life (leaving priesthood out of this!), and for the best pay. It would answer on every other score, too: it would resolve the financial worries; it would empower me to buy a new car; it would advance my preparation for priesthood; it would clear the way for my re-entry to the seminary; it would, finally, greatly assist my return, in a little over a year, to Europe, with my kids.

For all that this wonderful job was to do for me, dear reader, I was so deeply dejected that spring, so longing for a life that had somehow eluded me, that I was seven weeks, April 1 to May 23, telling Father Soane that I would take the job. I told him as well that I did not want to start until July 1, and I told him that I needed a minimum of two thousand a month. He granted both conditions without question, and I had only one last thing to do, at this point: I had to let Sacramento and the seminary know that I was taking another year out. I dreaded these communications. And as events were to play out, I dreaded them for good reason.

TEN

The business of formally withdrawing from the seminary program, which is what I now had to do, was a real downer for me. I had been on an officially-approved year's leave, during which I technically remained a seminarian, and there would have been no red tape, that fall, had I returned to the program: I simply would have sent to Milt Walsh an evaluation of my year out, gone through a routine re-entry interview, and then shown up for classes at the start of the semester.

There could be no question of extending the leave. I was either to return to the seminary at the end of August, or to withdraw from the program. I withdrew via three letters, two to the seminary and one to the Vocations Office, in Sacramento. I sent the letters June 13, not particularly thinking anything of it, but later that morning realizing it was a Fatima anniversary. I took some comfort in that, since I had, from the outset of my discernment toward priesthood, placed myself under Our Lady's banner.

There was little other comfort to be had, that typically bright, hot June morning in Marysville. I had known since Deborah's phone call that I was not returning to the seminary. Two months had gone by, and I had made no move to inform my superiors, either at St. Pat's or in Sacramento, because I was just too damned depressed to deal with it. It is hard to convey the sorrow of that spring; the sense of defeat. Any artist will understand how I felt, and I suppose, really, anyone who has ever faced the death of a long-cherished dream. It was genuine grief. I could have wept for my novels, for my audience, for my characters, whom I loved, and had created with such care, with such joy, with such astonishment, watching them "take life" through me, on the page. I could have wept.

I didn't weep. Not once. Not a tear. It's true I occasionally smoke a Marlboro with some of my boys, but my lack of tears was hardly the result of my being a macho man. I had no tears because I was so shocked and disoriented by what had happened that I had almost no connection to my own emotions over it. I was numb. Stuporous and numb. Losing my writing was like losing my best friend of twenty-three years; in fact, I had often described myself as a married man: I was married to my talent.

I suppose I had better just say this, to answer a question some of you may be asking: what about my other in-progress novels that spring, that summer? I had several manuscripts in various stages of development: didn't I want to get back to them, get them done, and start showing them in New York? The answer to this perfectly reasonable question is no. And the reason for that answer is that I no longer believed that "someone else is going to pick this up and give it (and Brawn) a well-deserved launch." Because my editor did not exist. There never had been any chance for me, or my novels, because "my editor" was a phantom. I could write twenty more novels; it would make no difference. New York and I were through.

How many people pursue anything for twenty-three years, without success, before throwing in the towel? I was what New York editors termed a "literary-commercial" hybrid; that is, a writer who was at once serious and entertaining. Editors prefer writers who are one thing or the other. They are not big on thinking out of the box. They have an inerrant capacity for predicting last year's best sellers. They want genre, or what sold last year, and I could not write to satisfy their expectations, and have any hope of satisfying my own. My standards were intrinsic to my work, and I would not violate them. It is true that my favorite novelists were mostly British and mostly dead, but it does not follow that I wrote like a dead British novelist.

I wrote intelligent and comic contemporary American fiction – and there was not an editor in Manhattan who knew what to do with me. Well, fine. I was not going to waste anymore of my time, love, energy or talent, pursuing publication.

But there was another reason I no longer wanted to complete THE BEST MAN, LOVERS AND OTHER LIARS, or THE DAY OF GRACE (my in-progress novels). I did not want to pursue them anymore because I believed that, in the spectacular failure of my efforts with GOLD COUNTRY, God himself was inviting me to lay it all down, to give it all up. I came to see, in the unparalleled lack of response from New York to GOLD COUNTRY, something beyond nature.

Why would God have created a novelist as ambitious as I was, and not also have created an editor for him? Good question. I more or less asked the Lord that question myself, sometime late that spring, when I took my Bible in hand and asked the Lord if there were anything he wanted to say to me, about my life as a writer; about the twenty-three years that had ended April 16. I let the Bible just fall open, as I sometimes do, when trying to know God's will. I let it fall open and let my gaze land where it would, on the page. It was Isaiah 49.

"Once I said to myself I have wasted my youth; in vain have I labored…uselessly spent my strength."

The passage – I read the entire chapter – amazed me. It spoke directly to my heart; it perfectly expressed the way I felt about my life, that spring. It did indeed seem that I had wasted my youth;

289

spent my strength for nothing. Of God, Isaiah 49 says "He made of me a sharp-edged sword and concealed me in the shadow of his arm. He made of me a polished arrow; in his quiver he hid me." Believe me, I was feeling very well hidden, that spring of 2002. But with Isaiah 49 as a lens through which to view it all, my struggle, my frustration, my sorrow, my defeat, acquired an air of the deepest consolation. To be deliberately shaped, by God, for some purpose, and at the same time, to be just as deliberately hidden – did that resonate with my experience, or what? Isaiah 49 did more. It told me that writing fiction was not a big enough job for me, that God's plans for me went beyond anything I had yet imagined. It also told me that as a writer, I was to expect resurrection.

I took Isaiah 49 to heart. I never doubted then or at any time since that it was God's own answer to me. And it was a hugely consoling answer: I felt very grateful to God, for being so gracious to me, to have led me to this passage, to have given me such reassurances. I also knew that any "resurrection" as a writer was going to come from God's hand, not mine. Not only could I NOT write, that spring, I no longer wanted to. It was over. My dream had died, and taken more than half of me with it.

Over the second half of that spring, I lost seventeen pounds. I have never been overweight, so this was pretty significant. I remember a summer morning in Marysville, visiting with two of my East Coast nieces, Seinin and Julie, who were then in their teens, and telling them, after they had commented on it, that my svelte physique was due to my "caffeine and alcohol" diet. My nieces thought that was great. I said it to make them laugh; but there were days that spring, that summer, when coffee in the morning and Heineken at night were all I wanted.

Five years later, on my first assignment as a priest, at the Catholic Community of Pleasanton, I spoke about this sense of loss, and the accompanying grief, in a Sunday homily. There was a large and active grief ministry in the Pleasanton parish, and leaders of that ministry, recognizing in my description of my emotions in 2002 all the classic symptoms of the stages of grief, asked me to come to the grief group, and talk about it. They said there was deep resonance between the pain of loss that I had felt as a writer, and the pain they had known, in losing loved ones, mostly spouses.

I was impressed with this request. After all, bad as I felt about my life in 2002, no one had died. I was aching over what had happened, but I kept it in perspective. Leave my writing out of it, and actually, my life that spring was pretty good. But as one of the women in the grief group was to say to me, "Well, Father, leave the death of my husband out of it, and I had a great year, last year!" I remember how accurately we were all able to describe one another's feelings, the evening I met with the Pleasanton grief group. The loss of a spouse can leave one feeling at sea, no longer sure what one's purpose or role is.

That is precisely how I felt, with the death of my writing. I had hugged the literary shore all my adult life, and I knew it well, knew its inlets and coves, knew its clear shallows and its deceptive riptides, knew its sandy beaches and its rocky cliffs. I loved that shore; it was my home country, and I had reveled in my "citizenship" there. In the spring of 2002, I lost sight of that shore. In the spring of 2002, I found myself way out at sea, on a raft, with no land in sight. As I had said to Lauren, that sunny afternoon in Berkeley, I no longer knew where I was going in life, let alone how I was going to get there.

The forced withdrawal from the seminary program underscored all of this. Milt Walsh was perplexed: loving and supportive, but perplexed. Father Coleman, the rector at St. Pat's, sounded almost as if he were grieving for my priesthood in the letter he sent me. I think he really thought I was not going to come back. Both Father Murphy and Sister Maureen had left the Vocations ministry, meanwhile, in Sacramento. I am not going to name the individual who was now in charge there. I will say only that he was NOT impressed with my decision to withdraw from the program, and essentially invited me to find something other than priesthood to do with my life. I wrote back that I had every intention of becoming a priest, and for Sacramento. And, in what may have been a fateful decision, I copied both of Sacramento's bishops, and the seminary, on that letter, as I would, on every letter sent to the Vocations Office, in the coming year.

I felt bad about the responses from the seminary, and I was disheartened, and annoyed, by the response from Vocations. But I wasn't too worried about it. Despite my withdrawal from the program, I figured I still had to look a good bet. My grades were almost straight A. I had stellar evaluations both at the seminary and in the parishes. I was to spend this coming year working a professional position in the Marysville parish under the supervision of a diocesan priest, and…I was still the nephew of Jim Poole. No one was gonna mess with me; I was fairly sure of that. Add to all of the above the fact that we seminarians were not exactly hanging on trees. It was and remains a sellers' market out there, where seminarians are concerned. Sacramento and St. Patrick's would take me back, I was sure. Meanwhile, I just had to get through this year.

***

That meant, among other things, bucking up. I remember my Aunt Rita telling me once, not long after Uncle Chuck died, that she was keeping herself busy on the probably-flawed theory that depression cannot hit a moving target. I adopted my aunt's counsel that spring. I already had my thesis back from Father Steve, with a number of recommendations for revisions. I was studying two languages – German, for my MA with the Dominicans, and Spanish, for the seminary, under the twice-a-week tutelage of Rafael Saavedra, Omar's older brother, and one of the most grown-up and responsible of my Marysville kids. I was involved in several ministries in the parish and some beyond the parish (i.e., Daria's RCIA program in Sacramento) and the kids and I continued with regular fundraisers.

I don't know if anyone beyond immediate family and close friends had any idea of my dejection that spring, but there were indications of it, here and there. On Friday, May 17, my great buddy Van, whom I'd met my first afternoon at St. Pat's, was ordained a priest for the Diocese of Oakland. It was an evening Mass, and I had every intention of driving down to Oakland that afternoon to attend it, and…I didn't. And the only reason I didn't is that my energy was so low. The thought of having to explain to the many seminarians and priest friends I would see there, that I was not returning to the seminary in the fall just…made me so depressed that I was willing to miss the happiest night of Van's life. I also missed a reunion of current and former Career Planning and Placement employees in Danville that spring, and I missed it for largely the same reason. Some of the best and oldest friends of my life were at that reunion. I cannot over-emphasize how unlike me this was. But that is how things were with me, in late spring, 2002.

The day I sent the letters to the seminary and to Sacramento, I called Daria and asked her to check my e-mail for me. I would do this occasionally, when for some reason I did not have access to a computer in Marysville. (I was not myself to own a computer for another two years.) I had very little personal correspondence via e-mail, at the time, and I would ask Daria just to check on e-mails of a business nature – those from parishes, the seminary, the Vocations Office, and of course, anything that might have come in from Milanka, at 206 Tours.

Milanka and I had had sporadic e-mail contact over the winter and spring, largely to do with re-scheduling pilgrims from the cancelled Italian trip. And sure enough, there was an e-mail from Milanka, when Daria checked for me. It had been sent four or five days before. It was not about rescheduling pilgrims. It was an invitation to lead a small pilgrimage to Medjugorje, at the start of July. The priest who had been scheduled to lead the group had had to bow out, and half the pilgrims had quit the trip when he did. But a handful remained, and they had no leader. It was a free trip to Medjugorje, if I wanted it.

I don't know what was wrong with me that morning. I hemmed and hawed about this offer. I told Daria that I needed to start my job in Marysville July 1, as Father Soane and I had agreed. Daria countered that Father Soane had been very flexible about my start date, which after all, was entirely true. She pointed out as well that, at my own request, I was only working part-time through the summer: I could double my hours later in July, if I wanted to make up for the time taken for the pilgrimage. I was still inclined to say no, and was trying to find the words to give Daria, who would always simply type whatever I said when we did this, like a secretary taking dictation.

"Dear Milanka," Daria said. "Wow! Yes, I would LOVE to lead this little group to Medjugorje next month!"

I listened to Daria, with a slight frown, and I listened to something else – the sound of her fingers on the keyboard. "Wait a minute!" I said. "You're not writing this are you?"

"I am. Why not? You're going aren't you? Of course you are!" She continued to type, and meanwhile let me know what she was typing. "I am sorry I didn't get this e-mail answered earlier, and I hope the trip is still available…"

I relaxed. Sure, sure, let Daria try to get me on the pilgrimage. Milanka had sent the email at the end of the previous week. No doubt she'd found someone else to lead the group by now. Still, I was surprised at Daria. She had never before taken it on herself to answer an e-mail for me.

We went through my other business e-mails. There were maybe eight or ten. When we had finished with them, Daria said, "Wanna see if Milanka has replied yet?"

I laughed. Daria's enthusiasm was precious. No way would there be a reply from Milanka already.

But there was.

Well, the response would be "Thanks for offering, Jim, but I have found another leader to take the group."

But the response was: "Hallelujah! You are going to Medjugorje!" I could hear Daria's smile, as she read Milanka's words.

I was not smiling: it is hard to smile, when your jaw is dropped halfway to your chest. "My God..." I said.

"I'll say!" said Daria. "Our God and Our Lady! Here it is the day, the DAY you send your letters withdrawing from the program, and Our Lady drops a trip to Medjugorje in your lap! What more could you ask for, by way of confirmation? This whole thing, this whole set of circumstances, is from God. It is God's plan, revealing itself step by step. How exciting! And what a way to start the year you have ahead!"

By this time, I had caught some of Daria's enthusiasm. I could not deny the timing of the day's events. I had had my letters written a few days before, just as Milanka had written her e-mail a few days before. But I could not bear to send the letters, until that morning. Immediately after the letters went out, immediately, in other words, after I took the irrevocable step of withdrawing from the program, I came in to Milanka's invitation, or, as Milanka would say, to Our Lady's invitation. From out of the blue, a trip to Medjugorje!

"She's rewarding you," Daria said, absolutely sure of herself. "She's telling you in no uncertain terms that she knows how hard this has been for you, but that you have done just exactly what you were supposed to do. I'm jealous! I wish God would give me such unmistakable signs!"

***

Not only did I get a free trip to Medjugorje that summer; Jorge and Miguel (aka Mikey) went with me. Some of the guys came over for a bbq the day after I'd gotten Milanka's e-mail. I told them that I was going to Medjugorje July 4. Their eyes lit up; they all wanted to know the how of it, since they all knew I had not planned a trip, and they knew as well that I was flat broke. I told them how it had come about. Jorge, who was making a lot of money, selling cars in Davis, said, "I'm going, too." Miguel, who was as broke as I was, said, "So am I."

I warned Jorge and Miguel that with the departure just three weeks off, they might not be able to get on the flights. And sure enough, they were waitlisted for one leg of the trip, Frankfurt to Split. They remained waitlisted for a few days, and I remember talking with 206 about the possibility of the boys taking a train from Frankfurt to Split, instead. Jorge meanwhile told me not to sweat it.

"If Our Lady wants us on this trip," he said, of himself and Miguel, for whose ticket he was paying, "she'll get us on that flight."

And the next day, she did.

And on the morning of July 4, Matt drove me and Jorge down to SFO, where we met up with Miguel. I remember that the airport was pretty empty that day; I imagine because of the holiday, but also, possibly, because there were rumors of another terrorist strike on America's birthday. Empty airport or no, we practically got strip-searched, going through security. Maybe my boys and I loosely fit some general profile to help the government identify potential terrorists, but the Filipina grandma receiving the same treatment at the next station over did not. I had not flown since the 9/11 attacks, and was dismayed at how long it took to get to the gate under the new regulations (and this was before the shoe-bomber, too).

(Do we live in a ridiculous world, or what?! SHOE bombers! SHAMPOO bombers! Saints preserve us.)

Well, anyway, we got to the gate and got on the plane, Miguel at the window and Jorge on the aisle. I don't mind the middle seat when I am between friends. I remember listening to the jazz station on the music program, and hearing that summer's biggest hit, Norah Jones' DON'T KNOW WHY. With its plaintive lament of poignant loss, it might have been my theme song, the first six months of 2002. Well, July is the seventh month of the year. And from Milanka's e-mail on, 2002 headed in only one direction for me: straight up.

***

It was a heaven-sent trip. I mean that literally. We met our little group – just an additional half dozen pilgrims – at Frankfurt, and we all flew on to Split together. A blue mini-bus met our flight and we started the drive down the spectacular Dalmatian coast. I remember Miguel dozing off and Jorge, busy with photos at the windows, unable to comprehend how Mikey could be asleep, when he might be seeing the Croatian coast again, for the first time in four years.

One of my pilgrims, Anthea, was a screenwriter from the East Coast. She had done a script on Catherine of Siena, and RAI, the Italian television network, was interested in it. It happened that, on the mini-bus, Anthea and I sat across the aisle from one another and started talking. What were the odds, I wondered, that I should have a pilgrim on this trip who was a serious writer?

It was mid-afternoon when we arrived at our pansion, and I decided to take a nap. I had been lying down maybe ten minutes, and just drifting toward slumber, when I heard my name, loudly and cheerfully called, out in the hallway. "Jim!" came the call again. I got up, a little disoriented from fatigue, and looked for my shirt, which I had taken off. Again, "Jim! Where are you?" A knock at my door. "What's taking so long? Are you naked?" I got my shirt on, and opened the door. Slavenka threw her arms around me.

"How is your mom?" she asked, after ascertaining that I was fine.

"She's probably put on her face, by now," I said, calculating the time in California.

As had been the case following the Kosovo conflict, Medjugorje this first summer after 9/11 was not super-crowded. There were plenty of people there, but mostly Europeans; definitely fewer Americans than usual. This was nice, as it meant the mountains were largely empty when we went to climb them. My first morning there, in fact, a Saturday, I woke early, around six, and went up Apparition Hill on my own. There was no one on the slope, so I decided to do the climb bare foot.

It was a sunny morning, but because it was still so early, the air was fresh and cool. I remember sitting at the apparition site, near the statue of Our Lady. I had never seen this statue before; it had been placed there since the last time I was in Medjugorje. I remember sitting there, with only a handful of other pilgrims anywhere in sight, and gazing out over the fields and the vineyards, over the villages themselves, all of which had grown since 1999. I sat there for a while, thinking about all that had happened in my life since our first climb up Apparition Hill, four years earlier. I was amazed to be there, that morning, and to be there with two of my boys! Only a month earlier I could not have foreseen any such thing. Good things, great things, can and do come to us, perhaps when we least expect them – but maybe, when we most need them.

Jorge and Miguel, now free, because of their age, to do as they pleased, in Medjugorje, were out late every night, and they heard from some of the young people there about Makarska, a tourist town on the coast, and they decided that they had to take a day out and go over, and I said it was fine. I only said it was fine after nixing a rental car, which had been Jorge's plan. I insisted that the guys take a cab, which I was willing to pay for. The drive in from the coast is along narrow two-lane roads and involves some steep climbs and hairpin turns, and I could not consider letting Jorge drive it in a rental car.

I remember the conversation, at the dinner table, with the rest of the pilgrims present, over this issue. I remember, too, Jorge's acquiescence to my insistence that he and Miguel take a cab. I remember that Jorge looked at me as if to say, "I will allow you to overrule me just one last time." He was, in fact, a good young man, to do as I insisted – not asked -- insisted. I don't know that, in the circumstances, I had any right to insist on anything. Jorge had paid for this trip entirely on his own. He had paid for Miguel to be here, as well. He was twenty-one and Miguel twenty that summer: I had no legal authority over them; only the moral authority I had exercised for the past six years. I really was concerned for their safety. When I said at some point that I had their parents to think of, Miguel blurted out, "Jim! My parents don't even know I am in Europe!" That is how much my boys had grown up, in the years since our first trip.

In any event, they took a cab. I no longer remember if I paid for it. I do remember watching, with the rest of the pilgrims, right after breakfast that bright Sunday morning, as the taxi, a brown Mercedes, pulled away from the pansion. Jorge and Miguel, smiling and satisfied, waved from the back seat. Makarska is a spectacular beach resort. It is about seventy-five miles due west of Medjugorje. I figured the guys would be there by noon, have most of the day, and be home in Medjugorje sometime after dark.

At dinner, which this group ate early, around five, one of my pilgrims, Jill, asked me if I had talked with Slavenka yet.

"About what?" I asked.

"About the boys," she said, looking a little apprehensive.

"No – why?" I asked, suddenly apprehensive myself.

"I should let Slavenka tell you, but…they have found a hotel and are spending the night in Makarska."

I absorbed this news, I felt, with a professionally-becoming calm. Inside, I was less than calm. "They talked to Slavenka?" I said.

"Jorge called her a couple hours ago," Jill answered. "They apparently found a place right above the beach, for a very reasonable rate."

"I see. I better talk with Slavenka."

Slavenka was only worried on one score: my reaction. "Jim," she said. "They are perfectly safe there. They have found a nice place to spend the night, and the truth is, if they spent the night sleeping on the beach, they would be safe. Please don't be upset. They are young and this is an adventure for them. We'll have them back tomorrow afternoon, well, okay, tomorrow night, because they will spend the whole day at the beach. I promise you, they will be fine."

"Suppose they don't come back, tomorrow night?" I said. I already knew what I would do in that situation; I wondered what Slavenka would recommend.

"If they don't come back tomorrow night," Slavenka answered, "you and I go over Tuesday morning – with our swim suits! We have a day at the beach, we collect Jorge and Miguel, and we all come back over here Tuesday evening."

I was cool with that. As long as the boys were safe, I was not about to begrudge them a night on the coast. I did want them back tomorrow night, though, and I only hoped they would come. I was convinced that the Blessed Mother herself had brought them here, and that she had brought them to Medjugorje, not Makarska.

The next day, Slavenka took us to Mostar, a city I had not seen on previous visits to Medjugorje, but a city I have not missed, on any trip since. Its Turkish Quarter above the blue-green Neretva River is enchanting. We had lunch at a café on a terraced slope overlooking the river, and listened to the call to prayer from five different minarets.

That evening, we climbed Krizevac. Most of my group went up quickly, but Anthea and I took our time. This allowed another American group to catch up with us. They were older, and Anthea and I had to help them on the way back down, which got us to the foot of the mountain after dark, and well behind our own group. Slavenka and the rest of the group were waiting for us with big smiles. "Miguel and Jorge are back at the pansion," Slavenka said. "They arrived an hour ago," said Jill. "They took a bus back!" "That saved them a lot of money," Slavenka added, impressed with the boys' resourcefulness.

The group had climbed Apparition Hill Sunday evening, when Jorge and Miguel were in Makarska. So, I took them up Apparition Hill, just the three of us, Tuesday morning; late morning of course – they had been out to Citluk Monday night. We decided to re-live our 1998 climb, when the three of us had gone up the hill barefoot. We decided, as well, to do the whole circuit – the entire hill and all fifteen decades of the Rosary.

It was only late morning, but it was already hot. It got hotter, as we climbed, and by the time we were making our way back down the slope, we were bathed in sweat. We prayed the Rosary the whole way, all fifteen decades. (This was just months before John Paul II gave us the Luminous Mysteries.) Miguel, of course, was capable of taking the stony path at the speed of light, but the fact that we were all praying together kept us together. As we came down into the village, and started along the main street there, just below the hill, who should pass us in her car, but Slavenka. She pulled over and waited for us to catch up to her.

I had asked Slavenka if she could arrange to get us together with Slaviska, from the 1998 pilgrimage. The boys had all had a case on Slaviska, and Jorge and Miguel and I would love to see her again. (Slaviska now worked for an import/export firm.) As we caught up with Slavenka, there on the road, she said, "Let me take you to lunch at the country club. I will call Slaviska, and if she is free, she can join us."

I would have liked a shower and a change of clothes, but it was not being offered, and in any event, Slavenka made no protest, with the three of us in her car, so maybe we weren't that unpresentable. We drove through the main tourist district of Medjugorje, and out into an open area which suddenly became lush and green – the country club. It is not really any such thing by American standards, but it is luxurious, for its greenery and its amenities, there in Hercegovina. Slaviska met us there, and the five of us had a long lunch, catching up, and laughing and talking over memories from 1998.

***

The next day we went to Dubrovnik. I mean, half of us did. The boys, Anthea and I. The boys had never been on the walls before, so we bought the tickets, and went up. I was taking photos of Miguel, seated on one of the cannons overlooking the sea when, "Oh my God! JIM SULLIVAN?" I heard, from stage right. Miguel and I both turned to look and – oh my God! Jennifer?

Jennifer, a lawyer, ran one of the departments at my office at Cal. We had known each other since 1980. One of her daughters, Ashley, just about exactly the age of the boys, came to Croatia each summer, to work with orphans from the war. Jennifer and her husband John, a judge, in the East Bay, had been coming to Dubrovnik each summer, as a result. Here they were all three: Jennifer, John and Ashley, on the wall above Dubrovnik, the same morning in July, 2002, that I was there. This story was talked about, at Career Planning and Placement, for a long time afterward.

I introduced Jennifer and her family to Anthea and the boys. We took pictures of all of us at the cannon, the sea behind us. Jennifer and John pressed us to come to lunch with them. I was happy to accept. We'd meet in an hour or so, after we had completed our respective circuits of the wall, at a restaurant Jennifer suggested. I assumed that the invitation was for me and Anthea. I cannot say why I assumed this. I cannot say why I turned to the boys, after Jennifer had left, and said "You're not invited." Honestly, I do not know what made me think that Jennifer was only asking me to lunch, that is, me and Anthea.

In any event, I had reason to question myself, when, more than an hour later, Anthea and I arrived at the restaurant. It was one of those wonderful out-door restaurants up the stone steps from the main square, and as Anthea and I came up the last of the steps, Ashley and Jennifer both greeted us with the question, "Where are the boys?" They were genuinely disappointed, as the guys had been, at my disinviting Jorge and Miguel. Ashley had very much caught the fancy of both the guys: who knows the influence that a couple hours of conversation over lunch with such an idealistic young woman might have had, with my boys? I will never know, obviously, since I so stupidly came between it all.

We had a great lunch, in any event. I told Jennifer that it was "just so cool" running into her on the wall above Dubrovnik; Jennifer said it was "beyond cool." Jennifer and her family loved Anthea, whose creative ambitions they could identify with. Both Ashley and her sister, Tara, had artistic inclinations. I was impressed, meanwhile, with Jennifer's knowledge of Dubrovnik, and even of this restaurant, where our party got extra attention because the staff knew and loved our hosts, and where Jennifer knew the menu so well she had no need to consult it.

Anthea and I spent the remainder of the afternoon at a couple of the churches, and buying post cards and gifts in the main square. At some point, a guy with a camera was running maybe twenty feet ahead of us and taking pictures and I asked Anthea if he were taking the pictures of us. "It happens all the time," Anthea said. "They think I am Andie McDowall." She did, in fact, look like Andie McDowall, and I was amused to think of the tabloid headline with the photos, "Andie and Mystery Man Spend Romantic Afternoon in Dubrovnik."

Miguel and Jorge, exiled to the sea, had spent the afternoon swimming; Miguel taking a leap at one point, from the rocks thirty or forty feet above the water, as if he were a young Croatian. Jorge got a photo of this remarkable moment, and you can see every muscle in Miguel's back straining to hold himself upright through the plunge. Had I known that this was how the boys would pass the afternoon, I would have told them to come to lunch, and been happy to pay for them myself.

I had promised the staff at the pansion that we would be back for dinner. (This was not Primorac; it was Mirjana and Iko's place, Pansion Pehar. I'd also stayed at Pehar, in 1999.) I am not sure why I thought getting back for dinner was so important. I don't even like eating at five or six in the evening – I'm a Latin, when it comes to dinner: ten o'clock is a good time for it. But I felt a sense of responsibility to the staff at the pansion and to the rest of the group; I felt we had to be back at the pansion between five and six, and so we left Dubrovnik sometime mid-afternoon.

I remember Miguel and Jorge crossing the white pavement of the central square, wearing board shorts and sandals and looking like vacationing members of the Mexican Olympic team. A beautiful girl, in hot pink and with long, blonde hair, approached them about the restaurant she was in the square to promote. Her name was Sanya (I am told it means "dream" in Croatian). Miguel was not interested in dinner, but he did ask Sanya if she wanted to take a photo with him. Sanya was happy to comply.

The guys asked me about staying in Dubrovnik. Miguel had become interested in dinner, after all, when it became clear that Sanya would soon be off work. They suggested that they could get a bus back to Medjugorje later in the evening. They had, of course, met up with a

number of young people out on the sea rocks as well, and had
already received several invitations for the evening.

Honestly, looking back on it all, I can't give the boys enough credit,
or myself too little. "No!" I fairly barked at them. "We're leaving
now. I promised Mirjana and Iko and Slavenka and everyone else
that we would be back for dinner. There is to be no discussion of
this. We are going back now." Anthea was standing to the side,
observing our interaction, and only later did it occur to me that her
sympathies may have lain with the boys.

After all, there was a compromise solution available: Have our cab
driver call Slavenka and tell her we had all decided to stay in
Dubrovnik for dinner, and would be back late tonight. It would
double the cost of the cab, but who cared? If I was afraid that the
boys would take advantage of being on their own in Dubrovnik, and
spend another night away -- and I was -- there was this middle
course, a course, which, actually, I would have preferred myself, had
I not promised everyone we would be back in time for dinner.

"Can we at least take a picture with Sanya?" Jorge asked.

We took several. I've had one of these shots, Miguel with Sanya,
there in the sun-drenched square, framed and on my desk ever since.
The typical response of those who do not know either Miguel or
Sanya, is, "Oh my gosh! WHO are THEY?"

When we got back to the pansion, the whole group expressed
surprise to see us. "We just assumed that once you got there, you'd
decide to stay 'til dark. What brought you back here?"

I avoided the looks I got from the boys. I saw a smile playing at the corners of Anthea's mouth. I shrugged and turned to Mirjana. "What's for dinner?" I asked.

***

The kids had missed Mostar, and I wanted them to see it, so the next day, we took a cab over; it is about a forty-minute drive. The guys loved the Turkish Quarter, Jorge in particular. He wanted to try one of the restaurants featuring Turkish or Arabic dishes, but Miguel and I were not so adventurous. We wound up at a garden restaurant which served, among other things, pizza, which Miguel and I had, and calzone, which Jorge ordered. There are a lot of shops with a lot of exotic gifts, hookahs and pipes and jeweled knives that look like miniature scimitars and heaven-knows what else, and the boys did some real shopping in Mostar.

As we crossed the broad, wood-plank bridge over the Neretva, returning to the cab, I pointed out to the boys the famous medieval stone bridge, lying in the water below. This bridge, a national treasure, had been deliberately destroyed during the war – far less for strategic purposes than to demoralize the people of Mostar, a large and important city in the region. Mostar suffered heavily during the war. It was not just near the front; for a time, it was the front. There are bombed-out buildings in Mostar even today, fifteen years after the Dayton Accords which ended the conflict in Bosnia. Other buildings carry the scars of strafing during the conflict. The bridge was to be lifted piece by piece from the water, over the next several years, and re-built. I was to walk across it for the first time, on a pilgrimage in 2007, with Will and Daria Young.

The last thing I had to do with Miguel and Jorge was get them up Krizevac. We did this our last afternoon. As it was about three o'clock, sunny and hot, there was no one on the mountain. Miguel went up barefoot; Jorge and I kept our shoes on, but Jorge carried a heavy rock on his shoulders, much of the climb. I was immensely proud of both them. We stopped at every station, where I delivered my typical off-the-cuff catechetical narrative on the Passion of Christ, and at each station we also said one Our Father, one Hail Mary and one Glory Be. We came to a point, way up the slope, somewhere around the tenth or eleventh station, where the goat trail, which is what these stony paths are, was blocked by, of all things…goats.

It was a place where the trail widens out, to thirty or more feet. The herd of goats – snowy white, actually rather pretty creatures – was spread out across the rocky ground in the shade of the pomegranate trees. We all three stopped and looked, first at the goats, then at one another. We took pictures: this was a first for us. The goats, maybe two dozen in all, made no move; they were clearly not afraid of us. I surveyed the path ahead and saw that we could easily pass through them, assuming of course that we would not freak them out, coming within a couple feet of some of them. I recommended that we proceed with deliberately slow steps, and that we make no sudden movements. The horns on the male goats looked…like something we did not want to mess with.

Despite being barefoot, Miguel led the way. He went right up through the herd, and not one goat so much as batted an eye. Jorge and I followed him as closely as we could. The animals were clearly domesticated, and evidently accustomed to seeing bi-peds on the mountain. We reached the top not long after that, and found one of the soda vendors up there, with his wares. I don't remember if the boys bought anything, bottled water or a Coke, or whatever. I do remember that the vendor, seeing us taking pictures, Jorge with Miguel, me with Jorge, Miguel with me, offered to take a shot of all three of us, and we handed him all three of our cameras. These are some of my favorite photos from all my years with the kids. It is hard to describe what it meant to me, to be atop Krizevac again, at last, with two of my kids.

Speaking of kids, two little, white, four-footed ones played a game with us, as we started back down the mountain. They ran along beside us, just a couple feet away, and then, when the boys would go to grab them, they would dart into the bushes lining the path. They would bound back out after a minute or two and run along beside us, til Miguel and Jorge would make another lunge for them – at which they would once again take cover in the bushes. After several minutes of this, Miguel leapt into the bushes after them, which evidently greatly alarmed them. For good reason. I have a couple photos which show these baby goats just inches from Miguel's grasping hands. The four-footed kids reversed direction at this point, and galloped up the hill, on the open path, for greater speed. The two-footed kid had much longer legs, of course, and was a college basketball star to boot. Miguel nearly caught the baby goats, more than once. It was fun to watch.

Our last evening, I was sitting at Columbo's, a famous restaurant in Medjugorje, with the other members of our group, watching Miguel and Jorge as they crossed into a gift shop on the opposite side of the street. What they were doing was saying good-bye to the young women working the cash registers. Some of these young ladies followed them out onto the street, where they exchanged hugs, and appeared to be giving them their addresses, or e-mails, or other contact information. My pilgrims and I looked to one another and smiled. Then, we watched as Jorge and Miguel entered the next gift shop. And the next. And the next. And the girls came out after them, hugging them, and handing them contact info. At this point, my pilgrims and I all broke up. This was even more fun than the baby goats.

We flew home the next day. A group of the guys met us at SFO – Matt, Ada, Pancho, Wally, Fonz. We went to a late lunch at a restaurant in Fairfield, and I distributed the rosaries and Benedictine crosses I'd bought the guys in Medjugorje. We talked about the trip Jorge, Miguel and I had just made; we talked about the trip we had all made, four years earlier. And we talked about the trip we were all now certain we would make, in 2003. The conjunction of events – my being unexpectedly in Marysville for the coming year, and this trip that Jorge, Miguel and I had just made, this trip that had been dropped into our laps from out of the blue – convinced all of us that, as Daria put it, God's plan was finally coming into focus for us: the long-desired and long-worked-for second pilgrimage was now just one summer off.

ELEVEN

About the year as evangelization coordinator, I need not say too much. The Marysville parish was thrilled, when Father Soane announced that I would be joining the staff for the coming year, before returning to the seminary to complete my studies. Though my withdrawal from the program may have caused consternation and doubt among some of my superiors, it did no such thing in Marysville, where the entire parish had believed in me and my vocation from day one. No one in Marysville (or Yuba City) was worried about me taking another year away from my studies, and especially not when it was to take a high-profile job in the Marysville parish.

Taking up a staff position at St. Joseph's, the parish where I had been baptized, made my first confession and communion, been confirmed, and had in adulthood served as a cantor, lector, Confirmation teacher, youth minister and more, was a gratifying business if for no other reason than that the rest of the staff was so glad to have me onboard. In particular during the coming year, I would work closely with Dale Walker, who was now running the young adult group, with Cindy Cannon, the parish DRE, with Ita Fuller and her husband Jim, who ran the office, and with Robert Haldeman, one of my kids from the 1998 trip, Alicia's older son, who now worked the front desk, at the parish office. Dave and Tish Offutt were still there, and were just as much behind me and the kids as they ever had been. I would also have the chance to work with Steve and Pam Souza, in adult faith formation and liturgy, respectively. Steve had been the founder of the youth ministry in Marysville: it was because of Steve's energy and vision that a youth group ever existed there. To some real extent, I owe the main narrative focus of this book to Steve. I only ever became a youth minister because Steve first built a youth ministry in Marysville.

These people were friends of mine. I had known them for years. I admired them, and worked easily and well with them. Karen Brown, who had helped me so much with the youth group when I first took it over, had since left the parish office in Marysville – but she had left it for the parish office in Yuba City, and several times during the coming year, she and I would get together for lunch, and joint-parish strategy sessions. Ro and I did no ministry together, but we didn't let that stop us from getting together for lunch, or from running down to Vallejo to see Father Leon. Finally, Sandy Coffey, who had offered me the job in April, was to work closely with me throughout the year. There were no "new-job jitters" for me in the summer of 2002. It was more like a very happy homecoming.

I worked part-time, July, August and September, this last being necessitated by the fact that I had a pilgrimage to lead, the second half of September. This was the Italian trip that had been cancelled because of 9/11. About one-third of the pilgrims had rescheduled for other dates and already taken the trip, but twenty or so of the group had wanted to wait to go in September, as we had originally planned, and we left for Italy September 16, a year less a day after the original departure date. It was one of the best pilgrimages I have ever made, with near-perfect weather; cheerful, reverent, easy-going pilgrims, and a great new hotel in Rome: the Tiberio, which has been my family's preferred Roman hotel ever since. We finished at breezy, sunny Capri, and I remember sitting back as the ferry headed for the Sorrento shore, and thinking what a remarkable year 2002 was turning out to be, considering that, in terms of my overall emotional state, it was the hardest of my life.

Maybe I needed all these deep experiences of grace, given that I was so shell-shocked that year emotionally. I had made my own effort to keep the graces flowing, at the lowest point of it all, during the spring, when I forced myself to sit down and think about, and then write down, every single thing in life that I had to be thankful for, starting with the fact of free breathing. This list, which I was to work on for a few weeks, eventually filled six or seven pages of legal-sized paper, one blessing per line. I would sit with the list, when feeling the need to buck up, and it did, in fact, invariably, buck me up.

There were mornings, a number of them, where I had to get up and slap a smile on my face, before going in to the office, but on those mornings, slap the smile on I did. My private sorrow about my writing that year was just that. My sorrow, too, about not being able to return to the seminary, was my affair. I was not going to inflict my sadness, which despite all of the blessings of the second half of the year, was still flowing right at the surface of my consciousness, on anyone. Marysville expected sunny Jim, and I made sure that was who showed up to work, each day.

The work was great – rewarding in and of itself, and to that extent, I am sure, healing. I am, in fact, a natural at evangelization, that is to say, the communication of the faith. Father Soane had me involved in every ministry in the parish that touched on evangelization: adult faith formation, RCIA, Catholics Returning Home, catechist certification, adult Confirmation, youth and young adult ministry, the school, and special events and programs (parish mission, faculty retreat, etc.). I realized that from out of the blue, I had been given the best job, for the best pay, in my life, and I will give myself this: I threw myself into it. With my thesis done and the novelist in me banished to oblivion, it was easy to throw myself into this wonderful

315

job. I had my Spanish lessons and my German to attend to, but other than that, the only extra-curricular activity I had going, in 2002-03, was getting my kids back to Medjugorje.

I told the parish of this goal from the outset, and as they had done before, the people of St. Joseph's swung behind us in everything we did. We made money right and left; every fundraiser we held was a success. My game plan this year was the same as it had been five years earlier: a mix of commissions and free tickets, fundraising, and a proposed $500 from each kid, which at this point, many of them could manage easily on their own. Though most of the kids were in college, at this point, several were working fulltime. Some were both working fulltime and going to school. They were moving out confidently into life, and they had joyfully embraced the idea (as I was billing it) of a "Five Year Anniversary Pilgrimage."

Friends are enormously important, when we are feeling the way I was feeling, in 2002. Some friends who really helped buck me up that summer and fall were Bill and Lynne Giovannetti, from the parish in Sacramento. They had known and revered my uncle, and when I came to the parish, they lost no time giving me an Italian welcome to their home. Their son, JR, had been in the youth group I started at St. Charles. Lynne and Bill deeply encouraged me to trust my circumstances; they had come, after all, from "a God who loves." Lynne and Bill knew of my need and desire to buy a new car, and sometime late that summer they gave me a promo package on the Chevy Monte Carlo, which included a gorgeous shot of a black Monte Carlo, which Lynne advised me to hang above my bed, with "trust. Trust. God knows your needs right now, Jim. God will meet them. How did Jesus Himself teach us to pray? 'Give us this day our daily bread.' You pray for that Monte Carlo. You need it, and God intends to give it to you."

In early November I took the Grand Am in to Al to be smogged. He called me back an hour or two later and told me that it would cost five hundred dollars, and that it was not worth doing: the car was spitting oil into the engine, and it could not be fixed, short of a new engine. This was the call I needed, to go out and start looking for a new car. I had asked Al earlier in the year what he would buy, if he were in the market for a new car. He'd said, "Jim, if I didn't have my family, and didn't need the Suburban, I'd buy that new Monte Carlo. It's sleek and smooth, with beautiful lines, and it's sporty, fun to drive. I'd get it in black, with a spoiler; put some rims on it…"

The Monte Carlo I bought was, according to who was describing it, cream-colored, champagne-colored, or the color of dirty sand. I liked the color, in any event, and I loved my new Monte Carlo. I remember parking it out in front of the office one day shortly after Thanksgiving, and Cindy Cannon, our DRE, coming in and saying, "Jim! Your new car looks like you!" That made me smile. I had to name it, of course, and I did: Thackeray. The reason I named the car for the author of VANITY FAIR is that the overall "take" I had on life, that year, was VANITY FAIR's take. Cynical, disillusioned, not expecting much, but laughing, and even, laughing with deep and genuine good humor. There's a point in the novel where Thackeray comes right out and declares Becky's good nature, despite her scheming, her social-climbing, her calculated charm and her cost-analysis approach to sex. The reason VANITY FAIR is my favorite novel is precisely the degree to which Thackeray got this emotional dynamic right: cynicism and good nature. I chalk it up to his Christianity. What does it matter that the world leaves us empty, given the promise of Heaven? Why should we not laugh at life's disillusionments, given the trifling value of the things of this world? Without an all-good and all-powerful God, such cynicism, embraced as a philosophy, would tend to bitterness. Whatever VANITY FAIR may be called, it may not be called bitter.

Nor was I bitter, that fall. How could I be, with all the astonishing grace that had been set flowing in my life, since the discouragements of the spring? I was graced through the job, through the recent pilgrimages, through the Marysville and Yuba City parishes, through my time with the kids, which was, as it had been, in 1997-8, just about constant. Nothing connected with this remarkable year could have been better for me, could have been more the medicine I needed, than the time I was getting with my kids. It was 1997-8 all over again, except from the perspective now, of all that had happened in-between. If I found myself feeling suddenly and unexpectedly sad, looking up, for instance, from my German grammar book, I would think of Miguel chasing those two little goats, and I would smile. I would think of several of the kids coming in as they had one Sunday morning, for the parish breakfast, after a late night at the Sacramento dance clubs, and with just three or four hours' sleep. "Don't worry, Jim," one of the girls assured me. "I'm not hung over – I'm still drunk!" These were my kids, all right. I smile at that memory to this day.

***

No, I was not bitter that year, but I must have been angry. I had to have been angry, because on Monday, December 9, I woke up simply furious – at God. God the Father. I have never in my life been angry at Jesus, and can't imagine I ever could be. I have never been angry at the Spirit, either. But my Father, oh boy. Sit down, faithful reader, and I'll tell you about it. This is the thing: I only got to know Jesus when I was a young man, at the end of my twenties, dealing with a deep personal crisis, and coming back to the practice of my faith, as a result. I met the Lord, as our evangelical brothers and sisters like to put it, and came to know him as my personal

318

Savior. I felt picked up and carried to safety by him. Seven years later, I got to know the Holy Spirit.

But the Father I had known all along. When I was a little boy, and I prayed to God, I prayed to my Father, not to Jesus, not to the Spirit. I knew my Father, as a child. I knew him, as a teen. I knew him even when I was away from the sacraments, for most of the decade of my twenties. When I prayed, in my twenties, it was to the Father. I have always known the Father's love, and I have never doubted its depth or its power. I was protected by my Father. I was guided by my Father. I was, frankly, indulged by my Father. When I wanted to fall into a swoon and tell God how much I loved him, I was talking to my Father. When I wanted to achieve something, and figured I needed grace to do it, I would ask my Father. And when I got mad at something, some set of circumstances, rather than at any one person, God the Father would hear from me.

And hear from me he did, Monday, December 9, 2002. Between going to sleep Sunday night, and waking up Monday morning, I had "gotten in touch with my anger" about 2002. I woke up simply furious, and I stayed that way 'til dark. I did not start the day with prayer, unless you want to call something along the following lines a prayer:

"You wanna tell me why I am in Marysville, this winter, Father, rather than Menlo Park? You wanna tell me what plan of yours was so precious that it required everything I have been through, this year, to accomplish it? You've got the seminary thinking I will never come back, and you have Sacramento Vocations suggesting I take up landscape gardening or long-haul trucking. I am forty-six years old and I am NOT aware of having done anything to deserve the defeats that you were content to hand me this year. All I have ever tried to do since coming back to the Church is to understand and accomplish your will, and this is the thanks I get?"

I enumerated every laceration, every humiliation, every denied hope or dashed ambition, from the first of the year til that morning, and then…I really got going. I raged at God, about the twenty-three years I had devoted to the talent he had entrusted me with. I reminded him of all the long and lean years of loving sacrifice I had put in, as a writer. I reminded him that I had only rarely complained all those years; that, in fact, I had rejoiced in my talent, and thanked him for the opportunity to practice it. I asked him if he had read any good books lately, because the morons New York was publishing sure weren't writing them. I continued in this vein, as I say, for hours. I did all of this in the privacy of my room, upstairs at Mom's, and neither Mom nor Trudi, who were in and out, all day, would have had any idea that I was…raging…upstairs, because it was all silent conversation: just me and my Father.

I knew waking up that morning that I would get nothing done at the office until I had had it out with my Father, so I did not go in to the office that morning. I did not go in that afternoon. I stayed there in my room, and, because constructive physical activity is a good place to go, with angry energy, I spent the next five or six hours cleaning up and re-ordering my room, to make it reflect the priorities of a busy parish staffer, rather than those of a graduate student/writer. I had files, I had books, I had stack trays, I had boxes of stuff to go through, keeping some where it was, storing some elsewhere, throwing some out. The room was not large, but I made use of every space, and it took me most of the day to have it newly arranged, arranged so that it would be an efficient home workspace for me, as evangelization coordinator.

When I had finished re-ordering the room, I went to my health club, the better to show my Father the strength of my anger, in banging all those weights. Silently, unknown to any of the other folks innocently working out at the gym, I was engaged in full scale Father-abuse: just furious, furious, at what had happened, maybe I should say, at what had NOT happened, in my life, in 2002.

As I was showering at the gym, I began to moderate my tone, in this daylong "conversation." (Obsessive monologue is a better way to describe it; no wait, better still: this unmitigated rant.) My anger had been volcanic all day, but now the eruption was subsiding, and I was beginning to notice the lava-scarred slopes, so to speak. I was beginning to realize how over-the-top (to continue the Vulcan imagery) my fury was. After all, hadn't I just last night gone to bed at peace with 2002, for all of its sorrows, but also, for all of its great unlooked-for and certainly unmerited graces?

I took a more conciliatory tack. "Look, Father," I said, lathering up in the health club shower. "I do not like being like this, and I cannot imagine you enjoy my company, when I am like this. I am sorry for abusing you. I need for you to do something for me. I need you to show me just what it was that was so important, here in Marysville, this year, that you went to such extraordinary lengths to make sure that this is where I would be, rather than back at the seminary, which as far as I am concerned, is where I should be. Please tell me why I am in Marysville this year. Because I just don't get it."

I didn't really expect an answer. Or anyway, I didn't expect an answer for several months or even years. I finished my shower, dried off, got dressed, and went out to Thackeray, actually having the graciousness to thank my Father, once again, for this wonderful new car. Then I drove over the bridge to Marysville – my health club is in Yuba City -- where I had to get up to church.

Father Soane and I had developed several Advent programs for the parish, one of which was a Monday evening prayer service at the church. The service involved the praying of the Joyful Mysteries of the Rosary, a reflection on that week's Sunday Gospel, and adoration of the Blessed Sacrament. These services started at seven, and were generally over about 830. I led the Rosary each Monday, but I had help with it. I had help from, as Father Soane had come to call them, "your rosary boys." It was Father Soane who had suggested I start involving the kids in liturgical services. This particular evening, Nelson and Lilin were helping to lead the Rosary. I remember thinking it ironic that they wanted to lead in English – each of them was fluent in both languages and my Spanish still had a long way to go. All the same, I managed. I knew the prayers in Spanish, and I was thrilled to have my kids leading prayer in any language.

Anyway, after the service, as was our custom, the guys and I went to dinner – in this case, to Applebee's in Yuba City. At some point Nelson said to me, "Jim, I've got something I need to say to you."

"Shoot," I said.

"No, I mean something important," Nelson said. "Something that is going to make everybody squirm and look away and not know what to say, and maybe even make me cry, but I have to say it."

I looked at Nelson. I turned to Lilin. Lilin and I both looked at Nelson.

"Jim," Nelson said. "I cannot tell you the difference you have made in my life. I cannot tell you. Jim, I have just come from church, where I led the Rosary before a hundred people. Do you know how amazing that is? I didn't even know how to pray the Rosary, before I met you. Now I am leading the parish, saying it."

Nelson went on. Because of our time together, he had led a youth group with over fifty members (Nelson had been president of the group, in 1997-8). Because of our time together, he had made his first confession and communion, he had been confirmed. Because of our time together, he had learned how to go to nice restaurants, read a menu, and behave like a young gentleman, rather than just being a kid, wolfing down burgers and fries at McDonald's. Because of our time together, he had been to London, Italy, Dubrovnik and Medjugorje; he had flown across the Atlantic and sailed the Adriatic. Because of our time together, he had gotten to know Jesus better, gotten to know Mary better, gotten to know the Church better...

You get the idea, dear reader. I listened to Nelson with huge eyes threatening at any moment to well up with tears – I was going to be the one to cry, not him. I listened to Nelson with an astonished gratitude, accompanied of course, by a pang of deep contrition, toward my heavenly Father. Talk about what I did not deserve! An answer, so immediate, and so unmistakable, to my demand, in the shower at the gym. I was a couple days later to tell Milt Walsh about it, and he said, "Like hearing your eulogy while you are still alive." That was a good way to put it.

What is more, before Nelson was through, Lilin had joined in. "Jim. Because of you, I pray the Rosary every day. Twice every day. I

pray it on my way to work and I pray it on my way home. I pray it
in Spanish. I pray it in English. Because of you…"

When the boys had finished, I told them what they had just done for
me. I told them about my day of rage, my day of beating up God,
my loving Father, and I told them about my request, of the Father, to
know why I was in Marysville this year. I told them, and my voice
broke, "God has answered my request."

Nelson and Lilin looked from me to one another, smiling deeply,
their eyes shining.

"God is good, Jim," Nelson said.

"You can say that again," said Lilin.

From that evening on, I never doubted why I was in Marysville. In
fact, from that evening forward, I was able to articulate my new
situation in these terms: I was back in Marysville fulltime, with a
fulltime job at the parish, the best job I had ever had in my life, for
the best pay. I had a full year to work with the kids toward getting
back to Europe, with nothing – not my thesis, not the seminary, not a
novel – to distract me. The kids and I were doing very well with
fundraising, and the whole parish was on board with our goal, just as
it had been, five years earlier. I had already this year had two great
pilgrimages, one of them dropped from the sky – and these trips
seemed to promise the trip that was at last coming into view: our
Five Year Anniversary Pilgrimage, our return at last to Medjugorje.
I looked at my new situation in these terms, and my heart was
flooded with gratitude.

I thought back to the afternoon I'd sat silently in my room at the rectory at St. Charles, dreading the possibilities for failure, with my planned year out. I thought, "If someone had told me that afternoon that these would be my circumstances, in 2002-03, I would have leapt to get here." Given my over-arching priority, getting my kids back to Europe, and leaving my novels out of it, these circumstances were the best I could have imagined. Indeed, I would not have imagined such circumstances, because I would not have thought them possible: I could not have seen such blessings coming.

Nelson and Lilin changed the way I experienced my own life that evening. And in that, they could not know the difference they had made for me.

TWELVE

On the morning of Tuesday, July 29, 2003, I was up at St. Joseph's, with a clipboard, checking off names as pilgrims got into cars and set off for the two-hour drive to San Francisco International. Mom, Trudi and my brother Dan were driving down with my sister Anne, in Anne's car. Because we had so many family going to Medjugorje, I was riding down with some of the guys. Several of them had already left – Jorge, Ada, Pancho, Nelson, Ravi. More than one dozen parishioners from Marysville and Yuba City were also going, including Pilar Perron, who had been with us, on the original trip, and Pilar's niece, Debbie, and Dale Walker, who had taken over the youth ministry from me. Our group was a nice size, twenty-six; neither too big nor too small. Though I had tried to interest Father Leon in making the pilgrimage with us, as our chaplain, he was unable to do so. He had been at St. Basil's in Vallejo now for over two years. It is a large parish and he was renovating everything; he was busy there. I did have a priest onboard, though: he was in the Bay Area and was getting to the airport on his own.

I was going to the airport with Fonz, Lilin and Matt. For some reason, Fonz had to replace his drivers' license that morning and he and his mom, Rosemary, were over at the DMV in Yuba City, getting that done. Fonz was driving us down in his big four-door pickup. Cat, Fonz's younger sister, was there with us, along with Fernando and their baby. Looking back on this narrative, it seems an outright injustice that Cat and Fernando have not yet had an introduction. Cat was too young for the youth group in its earliest years, but when she did join, about the time the group morphed into the Teen Rosary Group, she became one of its hardest-working and most reliable members. I don't think she ever missed a breakfast. Nor did her brother, or their cousins, and I used to say that, as long as I was sure that Cat, Fonz, Wally and Claudia were going to be there, I knew we had the breakfast covered.

In fact, our breakfasts all along, but especially that spring of 2003, had had more kids than we needed, to make them easy and fun. I have said this many times since, to those attempting to build a strong youth ministry: do NOT be afraid of fundraising. The right kind of fundraiser can be a powerful tool for group bonding, for solidarity and friendship among the young people, and for growing the group overall. And oh yeah – you might make some money! As we had done in 1997-8, we used the breakfast, our signature fundraiser, as a means of promoting the 2003 pilgrimage. When we announced the "last-ever" Teen Rosary Group breakfast in May, the parish arrived in such numbers that we ran out of food at both seatings, despite having deliberately over-bought.

I remember Cat and Claudia coming in and telling me, "Jim! We have to get five more plates together," and me looking at what was left, and shaking my head; then Lilin coming in and saying, "I have four people at the last table over who haven't been served yet," and then Pancho coming in, helping himself to a piece of bacon and saying, "Hey Jim! Are we planning to feed that family of six by the windows?" All we could do was serve up three of four final full plates, put together a few partial plates with what was left, and then direct folks to the "cold breakfast" which always accompanied the hot one; except that most of the fruit salad, most of the doughnuts and pastries, and even most of the cold cereal was gone as well. No one wanted their money back. "You're going to Medjugorje," people said, drinking the coffee and the orange juice that they had paid four-and-a-half bucks for. "We're happy to help!"

We were going to Medjugorje. Twenty-six of us. Ten of the kids. All male. I had known that Cat would not go, because of the baby. Jocelyn was only a few months old, that summer. Cat and Fernando came to see us off that morning just because they had been so much with us, in the months leading up to this long-awaited moment: the moment when everyone would be gathered at the church again, departing in separate cars this time, not a bus, for the San Francisco Airport. I had not guessed that Claudia and Alma would not make the trip. I was surprised and disappointed. Claudia was saving money to buy a house (my kids were growing up!) and Alma, up from LA for the big May breakfast, and very much interested in making the trip, all the same, did not go. Alejandra, Leticia, Vicky, Elva, Veronica, Talia and the other girls who had worked so hard for the Jubilee Year trip were still very much in touch with the old gang, but by the summer of 2003, they were long gone from the group effort to return to Europe. Several of the guys I had hoped might go had largely been absent from this final run-up to the trip, as well. Oscar and Cruz had children. Travis was in the military; so was Richard Haldeman. Omar, Rafael, Angel, JT, JD, Alvaro, Junior, Mike, John – one way and another, they were all pretty much beyond the group at this point, though again, they were all living in the area, and were in regular touch with us. Maybe the biggest surprise was Wally. Wally was at all the breakfasts, definitely still in the group. I don't remember, anymore, why he decided against the trip in 2003.

I had, in any event, ten young men on their way to Medjugorje that morning; three of them – Tico, Lilin and Ravi – for the first time. Sometime before ten o'clock, Fonz and Rosemary pulled up, with Fonz's new driver's license. We all hugged good-bye and then the boys and I set off. We stopped at a McDonald's somewhere in the vicinity of Woodland, and picked up Tico. I remember telling his folks, Jorge and Barbara, "Tico is with his cousin (Fonz) and with me; with my mom, my sisters, my brother, my niece and all of his best friends. Don't worry about him; he's with family." I am not sure what made me want to reassure Jorge and Barbara this way, given that Tico had already been in Europe with me, in 2000; but I did so reassure them, and it was certainly true, by 2003, that the kids and I, and our families, were extended family to each other.

At the airport, we were met by our priest. He was a young guy for the Diocese of Oakland, ordained just the previous year, with Saigon-matinee-idol good looks and a smile that lit the room. "Van!" I said, crossing toward the Lufthansa counters.

Van's presence on this pilgrimage was one of its sweetest achievements. I had long dreamed of having young seminarians as chaperones, on my next youth pilgrimage. My kids had only ever known a forty-something seminarian, and never mind that I looked thirty-something and often acted twenty-something: there is no substitute for genuine youth. I wanted my kids to bump up against a young man who was willing to make this radical commitment to Christ and to the people of God, and Van had long been on my list of potential candidates. It had taken us so long to bring this trip off, that Van was now ordained, and able to accompany us as our priest.

Van amazed me. He had no luggage for a nine-day trip, other than what he carried on his back, and it wasn't even that big a backpack. In addition to clothes for nine days, he had clerics and his alb in that backpack. He was dressed like any normal twenty-something on vacation, and my brother Dan, seeing me talking "with a kid in a ball cap," assumed that Van was one of my boys. I introduced Van to the guys and could see in an instant that he was going to be a hit with them.

I made a quick survey of the group as we got into line for our tickets, and then looked toward the terminal's glass-walled entrances, where, after a few minutes, I saw the last two members of our group arrive. Miguel, and my Goddaughter niece, Marisol. Marisol had graduated from high school a month earlier. This pilgrimage was my graduation gift to her. Marisol was so grown up that when she crossed in with Miguel, her hair up, smiling, her eyes shining, I thought she was Sara, her older sister, who had driven Marisol and Miguel to the airport. Sara was twenty-five that summer; Marisol eighteen.

Our group formed such a bulge in the line that the ticket agents opened a separate window and took us all at once, which was cool, as it meant we were all seated in the same section of the plane, and in sizable groups together. I sat with Marisol; she by the window so she could look out. Mari and I had given up our seats in the row behind, in order to accommodate a young mother with two children. The flight crew was very appreciative, and gave us a bottle of champagne, to say thank-you. We had a glass each, and then passed it back to the guys, who were seated together across a couple rows, in the middle section. They polished the bubbly off quickly, and so enjoyed it that they ordered more. Jorge told me sometime during the flight, when both of us were up and stretching our legs, that the cabin attendants liked them, and were "hooking us up." I could well imagine. There was a young man from Croatia seated next to them, and he joined in their in-flight revelry, and gave the kids lots of ideas about what to do, this time, in Makarska.

And we were going to Makarska. Eight of the boys and I. After the week in Medjugorje, we would go to Split and spend two nights, and then come down the coast, spending two nights each at Makarska and Dubrovnik. The dream the sixteen year-old Mikey had articulated to me, five years before – "I want to come back here and come to these beaches" – was coming true. I know, I know, dear properly concerned reader, Mikey's dream had included the option, uh, the certainty, of "committing lots of sins" on the beaches, and then going to Medjugorje, to confess them all. As it happened, because we wanted to be there for the Youth Festival, we would be in Medjugorje first, and then on the beaches. As for the sins, well, Dubrovnik is in fact one of the most Catholic cities on earth: it has over eighty churches. We could find a priest there, if Miguel were to feel the need of one, come the end of the pilgrimage.

I remember looking out the window, with Marisol, over Greenland. Greenland has always impressed me from the air. We'd left San Francisco mid-afternoon, but flying east, were heading into the night, and it was already maybe eleven PM in the Greenland time zone – Maritime, Atlantic, whichever it is. Yet, though the midnight sun was clearly setting over Greenland, the rugged terrain below us was lit up with a bright twilight; the snowy ranges glowed pale pink in the sunset.

"It's eleven o'clock at night down there," I said. "Amazing, isn't it?"

"Trippy," said Marisol.

***

At the Split gate at Frankfurt Airport, we met up with two other 206 groups that were headed to Medjugorje. The priest with one of the groups, Father Ed Chalmers, has been in Medjugorje every time

331

since that I have returned for Youth Festival. Ed goes for the festival every year. I am beginning to lean that way, myself. Combined, the three 206 groups had close to one hundred people. Our group had its own bus from Split to Medjugorje, something we were very grateful for, when we heard that the bus carrying the other two groups had mechanical trouble, and was a couple hours behind schedule, getting to Medjugorje.

Our group was not without its own little trauma, though. At the Bosnian border, the guard got on and asked to see everyone's passport, and when he saw Lilin's, he wanted to know where the Bosnian visa was. He didn't speak much English, and just kept repeating to a mystified Lilin: "Visa Bosnia, Visa Bosnia." Lilin resisted the temptation to reply with "Mastercard Bosnia, American Express Bosnia – what are you talking about?"

What the guard was talking about was that Lilin was travelling on a Mexican passport. Lilin is a permanent resident of the United States. He and his family continue to hold Mexican citizenship. You don't need a visa to get into Bosnia on an American passport. And you do not need a visa to get into Croatia on a Mexican passport. But you DO need a visa to get into Bosnia on a Mexican passport. I had called ahead for Lilin, to the Croatian Consulate in Los Angeles, to make sure he would have no trouble. How on earth it did not occur to me to check with the Bosnian Consulate as well, I will never know. I was working long, long hours, the spring of 2003, both with my job, and with pulling this pilgrimage together, and it literally never occurred to me to call the Bosnian Consulate. I guess I was thinking, "We come in at Croatia and we leave at Croatia; they will check passports there," and I was not processing further than that.

Lilin and I got off the bus, because without the visa, he could not enter the country. Miguel offered to get out and stay with us, but Slavenka, who was on the other bus, and who was contacted by the guide on our bus, asked Mikey to stay onboard. I was impressed, though, with Miguel's offer. He was feeling outraged for his friend, and Mikey has never been one to suffer injustice silently. But after all, the guard was only doing his job. This was 100% my fault. Lilin and I got off the bus, there at the border crossing which, though located in open country, was conveniently equipped with a bar-restaurant, a couple of shops, and other comforts of civilization. There was no hotel, and if Lilin and I were going to have to spend the night, I told him we would simply take a cab back to the coast, to Makarska, and spend the night there. Meanwhile, I was apologizing profusely to Lilin.

"Jim, do me a favor."

"What?"

"Shut up. This isn't your fault. This is friggin' Bosnia's fault. They think Mexicans want to come HERE illegally? Give me a break. It's a nice evening. Let's kick back and have a beer."

Slavenka had assured us that we would not be at the border crossing long. Imagine this: her brother-in-law was a highly-placed official in the Bosnian Foreign Ministry. She made one phone call, and a couple hours, and several Heinekens later, Lilin and I were in a cab, crossing the border, his tourist visa attached to his passport.

In the meantime, sitting on the restaurant's patio surveying the gentle hills beyond the border, Lilin said, "I'm a beaner, Jim. I'm not afraid of crossing a border on foot. We'll take that hill right over there, the lower one to the right. It'll give us cover in the open country before that bigger hill. Once you're on that bigger hill, you're in Bosnia. A wetback in Bosnia. That sounds like a title for one of your novels."

I sure was grateful to Lilin, for his take on this little misadventure. We had a couple hours there before all the paperwork was done, and during that time, I know I told Lilin that he was highly favored by Our Lady (as I believe he is) and that she had not brought him all the way to the Croatian-Bosnian border, just to have him spend the week in Makarska. It was like a mini-replay of the afternoon in Ancona, five years before, when Paul Delaney had reassured me of Our Lady's capacity to bring her plans off. One difference, though, is that Lilin didn't need the reassurance. He has deep faith, and an admirable ability to roll with the punches. It was a lovely summer evening, and we were enjoying our Heinekens, and one way or another, we were getting over that border, and that was enough for Lilin.

Lilin and I arrived at the pansion just as our group was finishing up dinner. Everyone cheered when we walked in. Once again, we were at Pansion Pehar, Mirjana and Iko's place: they remembered me from my previous visits, and gave me a big hug. I told Lilin that, since we'd missed dinner at the pansion, I would take him to dinner at the Dubrovnik Club, but Mirjana was having none of that. We were her guests; Slavenka had told her of the trouble at the border, sit down, sit down, have a glass of wine, dinner would be on the table in ten minutes.

We were actually in town a night ahead of most of the Youth Festival crowd, and so there was not much shaking, from the point of view of the young, in Medjugorje that night. So, dear reader, guess where the guys decided to go? After all, Ravi, Lilin and Tico were on their first visit to Medjugorje; they had never seen anything here before. The other guys felt obliged to introduce them to the bars and the youth clubs of Citluk. They were out late. They were all legal adults, and could do as they pleased.

And my candor about such things, beloved reader, is the reason I went to my brother Dan and suggested we add a publishing imprint, Catholic California Press, to his media business in Los Angeles. I do not mean to scandalize anyone. But I report situations as they are, not as maybe some of us would like them to be. I do not believe that any of the "Marian" presses out there would publish Father Brawn's account of his youth trips to Medjugorje. My kids are great. It is no scandal to me that they like dance clubs and late nights, and as these facts are part of the story, I'm not leaving them out. On the other hand, "progressive" Catholic publishers, perhaps intrigued with my approach to the young, and with my attitude toward pretentious monsignors, would, I assure you, balk at the thought of publishing a book that makes the case this one does for Marian devotion in general, and for Medjugorje, in particular. They'd think me a pre-Vatican Two troglodyte reactionary. For twenty-three years as a novelist, I had been rejected by the "commercial" New York fiction editors because I was too literary, and by the "literary" editors because I was too commercial. I might just as easily spend another twenty-three years, falling between the cracks, in Catholic publishing. And at my age, gentle reader, I ain't got the time. Hence, Catholic California Press. Necessity is the mother of invention.

Marisol resisted the invitation to Citluk, and stayed with us old folks. I was glad. She did not have another young woman to pal around with, on this trip, but she did have five members of her family, and in my family, we all like each other a lot. We all went up to St. James, after dinner, some to visit the bookstore, some to follow the prayer walk, which by 2003, was entirely paved and well-lit at night, some, such as Mom, Trudi and myself, to spend a little time in adoration, which is a nightly occurrence at the church. My family, Dale Walker and a couple of the other pilgrims all met up at Dubrovnik Club sometime later. Just as it had been in 1998, this nice outdoor restaurant right across the street from St. James would be our preferred social venue, on this trip.

I remember going to bed after midnight that night; pretty late, considering that we were just off the plane. I remember the sensation that came over me, as I was getting ready for bed: a combination of joy, gratitude, anticipation and release – release from five years' tension. Since the first time I had been here with my kids, nothing else in my life had meant as much to me as getting back here with them. And here, five summers later, we were. I praised God, thanked Mary and asked their angels to take care of my boys, who were young men now, and did not have to ask my permission, to go to Citluk. (Not, of course, that they ever HAD asked it…) I got into bed and remembered the first time, in early August, 1998, that I had laid my head on a Medjugorje pillow. I smiled, maybe even laughed, thinking about all the mis-adventures of that phenomenal first pilgrimage. Mom, Trudi and I had been on several pilgrimages since, but whenever anyone asked, we always told them that the best pilgrimage we ever took was the first one.

I drifted toward sleep, deeply content with how things had worked out. There was first the fact of this pilgrimage, which, though it had not repeatedly hung over cliffs, the way the 1998 one had, all the same did not close until just a few weeks before we were set to go. And exactly like the 1998 trip, this one closed when and as it did because Mama Warbucks stepped up to the plate. The kids and I had done well with our fundraising, and by May, deposits had been made for all ten of the guys who were to go. In addition to the breakfasts, we had held a bowlathon in May, and had had several other fundraisers during the spring. My plan was to bring it all home with our most ambitious fundraiser yet – a golf tournament in early July, but by mid-June, it was clear that the tournament was not going to make: we had not attracted the minimum number of players necessary to break into profit.

I was so sure of our success this summer, and so hell-bent (maybe not the best choice of modifiers!) to ensure that success, that I had been throwing big chunks of my own income that spring, into getting the kids paid for. When the golf tournament failed, I was, in the terms of the financial world, in an exposed situation, and there was very little time to regroup and come up with a Plan B. That's when Mama Warbucks took hold of the bat.

As part of an incentive program to get rid of pricier long-term faculty, and to assist the perennially-broke California state government, public colleges that year offered a substantial "early retirement" bonus to teachers who were eligible for retirement. Mom had always planned to retire in 2003 anyway. She got a fat bonus check from Yuba College for, as she put it, "simply walking out the door." She placed about a third of this check at the service of the pilgrimage, and my financial worries were over. The kids, who knew that everything was up in the air because of the failed golf tournament, could hardly express to me their admiration for my mom. "Your mom's a saint," they said.

What Mom is, and I suppose has been, all her adult life, is a missionary. And like any missionary, she's got Christian realism down. She knows what we are here for, and she knows that in the end, all of us are in one place or the other: shining in serene and radiant joy or seething with miserable and impotent rage. And, whichever destiny we choose, it's forever. Use that as your bottom line, and your priorities are quickly ranked. My mom takes seriously the need to help point as many people as possible in the direction of the first, the glorious, option. As for Mom's love for my kids, all I can do is hark back to the woman in Stockton, at Father Dean McFalls' healing Mass, in July, 1998, who had a "word" for me, from the Spirit. "I see a woman behind you, in this work. I see her very clearly. She has red hair. She smiles easily. Without her, you would not be able to do what you do."

I felt, as I say, release, that first night of this pilgrimage. Release from a tension that had lasted five years. But it was not just for the fact of the pilgrimage itself. It was also for the facts of my own life, which facts could not help but include all that had happened the year before with my writing. Something kind of symbolic had transpired with my writing, that spring. My friend Lisa, whom I had met at Cal in 1975, and who was and remains one of my best friends in life, had handed over to me, in March, a big box, a box marked "Jim's Books," a box containing full final drafts of my first five novels. Lisa was not rejecting me. She and her husband, Pete, whom I had also known since 1975 at Cal, when we were all undergraduates together, living at Spens-Black Hall, were re-modeling their home in El Cerrito (an East Bay city north of Berkeley). The room in which Lisa had kept copies of my novels was among those to be renovated, and Lisa needed to clear it out. She and Pete had minimal space for everything they had to store during the renovation, and wanting to make sure that my manuscripts were safe, Lisa returned them to me.

Feelings are what they are. They do not need to conform themselves to the objective facts of a given situation. How to describe the feeling that went through me, as I took my books back from Lisa? Since ALL THE ANGELS AND SAINTS in 1979, I had had no deeper nor more enthusiastic backer, in all my (frankly, dear reader, vast) acquaintance, than Lisa. "It's only a matter of time," Lisa had said to me, so many, many times, in the eighties, in the nineties. Lisa read each book as I completed it, gave me her feedback, and celebrated with me, as each one of my babies, each one of my novels, landed an agent, landed a realistic shot at commercial, New York publication. No one – no one – was more in the corner of Brawn, the writer, than was Lisa. Her devotion to my talent and to my quest was attested to by the fact that she alone, of all the people I knew, had a copy of the final draft of each of my novels, and kept them safe, in that book-lined room in her house in El Cerrito. I had always felt that in Lisa I had a sort of custodian for my novels, a Godmother, should something happen to me, or should my house (and my own original drafts) burn down.

Feelings are what they are. When Lisa gave me my novels back, I felt that they truly were orphans. I was dead, as a writer, and now their Godmother had also given my novels up. They were orphans. And when, that day in March, that I took the books back from Lisa, and shut them up in the darkness of the trunk of my shiney new Monte Carlo, I felt as if I were burying them. I told myself that I would take them to Liz; ask her to keep them safe, but I never did. I don't doubt that Liz, herself a writer, would have stored the copies for me; I don't doubt that Lisa would have taken them back, after the re-model had been completed. But I was where I was, that spring, a year after my self-surrender as an artist. I was unable to believe that anything good could ever again come, of any effort on my part whatever, as a writer. I took the books back from Lisa, not for a moment letting on to her how it made me feel. Because trust me, dear reader, Lisa would have been on that so fast it would have made your head spin; she would have found some new, safe place in her temporarily crowded house to store my typescripts. Lisa would have been appalled at my sentiments. She never has lost faith in me; she is like a sister to me. Never mind all that, I took the books back from Lisa; put them into the trunk of the Monte Carlo, and thought, "Well, that's that. Not even Lisa believes anymore. And if Lisa doesn't believe, then it is truly over." The novels rode around in the Monte Carlo's trunk for the next several years, all but forgotten.

All along of course, other developments had been underway, and all along, I had worked in with them; aware of the manner in which God had taken charge of my life. I am speaking in particular of my own "career" as a seminarian. This career had included my time as youth minister/graduate student/seminarian-at-St. Pat's/seminarian-in-residence-at-St.-Charles/evangelization coordinator. This "career" was now in its ninth year, but the road ahead at last looked smooth and easy. I had two years left at the seminary. Late spring and through the summer, I had completed the process for re-admission to the seminary program. It had been a simple business, where the seminary was concerned; just one re-admission interview with Father Coleman, the rector, accomplished in July.

It had not been so easy with Sacramento Vocations, where I filled out and returned the application they sent me, told them of my pilgrimage plans, so that they would know when I would not be available, then waited four or five weeks and heard nothing. When I called about it, I was told that I had filled out the wrong application. I had been unaware there was a "right" application, and in any event, had filled out the one Vocations had sent me. I asked them to send me the right application. I filled that one out and returned it, and also had two new letters of recommendation sent to them, as

requested. I heard nothing for two or three weeks. I dropped a line
to the office, reminding them of my upcoming pilgrimage dates, and
asking if they wanted to see me for the re-entry interview, ahead of
those dates. I heard nothing for another ten days or so, and then, the
day before I was to leave, I got a call asking me to come in for an
interview on Thursday. I explained that I would be in Bosnia on
Thursday, and asked if we could do the interview right after my
return. The answer was no. As I was leaving the next day, I had no
choice but to drive to Sacramento that very afternoon, for the
interview. I was annoyed by it, but at this point, annoyance was my
typical response to Sacramento Vocations, and I was not, in any
event, at all worried about it. The interview went smoothly, and as I
said to Mom when I came back in from it, that afternoon, "Well, at
least now I can go to Europe sure that I have dotted all my i's and
crossed all my t's, where returning to the seminary is concerned."

Really, it was kind of amazing, the symmetry of it all. Ten days after
we returned from the 1998 pilgrimage, I was at St. Patrick's, a brand-
new student. Twelve days after we returned from this trip, I would
once again be at the seminary, beginning my next-to-last year of
studies. I felt deep peace and joy, a serene and happy anticipation, at
the prospect. And it was in the embrace of such feelings that I
drifted into sleep that first night of this pilgrimage, the pilgrimage on
which, at last, I had my kids back in Medjugorje.

***

Thursday, our first full day in Medjugorje, the kids and I skipped
breakfast at the pansion (which most of them were not awake for
anyway) in favor of reviving a tradition from five years before:
breakfast at the Dubrovnik Club, where for the equivalent of three or

four dollars, you could get a very good American-style breakfast: a ham-and-cheese omelette, for instance, with orange juice and coffee, or strawberry crepes with whipped cream and bacon. We went to the English Mass later that morning, did some shopping along the main drag, and then a bunch of the kids and I met up with a bunch of the kids and Van, and had a late (one or two PM) lunch. It was at this lunch that I first caught wind of the plan being developed among the guys, to leave for Makarska, the next day, and basically, to spend the weekend there. I did not get many details, but ascertained that Jorge was the mastermind of this plan, and I decided I would talk with him about it, later. The plan did NOT please me.

Late that afternoon, we climbed Apparition Hill. Van wore his clerics, which I thought very brave of him. Esteemed reader, please understand me: Medjugorje is HOT in the summer. True, there was a high, thin cloud cover that afternoon. But it still had to be close to ninety, as we started our ascent. Van led the first decade of the Rosary, and we took turns after that. Some of the guys were going barefoot, and some not. As we neared the site of the apparitions, I wanted to ask Van something and couldn't find him. I looked back down the trail and saw him, coming along slowly, smiling, an older female pilgrim on each arm. Van was not just a hit with the kids. The whole group loved him.

Somehow, my niece Marisol got separated from the main group, as we were coming back down the hill. I do not really know how this happened. Youth Festival was just starting that day; most of the thousands who would be attending were still getting settled into their pansions that afternoon, and almost no one else was on the slope when we were. But somehow, Marisol did get separated. And, not unlike Mary and Joseph in the story of the child Jesus in the temple, Mom, Trudi and I assumed that Marisol was with Anne and my brother Dan. Anne and Dan, meanwhile, assumed she was with us. We all got down the mountain and walked back through the vineyards to the pansion. No doubt many of us did as I did – went upstairs and showered and changed clothes. Maybe an hour later a lot of us were assembled downstairs, just to visit for a bit, before dinner, and…Anne asked me if I knew where Marisol was. Anne and I are Mari's Godparents. We were thinking not just of Marisol, but of Liz, our sister: Marisol's mother. And we were feeling a nasty combination of worry and guilt, and feeling both big-time.

Anne and I decided that she and Dan would go back up to the hill, to look for Marisol. This was largely due to the fact that I had a meeting with Slavenka, just at that moment, to iron out some difficulties that had arisen with return airline tickets for Pancho and Fonz: somehow, we had Pancho returning with the main group, which he was not doing – he was staying for the trip down the Croatian coast – and we had Fonz returning with the group of us who were going to the coast. Getting this straightened out took some time, and it also took $300; but I was prepared for that: I had learned from my very first pilgrimage how important it is that the group leader have an emergency stash of cash, precisely to deal with such contingencies.

As Slavenka and I were getting together, who comes in but Marisol – a full eighty or ninety minutes behind the rest of the group. Fortunately, Anne and Dan had not set off yet. Mari was not troubled. She had "gotten lost" on Apparition Hill, all right, but only in order to…find something. Find what, you quite rightly ask, inquisitive reader. I asked too.

"I don't know," Mari said. "I don't know yet. I am just really glad for the time I had alone up there, on the hill. I was only freaked out for a few minutes. After a while, it was hella cool, up there. I could feel God up there, man. I wasn't scared at all. I am really glad this happened."

I looked at Slavenka, who looked at me, smiling. I was, in any event, greatly relieved to have Mari back at the pansion, and that she had gotten down before dark. Anne was across the lounge and Marisol went over to her, and started to debrief.

Thursday night was the real start of Youth Festival in Medjugorje. The streets were thronged with pilgrims, and the vast majority of them were in their teens, twenties and early thirties. The youth party along the street and in the cafes was so huge that the boys decided there was no reason to leave Medjugorje, and so we were all in town, that evening. We went to evening Mass and most of us also spent some time after it, at adoration. After that, the family and I, and certain pilgrims so inclined, found our way to Dubrovnik Club, where Anne and I took up with three Irish pilgrims who were to become real companions to us, on this journey. They were two women, probably in their mid-thirties, and a man about the same age, he being in a wheelchair, and not temporarily. He was living with a permanent disability. I cannot remember his name, nor that of the second of the women; but I do remember the one I met first, who had raven's wing black hair, and an almost hauntingly beautiful face: Gemma.

Gemma had a special devotion to the souls in Purgatory. She was so connected to them through prayer and sacrifice that she understood herself to have been given insights into some of their circumstances.

344

In particular, she was praying for a Native American woman who had perished in an army massacre, near the end of the nineteenth century. This beautiful woman, Gemma told me, "was trapped in the horror of the moment of her death," and it had been laid deeply on Gemma's heart to try to win her release. I pray for the souls in Purgatory, but I must admit I never think about what it may be like for them. Gemma's empathy impressed me.

Gemma also told me that she and her companions had seen me as I entered the restaurant and smiled, agreeing with each other that I had to be a priest. Out of costume, but no doubt, "that guy is a priest." Gemma's observation brought to mind a conversation with one of my literary friends, Meredith Moraine, from fourteen years before. Meredith and I had met at the Squaw Valley Writers' Conference at Lake Tahoe, in August, 1989. We were in the same "critique group" which met every morning for three hours all week long. Meredith told me that she looked across the table at me and thought, "Gee, what a nice-looking young seminarian." This was nine years before I was to start at the seminary. But Meredith is a gifted novelist, I suppose, precisely because of the accuracy of her emotional radar. I myself did not guess, in 1989, that I was a future seminarian. And I was unaware that I was giving off any such vibe! I was less surprised, needless to say, by Gemma's intuition about me, in 2003. In fact, given my recent experiences, I was deeply comforted by it.

While all of us were enjoying the scene at the Dubrovnik Club, Van was off at the homeless shelter, visiting the residents.

"Homeless shelter?" I said, when he joined us near the end of the evening. "Here? In Medjugorje?"

345

"Yeah, right over there," Van said, and pointed in the direction of the shelter, which was somewhere off the main street. (I never did go looking for it, dear reader.)

I looked around the group. Mom and Trudi had been here before; Gemma too. I had been here five times, and never knew that there was a homeless shelter – or any need for one – in Medjugorje.

"How many people are there?" I asked.

Van didn't know. He had talked with "a few."

I shrugged, and ordered two Kaltenbergs –one for Van, one for me.

That night, a group of us sat out on the little patio at the back of the pansion, talking, until four AM. I mean, that is when I went to bed. I don't know when Anne, Marisol, Dan, Dale, Debbie or the boys went to bed. I remember that shortly before four, a few of us walked a couple blocks to a bakery that was just opening up, and got some bread, maybe some pastries, I can't remember, and brought it back to the group on the patio. We must've gotten hungry. It was a serene night, with lots of stars and perfect temperatures, a light breeze and no humidity; just right for a long and lively conversation about life, about faith, about the journeys that had brought each of us to this moment, and this place, the patio at Iko and Mirjana's in Medjugorje, this lovely summer night. I enjoyed the conversation that night. With this group of pilgrims, there were to be several more like it.

***

The next day, after the English Mass, the kids were all taken up with the plan to go to Makarska. Miguel and Jorge had arranged it all the day before, with Slavenka. There were several young people who were not part of our group who were also going, and Slavenka had reserved a mini-bus, one of those little conveyances that can hold fifteen or twenty people. I had talked with the guys who were going, and had expressed dissatisfaction with the idea: "We will be on the coast all next week, including two nights in Makarska."

"Yeah, but this is the weekend, Jim!"

"We will be on the coast next weekend –"

"In Split, not Makarska –"

"Split is a lot more cosmopolitan than Makarska," I argued.

"But Fonz and Tico won't be on the coast with us. This is their only chance to see Makarska."

"What about Lilin?" I asked. The visa Lilin had was a one-time entry document; he could not leave and come back, without getting a new visa. "You guys just planning to leave him here?"

"Hell no! He can come with us."

"Then you must be planning to leave him in Makarska."

They knew about the restrictive visa. They were just being unrealistic about it, because it suited their purposes. Sure Lilin could go to Croatia with them. Slavenka would have to send another state official to the border, to get him back into Bosnia.

I had a right, this summer, unlike the last, to weigh in on anything they did: they were here because of fundraisers I had arranged, and because of my family -- my money and Mom's. I had asked the guys for $500 each for the trip, and they had all but a couple managed to come up with it. But this was a $2,600 trip. So, I argued with them. In the end, though, I did not feel I could hold the guys in Medjugorje. I expressed deep unhappiness with their plan, and let it go.

Ironically, considering they would not be with us on the coast the following week, neither Fonz nor Tico wanted to go to Makarska. Fonz just flat-out was not interested. Tico decided against it when he realized that Lilin would not be able to go. Nelson and Ada both wavered, as well. At one point, neither one of them was going to go. But when the bus came to the pansion, right after lunch, they got on it. So seven of the guys, plus some other American kids whom they had met the first two nights in town, went to Makarska Friday afternoon, and stayed til Sunday evening.

While I was feeling – vexed – at this situation, I ran into Van downstairs at the pansion. He was with some old guy in an off-white, sort of cream-colored, habit – not Dominican; I know the Dominican robes. The old guy was thanking Van in broken English, shaking his hand with both hands, and evidently taking his leave.

"Who's that?" I asked, after the old monk had left.

Van told me his name, but I do not remember it.

"What was he thanking you for?" I asked.

"I let him have my room last night," Van said.

"WHAT?"

Van shrugged. "He didn't have a place to stay," Van said. He told me the old monk was from some central European monastery, and that, like many European religious (apparently) he had simply come to Medjugorje expecting to be taken in at one of the pansions free of charge, since after all, monks don't have money. But it was Youth Festival, and there were thirty-five thousand people in Medjugorje, and…there was no room at the inn.

I looked at Van. First he finds a homeless shelter here; then he finds a homeless monk, and gives him his own bed!

"Where did you sleep, last night?" I asked.

Van indicated one of the sofas in the lounge.

I rolled my eyes. I had known Van five years, but this – instinct – toward the vulnerable was new information to me, about his character. Of course I admired him for it. But I was glad not to be blessed with the instinct myself.

"Van," I said. "You have seen my room. You know they gave me a triple, because I'm the tour leader, and they always give me a nice room. I have two extra beds. I am not offering either one to a homeless person or to a wandering monk. But should you give your bed away again, I offer you one of mine."

Van smiled.

"Hey, Jim."

I turned around. Tico, Fonz, Lilin; my good boys; the ones who had refused Satan's invitation to the beach.

"We're gonna go up Apparition Hill again," Tico said. "Wanna come with us?"

I grinned. "That's a date. When?"

"Right now," said Fonz.

"It's gonna be hot," I said.

"Yeah, that's why we wanna go," said Fonz.

"We wanna sweat like bleep bleep bleepers ," said Lilin, and I will let you use your imagination, gracious reader, as to his exact words. These were my good boys, all right, but their language did not always betray it. "We wanna offer it up for the souls in Purgatory, and for those bleeping bleepers headed over to the coast."

"We don't want any tragedies on this trip," said Fonz. "Don't want anybody drowning, or breaking his neck in a diving accident at Makarska."

"We figured we'd put some sweat and prayers into it for the guys," said Tico. "Load 'em up with grace, for the weekend."

I was beaming. So was Van. I set off with my three saints-in-the-making. Van set off on his own – to rescue someone from the gutter, no doubt.

The boys and I took the climb barefoot. "Those bleeping bleeps better bleeping appreciate this," said Lilin.

I was laughing. I could not get over these three. They not only wanted to climb barefoot, they wanted to go to the top; they wanted to say not just the Joyful, but also the Sorrowful Mysteries, for their buddies, and for the weekend on the coast. It was hot, and we were drenched with sweat, by the time we got through with the Sorrowful Mysteries. The guys had asked me to narrate the Mysteries as we climbed, so no matter how hot it was, no matter what my feet felt like, and no matter how wet my shirt was, I was enjoying myself. I love diving into the Mysteries of the Rosary, and never more so, than with the young.

When we had finished with the Sorrowfuls, way, way up Apparition Hill, we had the option of circling around the back of the mountain and completing the Rosary circuit (with the Glorious Mysteries) or simply heading back down the hill. I was pleased with the guys' decision to head back down the hill.

"That's enough for those bleepers," Lilin said.

"Shall we put our shoes on?" I asked.

"Hell no!" said Fonz.

"What kinda tenderfoot are you, Jim?" asked Tico, genuinely surprised that I had made the suggestion.

"Those bleepers need us to stay barefoot all the way down," said Lilin.

We came down the mountain barefoot, offering it up for the Seven Sinners on the coast.

***

Naturally, Fonz, Tico and Lilin met young people that weekend. Medjugorje was filled with thousands and thousands of teens and twentysomethings. The city was short seven of them, of course, but that didn't matter to anyone but me. Among the young people the guys met that weekend was a simply breath-takingly beautiful Irish blonde, about the same age as the boys, named Chiara. (The pronunciation is along the lines of kir-uh, but that does not really nail it.)

"Oh no," I thought, when the guys first told me about her. "Not another Irish girl!"

But Chiara was different than the hearty Irish lasses from 1998. She had arrived in Medjugorje sometime early in the summer, planning to stay just a week. She decided to stay a second week, and then for a whole month. At Youth Festival, she had been in town six weeks, and was not yet sure when she would leave. You hear about the young doing this sort of thing, in Medjugorje. Chiara was, as I say, a simple knock-out, easily the Celtic opposite number of gorgeous Sanya, whom Jorge and Miguel had briefly met, the previous summer, in Dubrovnik. But though she cannot have been unaware of her beauty, she really seemed unconcerned with it.

Chiara had the guys at adoration Friday night, and again, Saturday night, and again, Sunday night, when my seven devil boys had returned from their debauch-by-the-sea. I found myself wondering if maybe Our Lady had not sent an angel among my boys, to help them achieve the proper focus and intent, with their days in Medjugorje.

But...angels don't drink, and Chiara could, and did drink. She'd be at a table with all of us, at Columbo's, at ten o'clock at night, and suddenly pulling a lace shawl over her bare shoulders, say, "Let's go to the church for adoration," and...knock me over with a feather, my dear equally incredulous reader, half the guys would leave their drinks and follow. I had never (and never have since) seen anything like it.

Chiara shared with me Saturday evening that she was very disappointed that I had let the guys go to Makarska. She had apparently met them all briefly, Thursday night, and hearing our story from them, had been much inspired: what an amazing group of young men! To discover from Fonz, Tico and Lilin on Friday, that most of the guys were in Makarska for the weekend, forced Chiara to reassess her initial set of impressions. She was very sorry to think that they had come all this way, after all this time, only to abandon the Blessed Mother for the beach, at their first opportunity. She told me she could see their potential, and she assured me that, had I put my foot down, the guys would have stayed in Medjugorje.

She may well have been right.

"When they get back," Chiara pleaded with me, "make them go deep here. They have such deep faith. I could sense that in them almost immediately. There is so much here for them, Jim, if they will only take the time to go deep with it. God has great plans for them. They're not here a second time by accident."

"You can say that again," I said.

In fact, I much appreciated what Chiara had said about the profundity of the boys' faith. Heather Higgins, who had been my assistant with the youth ministry in the early years, once said exactly the same thing about them. We were at a wedding in Marysville, and a number of the original members of the St. Joseph's Youth Group were there. I had taught most of these young people for Confirmation, but I had not been their youth minister. We were at a table at the reception, and the subject turned to my kids. One of the guys said something about how rough and rowdy my guys were, and he didn't mean it as anything but an observation: this young man had become good friends with several of my boys. Heather said, "Yeah, they're a little wild, but they have such deep faith. Such deep, deep faith. It takes you by surprise. God has plans for them."

Chiara had intuited this truth about my boys – their deep faith – from a brief meeting Thursday night. I could only hope that the Magnificent Seven on the coast would spend some time with this young lady, on their return.

***

Meanwhile, the rest of my pilgrims were going deep, in Medjugorje, and were getting a lot from the effort. Marisol went back up Apparition Hill on her own, Friday, and again, Saturday. In fact, she was so drawn to the hill, that she went every day but one – the day we went to Dubrovnik. More than once, she climbed the hill twice in the same day, sometimes alone, sometimes with others, sometimes barefoot, and sometimes not. She had indeed "found" something up there, getting lost that first climb.

Marisol's response to Medjugorje was more than I had hoped for. My Oakland nieces have all got deep faith, too. But they are worldly, sophisticated, politically aware and culturally astute young women. They question a lot, including plenty of things about the Church. They will never be pray-pay-and-obey Catholics. I really didn't know what Mari would think of Medjugorje; she had told me a year or so earlier that she wanted to go on one of my Italian pilgrimages with me, because she treasured Italy for its art and its history. If I had been leading a trip to Italy, that summer, I'd have taken Mari on that pilgrimage, rather than to Medjugorje. But Marisol was lapping up the experience of Medjugorje: attending all the talks by the visionaries, going to Mass and adoration, saying extra rosaries with her aunts, or my brother Dan, as they would walk through the vineyards on their way here or there. Marisol "got" Medjugorje fast. As her future-priest Godfather uncle, I could not have been happier.

My siblings Anne and Dan were having a similar experience: it was the first time for them in Medjugorje as well. Dan's big venue was Krizevac. He climbed it a couple times, mid-day, on his own. People have – experiences – on Krizevac that they do not have anywhere else. I have never had anything special happen there, but lots and lots of Medjugorje pilgrims have. My brother is one of them. He saw the dance of the sun, one afternoon, on the mountain. "Jim," he said, "the sun just went OFF." He did not mean it turned off. Just the opposite. It went wild, spinning and changing colors, and throwing off great waves of multi-colored photons, and so forth. I can't really describe this phenomenon, because I have never seen it.

Dan came down the mountain after a long period of prayer at the top, and everyone he met, all the way back into town, he said, "had a glow around them, this shining light was all around them, like an aura, like an all-body halo." Dan said that even the rocks, the trees, the bushes, the birds, the whole mountainside, was sort of pulsing with light, with some kind of serene radiance. "Grace is tangible here," he said. I remember turning to Mom when Dan told us this, my eyebrows raised. Mom just smiled. My brother was definitely "open" to the Medjugorje experience.

My sister Anne took a lot of interest in the visionaries, and what they were saying; she compared and contrasted the Medjugorje messages, the secrets, the general ambience, with her experience of Fatima and Lourdes, several years earlier. She was not big on the "fear factor" that she discerned at both Fatima and Medjugorje. She told me that Lourdes was her favorite Marian site, because of its joy. I have to agree that a fascination with the secrets of Medjugorje misses the point. As I said at the outset of this book: the secrets are for the future. There is no reason to speculate on them, or worry about them. The message of Medjugorje is what matters, and it is a message of deep hope and ultimate joy. Anne and Marisol talked a lot, both on the pilgrimage, and afterward, back in California. I remember Mari telling me, that first autumn after the trip, that when she got upset or worried about something, she would call Anne, start talking, and one or the other of them would say, "Let's give this to Our Lady," and right there over the phone, they would say part or all of a rosary together.

I don't know if Mom saw the sun dance, this trip, but I know that a number of my pilgrims did, including my sisters, my brother and my niece, all at the same time. They were walking back through the fields from a public apparition up at Cenaccolo, the center where all the young ex-addicts help other young people get off drugs. Marisol told me that she and my siblings were walking along, saying a rosary, and all of sudden, "the sun just started doing its thing, man. It was hella cool, man, really beautiful. I was practically in tears."

Someone who had not come to Medjugorje particularly open to the mystical phenomena which occur there, was Tico. When he had been in Rome with us, three summers before, Tico had bought one of those special Jubilee Year rosaries. It had a silver chain. He and I had been at dinner, a few weeks before we left on this trip, and he mentioned to me that he did not believe rosaries were actually turning gold at Medjugorje. I reminded him that this had been the experience of several of the guys, on the 1998 trip. I told him as well that I had several rosaries that had changed color.

Tico was not buying it. "It's something in the metal," he said. "Something in the rosaries they sell in Medjugorje. They treat them with something that makes them turn gold later."

I laughed. My first rosary to turn had been bought in Boston in 1994. Three years later, while talking about my work with the kids, at my prayer group in the foothills, the rosary simply turned gold. Take it or leave it, I told Tico, that is what happened. As for the rosaries the guys had, in Medjugorje, in 1998 – I had bought all of them in Sacramento, a month before we left on the pilgrimage.

Tico resisted my arguments. I shrugged. As I have said already, it makes no difference to me, whether people believe in the mystical elements of Medjugorje. They're not important. What's important is the message. Know that God exists, Our Lady says. Know that Jesus is your Savior. Convert your heart to peace. Take that to heart, and you don't need anything else from Medjugorje.

All the same, "Bring a silver rosary," I advised Tico.

He brought his Jubilee Year rosary; the one he'd bought in Rome.
Before leaving California, he had shown the rosary to his folks and
his sisters – "It's SILVER, right?" Everyone agreed. It was silver.

Saturday morning, at Cenaccolo, we were standing on the grass
cheek-to-jowl with nine million other pilgrims, while inside, one of
the visionaries was having a public apparition. I will be honest with
you, trusted reader, I am NOT into these public apparitions. Don't
get me wrong: of course I believe in them. I just don't see what the
point is, in having everyone in the western Balkans converge on that
one spot where one person, the visionary, is going to see the Blessed
Mother. You're no holier because you are within a few hundred feet
of Mary. You can be a LOT closer to the Blessed Mother than that,
anywhere on earth, anytime you want to pray. You can be in her
very arms, in prayer.

My lack of enthusiasm notwithstanding, I of course had to be at
Cenaccolo that morning: I was tour leader; it was my job to be there.
All nine million of us were praying the Rosary. I was standing near
some slender but leafy trees, hoping that their shade would not fail
me, as the sun climbed higher (it was mid-morning). Anne sidled up
alongside me with the news, "Tico's rosary just turned gold."

I turned to Anne with wide and smiling eyes.

"He's freaked," Anne said. "But it's a good freak."

***

The three 206 groups went up Krizevac together, Sunday morning. It was light when we got to the base of the peak, so maybe we went up around seven or eight. There were a lot of us, as mentioned before. The priests led the prayers at the first three stations, and then we took turns with it, among the rest of us. I remember watching Father Ed Chalmers and really, really liking him. He had a truly "fatherly" way about him: he is the kind of priest Bing Crosby used to play. We need more like him. I lost track of Van more than once. Every time I stopped to look for him, I found him far down the trail, looking like a Southeast Asian angel, albeit fresh from Gold's Gym, an older lady pilgrim on each arm. Van was always smiling and he was never in a hurry. I think he's gonna live to be one hundred.

The Seven Sons of Satan returned from Makarska Sunday evening, just as promised and right on time. They had had a blast on the beach. Among other exploits, they had told all the European girls that Ravi was actually from a titled East Indian family, a member of the Punjabi aristocracy. They evidently carried the ruse off rather well. We have all called Ravi "the Prince," ever since.

I got together with them in an upstairs meeting room, and told them that they were required to do two things, over the next several days: attend Mass with the group each day, and climb Krizevac with me. The rest of their time in Medjugorje was up to them. They knew where the church was. They knew where the confessionals were. There was adoration at the church every night. There were talks at the church every day. There was the spectacular Youth Mass every evening. They were welcome to re-climb Apparition Hill. There were plenty of opportunities for grace here, and they knew it. They were grown-ups, they could make their own decisions. But two things they owed me: daily Mass with the group, and Krizevac, with me.

"Jim! Do you think we would come here and not climb Krizevac?"
Miguel, outraged at having his piety impugned.

"I'm goin' up barefoot," one of the guys said.

"Me too," said another.

"I'm goin' up naked," said another.

"In any event," I said, "we're going up. We're going up when it is
hot. We're going up when there's no one else on the slope. We'll
figure out when, later. It can't be tomorrow. We are going to
Dubrovnik tomorrow."

This news brought a collective hoot of approbation from the
Makarska Seven.

***

The next day we went to Dubrovnik. That is, most of us did. Dan
didn't go; he did not want to take any time away from Medjugorje.
Dale didn't go, either, and for the same reason. Tico and Lilin did
not go. Lilin could not go, because of the way his visa had been
written up. I had not been consulted when his visa was being taken
care of, and we only understood its restrictions when we got to
Medjugorje, and Slavenka, looking at what had been done at the
border, explained them to us. Because Lilin could not go, Tico
would not go. This was a big deal, because Tico was not part of the

group of us, going down the coast the following week. If he didn't see Dubrovnik now, he would not see it at all. Tico didn't care. He was not going to leave Lilin on his own in Medjugorje. Fonz considered staying for the same reason. Tico urged Fonz to go, however, and Fonz, who of course had seen Dubrovnik, in 1998, did not need a lot of persuading.

There was a huge traffic jam at the border, so huge that we backtracked a bit, and took a separate route through the mountains, rather than down the coast, to get to Dubrovnik. We missed a lot of the spectacular coastal scenery as a result, and I hoped that we would come back up via the coast, so that my first-time pilgrims would not miss it. I have seen some magnificent coastlines in my travels, and I live in a state famous for its dramatic seascapes, but for my money, nothing beats Dalmatia.

We had the usual city tour with a delightful local guide whom I tipped outrageously because half the pilgrims were kids who would not think of it. She went away smiling. I always like to have my local guides go away smiling, because I figure there is an excellent chance that they are going to see me again, the next summer.

Slavenka had come down with us, and was to spend the rest of the day with us. But she had not accompanied us on the tour. Nor had Jorge and Miguel. Rather, Slavenka had met up with two girlfriends in the old city, and, with Jorge and Miguel, they had taken a table at one of Dubrovnik's many outdoor cafes. They spent the better part of the morning there. If you infer from this, dear reader, that, following the 2002 trip, Jorge and Miguel had become favorites of Slavenka's, I would argue that you have drawn the correct inference.

In any event, I owed them this indulgence, after dis-inviting them to lunch, as I had the previous year, with Jennifer and her family.

We had Mass at St. Blaise, one of the four principle churches of the old city, and I watched my buddy Van up there, young and smiling, at that ornate and ancient altar, and I smiled. After Mass, we were free for several hours. I had learned from my experience the previous summer: we were not leaving Dubrovnik today until six PM. Most of the guys went immediately to the beach. They were hungry. There were restaurants at the beach. They wanted to spend the rest of the day at the water. Matt, my family and I, together with the rest of our group, went up the stone steps from the main square, found a restaurant that looked good, and had lunch.

After lunch, I told folks where to go, depending on what they wanted to do. Some went into the old city, to shop. Some went to the beach. Some went back to re-visit some of the churches, and the Franciscan monastery, which we had seen that morning, on the city tour. Matt, Marisol and I went up on the walls. Matt and Marisol were suitably impressed with Dubrovnik, from its walls.

"This town is off the hook," Marisol said, videotaping the view of the yacht harbor, from maybe one hundred feet up.

I was glad to have Marisol's enthusiasm. She had told Anne earlier in the morning that it felt weird to be gone from Medjugorje; to be unable to go up Apparition Hill. She felt as if she'd let the Blessed Mother down. Anne countered with the fact that we had already said two rosaries on our way to Dubrovnik, and very likely, would say two more, on the drive back to Medjugorje: "The Blessed Mother is not displeased with your efforts today, girlfriend." Mari nonetheless felt that she had maybe abandoned a higher calling for the day, in coming to spectacular Dubrovnik. "I could have stayed in Medjugorje, missed all of this, and offered it up," was Marisol's take. I was not at all unhappy to hear such sentiments from my niece: they evidenced a true Catholic sensibility. All the same, I wanted her to enjoy Dubrovnik. And she did.

We went to the beach, after the walls, getting there in the later part of the afternoon. We would not have all afternoon at the beach, as the boys had had, but we would have a good couple of hours, and that was enough for us. Mom, Trudi and Anne had come down to the beach after lunch, and were seated comfortably at an open-air restaurant above the sand, where they could see everything. Marisol joined them. Matt and I went down to the changing rooms and got into our swimsuits.

On the beach proper, we found Van, looking like he'd just stepped away from a Ralph Lauren shoot, in board shorts and dark glasses. He was guarding the area where the group had set up camp – a lot of towels and water bottles and cameras, etc., spread out luxuriously over the decidedly non-luxurious-thin-and-pebbly-sand of the beach itself. Van was keeping watch while the boys, all of them, plus Slavenka, and her two friends, were having a ride on the "Banana Boat."

"Banana Boat?" Matt and I asked.

Van pointed out over the blue-green water.

Sure enough, way out there, several hundred feet from shore, was a speed boat pulling an inflatable shaped arguably like a banana, and on the banana were…all the guys, plus Slavenka, plus her two girlfriends, whom I had not yet met. The banana boat ripped right along behind the speed boat, rapidly rising and falling on the waves. We could just barely hear the hoots and hollers of the guys, as they rose up and plunged down with the Adriatic swells. Matt and I laughed.

"I wish I was out there," said Matt.

"Me too," I said.

All at once, the banana boat went bananas: it came down hard at an angle and threw almost everyone into the sea.

"Whoa!" said Matt.

"Golly gee!" I did not say. I said something else, but it was unpriestly of me. I was thinking of course, "They are way out there: I can't get to them in time, if one of them needs help."

None of them needed any help. They came ashore laughing and reporting an exhilarating ride. They would have done it again, except it cost too much. And on this, I will give my boys a lot of credit. They know how to curb their appetites. Everything to the max, but nothing beyond that; nothing to excess.

Van, Matt and I went into the water, now that the guys were back to guard their stuff. The water was great: the currents were at once both warm and cool, and there was, even here in the surf, that fabled Adriatic clarity. Not quite swimming pool clear, but clear; clear at thirty feet down, so that you really have no idea, 'til you're way out there, just how deep the water has gotten.

We took lots and lots of photos. Van and Slavenka feature prominently in them. The guys all wanted to know where Van worked out: he told them he did not belong to a health club. He just did sit-ups and push-ups every day. (Oh! To be twenty-eight again!)

"You know what, Jim?" Nelson said. "I don't think Van really wants to be a priest."

"What do you mean?" I said.

"He's too cool. He's way too cool to be a priest."

"But he is a priest."

"We just think he wants to have fun," said Fonz.

"Does that mean he would not want to be a priest?" I asked.

"You know what we mean," Fonz said.

366

I did know. They had never met a priest the likes of Van Dinh before. That fact had me smiling, the rest of the trip.

We came back up from Dubrovnik along the coast, and I was glad, as I really wanted Marisol to see it. "Hella cool," she said, of the Dalmatian shoreline, her camcorder going.

We were in Medjugorje before dark. Mirjana served dinner at nine. This, I thought, was the right way to do a day in Dubrovnik.

***

The excursion to Mostar on this trip was different than any other I have made, in that Slavenka, who lives there, invited us in to her home, that afternoon. We met two of her three children, but her husband, a physician, was working. After seeing Slavenka at home, we did the usual Mostar thing: Slavenka took us to a mosque, where the young attendant, a Bosnian with blue eyes and fair skin, was very pleased to show us around. Mostar itself is a predominantly Catholic city but a plurality, if not outright majority, of Bosnians are Muslim. After the mosque, we crossed the broad plank bridge to the shops and galleries on the opposite side. My family had not seen the Turkish Quarter before, and they loved it. (Though Dan, again, had chosen not to leave Medjugorje, that afternoon.)

There are good restaurants on the slopes rising along both sides of the Neretva. The setting is very green and well-shaded from the hot Balkan sun; these are really nice places to kick back for an hour or two. We decided to go to a restaurant back across the river. Mid-way across the bridge a small crowd had gathered. This told me,

Jorge and Miguel, who had been here the previous year, what was about to happen, and we went to the rope-rails of the bridge to watch, calling on the rest of our group not to miss it. A moment later a Speedo-clad Bosnian youth, about the same age as my boys, went over the side of the bridge, keeping his toes pointed firmly toward the water, what, sixty, seventy feet below? I don't know how far. Only that, if he had been my kid, I'd have had a heart attack. He went down ram-rod straight, disappearing into the blue-green, swift-flowing water with such precision that he hardly made a splash. When he came up a moment later, several yards downstream, the crowd on the bridge erupted in cheers and applause. The kids make fifty bucks (or thirty euros) for each jump. The cool blue water that hot afternoon looked very inviting, and as he came up on the shore, the boy was grinning, waving up at us. Nice work if you can get it – and if you can survive it.

My family and I had lunch at one of the terrace cafes above the river. While we were there, the call to prayer went out from the two or three mosques that are right there, at the river. If you have never heard the Moslem call to prayer, I am here to tell you that it is really beautiful. The experience was not diminished by the fact of a tinny background Euro-pop rock coming from the restaurant's speakers. In fact, the combination of sounds intrigued us; call it a direct experience of the post-modernist sensibility. Marisol felt that Mostar, too, was "off the hook."

***

This was the first time I had been in Medjugorje for the full Youth Festival: in 1998, we had arrived just as it was ending. I had never seen the Youth Mass in the evenings, 'til this trip. It blew me away.

368

For those of you unfamiliar with the lay-out at St. James, there is a huge open area behind the church, with a stage that can be used for talks, for concerts, or, as in this case, for saying Mass. At the seven PM Mass, during Youth Festival, this open area is filled with tens of thousands of young people, and they come from all over the world. Many of the groups bring their home country flag, and you see, among many others, the banners of Brazil, Kenya, Korea and Australia, as well as those of most European nations. The Maple Leaf is always there, as is the flag of Lebanon. The Stars and Stripes are usually there, though – despite the huge number of American pilgrims – you don't typically see more than one or two American flags out there above the crowd. The first night we were at this Mass, some of the kids pointed out the Mexican flag; Chiara showed us the Irish.

The evening Mass at Youth Festival could serve as a model for vibrant youth liturgy the world over. The music is great, and when the whole crowd sings, it can lift you off your feet. Young people from various nations serve as lectors, and read the petitions. Communion can be distributed by as many as three hundred priests. The Mass itself is in Croatian, and so is the preaching, but you can purchase a headset for translations. I never have. The Mass is the Mass. I never understood it in Latin, as a little boy, and yet, of course, I DID understand it. Same thing here.

Some of my pilgrims were at the evening Mass every day, but I wasn't. Our group had private Masses all over town – at one of the convents, at the orphanage chapel, and so on. I did attend the evening Mass a couple times, though. Mom and I and some of the kids stood at the rail overlooking the great sea of worshippers seated on the benches below. By the time we would get there, there was no room to sit in the crowd, not that I'd have wanted to, anyway. I am not big on being in the middle of a crowd, not even a crowd gathered for Mass.

Toward the end of the evening Mass, we'd deputize two or three of the kids to go across the street and stake out a couple tables at the Dubrovnik Club; if we didn't, lots of luck finding a place to sit, that night. One of the things that really amazed me that trip (and on each since, as I have several times been back at Youth Festival) was the sheer numbers of young people in the city. Not just the restaurants and bars, but the gift shops and the ice cream and soda stands were packed; the sidewalks had the foot traffic of midtown Manhattan at lunch. It was phenomenal.

The one real drawback to this is that, if you go to the mountains at the "popular" times, especially dawn, you can find yourself climbing a stony goat path in a crowd, in a sea of pilgrims, hundreds if not thousands deep. It is the fulfillment of a vision Pope Pius XI had, of huge numbers of pilgrims streaming up a hillside to a large cross, somewhere in the Balkans. I cannot take the time here to detail Pius' vision and how it helped bring about the erection of the great cross atop Krizevac, in 1933. But it is cool to think of it that way; to realize that you are participating in the fulfillment of a pope's mystical grasp of a future reality. And though the huge numbers of pilgrims streaming up that Balkan hillside is in itself a great thing, it does not make for the most prayerful or serene experience, if you happen to be in the midst of the crowd. I prefer to climb the mountains in the middle of the afternoon, when you are not likely to run into anyone but the goats.

***

And that is what the guys and I did, our last day in Medjugorje. Actually, as it was the same day we had gone to Mostar, we climbed so late in the afternoon that it was evening by the time we reached the top. Still, we were fortunate in that the mountain track was almost deserted. Miguel and Tico went up barefoot. We took our sweet time, going up, not just because we were praying at each station, but because we were busy remembering the 1998 climb. I would no doubt have badgered the guys to climb Krizevac with the main group, on Sunday morning, had they been in Medjugorje on Sunday morning. But now, Krizevac being something of the crowning achievement of any Medjugorje pilgrimage, and the guys bringing forward so many memories, from the first climb, it seemed very right that we were going up the mountain by ourselves, and on our last afternoon in Medjugorje. It was Wednesday, August 6, the Feast of the Transfiguration; that is, the feast of a transformative, mountaintop experience.

About one-third of the way up I saw Tico, who was a few feet ahead of me, stop and smile, looking out toward the western sky, where the sun was. He tapped Miguel on the shoulder, and indicated the sun. Miguel looked, and smiled, and kept looking, as did, one by one, all the rest of the guys.

"You have to be patient, Jim," Ada was once again saying to me, as I was once again protesting that I, at least, could not look at the sun. All I was seeing, when I looked at the sun, was the sun.

"You gotta look slowly toward it, turn slowly into the full view, give the disk time to cover it, and then it happens," Ada assured me, not meanwhile taking his eyes from the spectacle.

I didn't care about seeing the miracle. After I had tried a couple times to see it and it didn't happen, I was content to take pictures. After all, precisely this had happened, five years earlier. But I had not had my camera, then. This time, I did. I took several shots of my boys, all of them, standing transfixed on the goat path, staring at something which, from the photo, you cannot identify. You can only tell that they are all looking at the same thing, and I am their witness that what they were looking at was the sun.

"Wow," said Ada. "Did you see that? That purple?"

"Awesome," Nelson said, smiling.

"Ho! That was cool!" said Fonz.

"Try taking a picture of it, Jim," said Matt, not looking away.

I kept taking photos, but not of the sun. Pancho, rapt like the others with what he was seeing, all the same did have the presence of mind to point his camcorder directly at the sun. He watched the miracle through the camera, but when we replayed it later, all the video shows is the sun.

Go figure. Because of my Catholic faith, no explanation is necessary. Short of the faith to accept miracles, I suppose, no explanation is possible.

The question, "Why this miracle? Why this business of the sun, spinning, dancing, throwing off waves of colored electro-magnetism?" is certainly not one I can answer. It is a small-scale re-enactment of the great miracle at Fatima, in 1917, and I suppose it is connected to that. I suppose that it tells us that Medjugorje is connected to Fatima, and that anyway, the dancing sun is Our Lady's signature miracle, a way of reinforcing the fact that it is, indeed, Mary, at Medjugorje. But why Our Lady ever chose this particular miracle to begin with, well…ask her.

By the time we reached the top, the sun was setting. It cast a pink-gold glow as a backdrop for our pictures, and I got some great shots of the guys up there: our triumphant second ascent of Krizevac. It was an emotional moment, and a couple of the guys had tears in their eyes. If I were to identify them, I would be found strangled in an alley, shortly after this book appears, so never mind which ones. It was a big moment for all of us. We prayed, we thanked God, we did a group hug and a group hurrah!, and after some more photos, we started back down, as a blue dusk was falling across the mountain. We got down just before dark.

***

The fun of our last night in Medjugorje shows up in the photos. For some time, most of us were at Columbo's – Anne and Marisol, Dan and Dale and Debbie. Chiara was there, with her California body guards, Tico, Fonz and Lilin. Nelson and Pancho crossed the street from the shops where they'd made some last-minute purchases. Matt and Ada were at their own table, with several European girls.

Miguel, Ravi and Jorge turned up about half an hour after we'd arrived there, Miguel trying to hide out from a Polish girl who'd "gone ballistic." She evidently felt Miguel to be guilty of some huge romantic betrayal, though clearly, in Mikey's eyes, it was all in a day's work. The girl eventually found him, and "Migwell, Migwell," I can still hear her plaintive and charmingly accented pleas, "why you were not there this evening? I looked for you everywhere!"

Migwell's wide eyes and palms-up gesture could have suggested anything, from guilty surrender to "What are you talking about, girlfriend?" to "Have any of you ever seen this young woman before?" Neither Jorge nor Ravi did anything to help him out; Marisol was holding back a broad grin, and Dale had to look away to keep from laughing.

Sometime later I found myself at the Dubrovnik Club with all my family. We had been joined by some Californians from another group, whom we had met earlier in the week, and Gemma and her companions were there, too. We stayed late, kept our waiter busy, shared stories and took lots of pictures. Everyone wanted to be sure that they would get an invitation to my ordination. I cheerfully promised to provide same, meanwhile reminding all of them that that happy event was still two years off. We all promised to stay in touch, and when I think of Gemma, in particular, I wish we had.

THIRTEEN

Slightly over half of our group returned home on Thursday, August 7. They had an early flight out of Dubrovnik, and had to be off from the pansion by something like three in the morning. Mirjana and Iko had "breakfast" for them at two AM, and I was there to say good-bye to everyone. I was still up; I would not have made it, if I had gone to sleep first. If I haven't said this already, two AM is a very normal "lights out" time for me. My natural rhythm, in fact, seems to be to go to bed about two and to rise about nine.

Eight of the guys and I were staying another week, for the excursion down the Dalmatian Coast. We were starting at Split. Mom, Trudi and Anne were going to Rome for five days. They had a one-hour flight from Split to Rome, that afternoon. We were as a group taking a mini-bus to Split, late Thursday morning. I appreciated the convenience of the travel time. We took a back route to Split, not one I am familiar with, and like the back route to Dubrovnik, earlier in the week, it kept us away from the coast 'til we were nearing Split itself. At the airport, we said good-bye to my family, amid big hugs and lots of thanks.

"Your mom's a livin' saint," Lilin said, as we pulled away from the airport. "And not only that, she's fun to be with."

Our first two nights were in Split, so we went straight to our accommodations, a bed and breakfast just half a block up from the waterfront promenade. It was a great place: four big bedrooms, one bath, all along the same bright, high-ceilinged corridor. We were on the second floor, but the ground floor seemed to be used only as an entry to the long and curving stone staircase. There may have been storage there, but there were no guest rooms, and I was glad. I didn't want us waking anyone up. The proprietors, a gentle, smiling older couple, spoke neither English nor Spanish, but fortunately they knew German, so we were able to communicate easily.

I took the bedroom at the end of the hall, and the guys split up among the others. I had to go see Ratko, who handles ground operations for 206 in Croatia, about paying for our nights here in Split, and getting vouchers for the Dubrovnik hotel. Ratko's office was right around the corner from our bed and breakfast. I mentioned to Ratko that I was a little worried about our hosts. I knew that we had been described as "nine pilgrims from Medjugorje." "But Ratko," I said, "I cannot imagine, based on that description, that these sweet old folks were expecting me and my boys." Ratko, jolly and middle-aged, with dark hair and bright eyes, waved my concern away. "Relax," he said. "Marito and his wife will love your boys. Doesn't everyone?"

When I came back in, the guys were all gone. I decided to do something I had wanted to do since that morning five summers earlier when I'd first glimpsed the Split waterfront from the deck of the Sansovino: I walked the length of the promenade. We were very well situated, just a block from St. Francis of Assisi church, and as I say, half a block up from the promenade. Split's waterfront is gorgeous. It is lined with Canary Island date palms (the same kind of palm as at the seminary, and along another urban waterfront: the Embarcadero in San Francisco). There are artfully laid-out strips of lawn and bright flower beds. The long curve of the harbor provides a striking set of views from any point along the promenade. There are lots of shops and boutiques, and many cafes and restaurants with outside tables. There are plenty of street vendors selling everything from tourist trinkets to iced orange juice, which just at that moment, sounded good to me. I went into a bank and changed some dollars for the Croatian kuna, and bought the biggest iced orange juice I could get. It was a bright and hot afternoon.

Split is amazing. Turn up any street from the promenade and walk a couple of blocks and…you are in Roman ruins. Split was founded by Diocletian (circa 300 AD) as his retirement villa/port/compound. Some of the original structures still exist, and even where they have been gutted, leaving nothing but a colonnade, for instance, modern Croatian Split has incorporated ancient Roman Split into itself. There is a vast open-air bazaar amid the classical ruins. There are jazz bars and cafes, too, among the ruins, with lots of outdoor seating, to accommodate the many tourists in the California-like summer: long, hot and dry.

I was on my own well over an hour, but was cool with it: I like time alone, period, and maybe especially, if I can get it, when I am travelling. In fact, being out on my own in a new city had been one of the deepest joys in travel for me, in my twenties, in my thirties. It started with New York, the summer of 1979, when I was twenty-three. Never mind the crowds: I think New York, well, Manhattan, is a great walking city. I later walked Chicago, New Orleans, Atlanta, Boston, D.C., Princeton, New Haven; also Hamilton, Bermuda, which though a physically small place has got a big-city feel, especially when the cruise ships are in port. I spent some adventurous afternoons finding my way around Tokyo, when I was there for Taizo's sister's wedding, in the spring of 1986, and of course, I explored every European city we visited, when I travelled to Europe with Uncle Jim, in 1989. In the years since 1989, much of my travel had been pilgrimage; and of course, when I am on pilgrimage, I am working. The simple pleasure of setting off on my own and exploring a new city was something I had lost touch with, over the past few years. So, walking Split on my own that hot, sunny afternoon brought back a treasured set of memories. It made me feel downright young again.

The guys and I met up later that afternoon at the house. They had twice sent runners down to the house, to bring me to them, only to find me not there. They were concerned that I was alone. I appreciated their concern. They had been up in the Roman section as well, and…"Jim, this town is off the hook!" "There are fat-ass Roman ruins here!" "Have you seen the waterfront?" "They have bars and restaurants right there in the ruins!" "We found a McDonald's!"

The guys loved Split so much that they asked me about staying on an extra night or two, with (as we were already calling our elderly hosts) Mom and Pop. The next stop was Makarska, but all the guys but Lilin had already had two days there, and, in fact, we had not been able to secure reservations in Makarska through Ratko, ahead of time, a fact which made me a little nervous. I had the experience of the boys, of course, both last summer and this, with impromptu trips to Makarska, so thought it likely that we would have little trouble finding accomodations, once we got there. But as we did all love Split, and since where we were staying was well-priced, well-situated and comfortable, I talked to Ratko about adding a third or even fourth night here. But the rooms were already booked, which given the location – we were within easy walking distance of everything you want to see and do in Split – was no surprise.

Something that did surprise me was coming in, with Lilin, early in the evening, our first night there, and finding the guys all busy with their preparations for a night in the clubs – Pancho just out of the shower, Jorge just ready to go in, Ravi at the mirror with hair gel, Ada and Matt having a pre-party Corona, and so on – and finding our "Mom," our gentle and smiling Croatian hostess, in the middle of all the hoopla, ironing a shirt which I recognize as belonging to Nelson, who was bopping back and forth between the rooms bare-chested. While I was taking in this set of facts, who pops into the room and hands "Mom" a shirt but a bare-chested Miguel. "Mom" smiled, took the shirt and said, "Grazi…" (She and Marito also spoke Italian, so that, speaking slowly enough, they and the boys could communicate with each other, Italian to Spanish and vice versa.)

I followed Miguel into the hall. "Mikey! What the Hell –" I said, and indicated our hostess at her work.

"Jim!" Miguel said. "She offered to iron them for us!"

"Jim, we were gonna do our own ironing, like always," said Nelson, coming into the hall from one of the rooms. "She saw Pancho get the ironing board out, and she just came in and took over."

"Yeah, she pushed Pancho aside, grabbed the iron from him and threatened him with it!" said Ada, from behind Nelson. "She's a mean old bat! Very territorial."

I turned to "Mom," who of course, had understood none of this. She was smiling. "The young men are going out for the evening," she told me, auf Deutsch. "They want to look their best."

I insisted that they could iron their own shirts. (As in fact the boys can and do: it is a guaranteed part of the trip, whenever we travel together, this hour or so of prep for the evening, which includes ironing shirts. I have never learned how to iron myself, and was impressed to discover that my buff, athletic, macho kids knew the skill.) I explained to "Mom" that the boys knew how to use an iron.

She just kept smiling, and waved my concern away. This service, like breakfast in the morning, came with the rent, as far as our Croatian Mom was concerned. She said something in Italian, the only part of it that I got was "di collegi," (and I do not know if I spelled that right). She looked up from her work and shot me a wink, maybe remembering that it was German, not Italian, that I spoke. "Sie sind sehr frohlichen Jungen," she said, which pretty much translates, "These guys are a lotta fun."

I thought of the won-over waitresses, at Black Angus and Red Lobster…

About our two days in Split, I am not going to give a lot of details. We went to the beach – mostly rocks: Split is a resort city, but it is not famous for its beaches. We went shopping, wandering through the huge open-air bazaar and the commercially-developed ruins. Anyone who thinks girls have a corner on shopaholism needs to spend a morning in the Split bazaar with a few twenty year-old males. I normally hate shopping, but Split's bazaar, Roman columns hung with bright sales banners, stalls selling sandals and beach towels set up in the shadow of an ancient aqueduct, and so on, kept me smiling the whole morning.

And the city is every bit as attractive at night as during the day. The nights included walking the promenade, having a drink or two outside, at one of the cafes, going "inland" to the ruins for dinner, and then back out to the bustling promenade. I went home by midnight both nights, but the guys found a huge disco at the far end of the promenade that kept them out much later.

Given the advanced age of our hosts, I went to bed each night in Split, ready to leap up and scold the guys in fierce whispers, if they came in laughing and loud, at some ungodly hour. In fact, I did not hear them come in either night, and if I didn't, it's a cinch Mom and Pop, who lived upstairs, didn't. The second night, Ravi and Jorge somehow got separated from the guys with the keys, and when they came back to the bed and breakfast, around four in the morning, they had to toss pebbles through the windows, to get one of the other guys to come down and let them in. I heard about this from Marito and his wife (I cannot remember our hostess' name) over breakfast the next day.

"Steinen," they told me, "durch die Fenster." Stones, through the window.

I thought they'd broken a window, and it showed on my face. "Wieviel kostet –" I started to ask, wanting to know the price of the window.

The old folks chuckled, assuring me the windows had been open. "Di collegi" out in the street had needed only to hit one of the other collegi, up in bed, with one of die Steinen. This, fortunately, Ravi and Jorge had managed to do, and so they got back into the house, for what was left of the night. Marito and Mrs. Marito quietly beamed, telling the story. These were, indeed, frohlichen Jungen. But if I may say so, Marito and his wife were frohlichen Altern.

I did have one real moment of angst in Split. It happened during the "prep hour" our second evening in town. I came in with Lilin and Matt – we'd been out getting film – to find Jorge, Miguel and Ravi, still dressed for the beach, standing on the balcony of one of the rooms, pouring drinks from a couple of bottles, talking excitedly and, I suddenly noticed, passing a gun back and forth between them.

"What the Hell," I started.

"JIM!" Mikey said, in a voice full of excitement and...something else...I couldn't identify it yet. "Come here, come here."

"Shhhh," said Ravi. "Keep it down, keep it down. We don't want anyone calling the cops on us now!"

"Quiet!" Jorge said. "Don't say anything like that, man!"

"Let me see that –" I said, pointing to the gun, which Jorge was holding. "Where did that come from?"

"We bought it, man!"

"Let me see it –"

"No, no man," said Jorge. "We're just trying to figure out where to get rid of it –"

"What?"

"Listen, listen," Miguel said, taking my arm and pulling me in close. "This is serious, Jim, it's serious."

Alarm. That was the something else I heard, in Miguel's tone.

Long story short: the guys had bought the gun in a side-street shop, had gotten on a city street car to go to the beach, had not understood how to pay for the ride, had gotten off at the beach, ignoring the demands of the driver that they pay, had been approached by police, one of whom started to search Jorge's bag, so that out came the gun, in Jorge's hand, off went a shot over the heads of the police, ducking for cover went the cops, and all three of them – Jorge, Ravi and Miguel -- took off running, disappearing down an alley, around a corner, up a street, and into a broad and busy boulevard, where the cops lost them. Now…they had to get out of Split, because the cops were looking for them –

"Get out of Split!" I said. "Get out of Croatia altogether! Oh my God!" My mind was racing, and it went in one direction only: protecting my kids. The boys hadn't killed anybody, after all. They hadn't even hurt anybody. They had only acted incredibly stupidly. I was not, in the circumstances, the least bit concerned with furthering the cause of Croatian justice. I had one concern in this affair: getting my boys back to California as fast as possible. I asked them a series of yes or no questions. Did the cops ask your names?

Did you give them your real names? Did you tell them where you are staying? Did they see your passports? Do they know you're Americans? The answers to these questions were an uneasy mix of yes and no.

"We've gotta get outta here, Jim!" Jorge said, his voice filled with anxiety. "We just – I don't know, man – we just gotta figure this situation out –"

"It's bad, man," Miguel agreed.

"It's messed up," chimed Ravi, shaking his head and pouring himself another drink. "Hella messed up."

I took a deep breath. "We need to figure out getting to the airport and getting back to the States," I said, meanwhile wishing that I could see Ratko, tomorrow, about changing our return flights. But tomorrow was Saturday, and anyway, Ratko had gone to Trogir, a resort a bit up the coast, for the weekend. I had no way of reaching him before Monday.

Who could say? Maybe it would be better to stay with our original plan, and to travel inconspicuously down the coast to Makarska and Dubrovnik, rather than to try to change the tickets right away and leave from Split, where the boys were being looked for. We did not want to red-flag anyone that "those three American kids with the gun" were trying to get out of the country…

While I was considering how best to proceed, the boys continuing to drink and talk in their breathless excitement and fear, Jorge pulled out a cigarette, and offered it to me. I have never been a smoker. But it's weird. I will sometimes light up, with my boys. Call it inculturation. (Although you raise a legitimate issue, perceptive reader, to ask just WHO is being inculturated here, and into WHAT culture…) I accepted the cigarette, and the light, which Jorge next offered –

From his "gun."

I was drawing on the cigarette to get it lit before I realized what was up. I stopped, the cigarette between my fingers, and looked at Jorge, who gave himself away only in the twinkle in his eyes. I turned to Miguel, who was grinning broadly, and before I could turn to Ravi, he was slapping my back and laughing out loud. An eruption of laughter took place behind me, as well, for the rest of the guys had convened in the room, to witness the charade.

"You frohlichen collegi," I said. And if you believe that was my actual response, I have a bridge in Brooklyn I would like to sell you. What I in fact called them made the guys laugh even harder.

"Let me see that," I said, a moment later, reaching for the "gun." Jorge aimed it straight at me, and "fired" again. Out shot the cigarette flame. The guys were practically doubling over. They were immensely pleased with themselves.

It was one real-looking "gun." The last day of the trip, when they x-rayed Jorge's luggage at Dubrovnik airport, they pulled him out of line and questioned him for a quarter of an hour. They did not return the lighter to him. "Bleepers," Jorge said of them, as we headed toward the gate. "They're probably fighting over who gets to keep it."

As we were leaving Split, late Saturday morning, "Mom" and "Pop" wrote down their names, address, and telephone number. I probably still have all this info stored away in some "safe" place – so safe that I have long since forgotten where it is. Anyway, they assured us in German and Italian that we were welcome back anytime. They hugged all the collegi good-bye, and we set off along the promenade for the morning bus to Makarska.

***

Not only did we have no trouble finding a place to stay in Makarska, we had our choice. At the bus station in Makarska, we split up into three parties, two to go out looking for a place, and the third, Ada, Matt and myself, to guard our bags at the station. I had a little nervousness about the whole business, and was prepared for us to have to split up into two or even three different places, in terms of accommodations, but Ada and Matt weren't worried at all.

"The Blessed Mother is in charge of this trip," Ada said. "She brought us all over here together and she'll keep us all together." Ada had made himself at home, arranging some of the bags so that they practically constituted a chaise longue.

I appreciated Ada's serenity and confidence, but after all, it was Saturday morning in a beach town, and not just any beach town: it was Saturday morning on "the Croatian Riviera."

But Ada was right: both of our scouting groups came back with places that had room for us. One of the groups had found two places. All the accommodations came in roughly the same, in terms of rates. We decided on the one that was closest to the beach, which came as well with an offer of taxi service. It was a small (three story and maybe ten-unit) condominium block, and what we got was a three-bedroom, three-bath condo with a living area that could be converted to a fourth bedroom (for me). There was a kitchen and a dining room, as well. We were right at the middle of the spectacular Makarska beach, about a hundred feet up from the beach promenade. Our host, a young man named Iko, lived with his family right next door. Since the end of communism, many families in Makarska have begun to invest in tourism.

I had seen photos of Makarska, from Miguel and Jorge's excursion the previous summer. I knew it was a magnificent setting. The photos, breath-taking as they were, did not do justice to the place itself. The city lies on a broad, semi-circular bay, a bay lined by the beach, which is sandy by European standards, rather than stony. (There is actually a second bay, as well, a bit to the south, and that one has the marina.) The beach is, I'd guess, two or three miles, curving around the blue-green water. The city rises from the beach across a shallow sea plain toward the lower slopes of a spectacular mountain, six thousand feet high: Biokovo. In the summer, the mountain is bare and dry, with just Mediterranean scrub for vegetation. In the winter, snow covers the peak, while on the beach, fan palms glisten in the sunlight. Biokovo frames Makarska, and especially given the clarity and color of the water, all but guarantees great photos, no matter where you are on the beach. The beach's long promenade is lined by oleander, by hibiscus and by a type of bougainvillea that I have never seen in California, or Bermuda, or Venezuela, or Mexico: I have seen this dense, light purple bougainvillea only in Mediterranean lands. There are casuarina pines, and Italian cypress along the promenade as well. It goes without saying that the promenade has many restaurants, bars and clubs. Makarska is a beach town, and tourism is how it lives.

Our host, Iko, with whom I became quite friendly, apologized, getting our things from his car, that the accommodations were "not first class." I suppose they weren't, by American first-class standards, but they were more than roomy and comfortable enough for us. I was with a bunch of twenty-one and twenty-two year olds. THEY didn't need the Sheraton. And I've never needed it.

Anyway, I need say less about Makarska than I did about Split. Three days in Makarska were spent the same way. Get up late. Have lunch along the boardwalk/promenade. Get out to the rocks at "our" end of the beach, where there was a great diving spot. Spread our towels, splash into the cool, clear sea, and soak up the sun. For several hours. Come back along the boardwalk for dinner at one of the outdoor restaurants. Go back to the condo for the "prep" hour and then – the boys were off to party. Their stamina impressed me; Iko, too. I was coming in from Mass one morning (Makarska has several churches, and the Sunday Mass I attended there was out-the-door full, a fact which reminded me of the adage that where sin abounds, grace abounds all the more). I was coming in from Mass, as I say, one morning, and Iko told me that the boys had come in, just ahead of me. He meant, they had come in for the "night." It was probably about eight-thirty in the morning. Iko told me he saw the guys set off for the clubs each evening, and then saw them return each morning, and he meant MORNING. He and his wife, a beautiful young Croatian woman who worked as a police dispatcher, and their little boy, would be having breakfast on their patio, when they would see the guys coming in. Iko thought they were great: "They are full of joy," he said. "Among other things," I agreed.

In fact, the guys told me that the clubs closed at dawn. With other young people, they would then hit the beach, swim a while, then come up to the restaurants and have breakfast. This would get them back to the condo around eight. They'd crash til one, maybe two in the afternoon, then start the whole cycle again.

You're only young once. As long as the kids were safe, I was cool with their schedule in Makarska. I could not have prevented them from it, in any event, but it is also simply the fact that I agree with Gino: "They need to feel their strength." Full-scale adulthood, with all of its decisions and challenges, was, for all of them, just around the corner. Now was the hour, and Dalmatia was the place, for them to close the dance clubs, and to go swimming in a translucent sea, by the dawn's early light.

In my concern for them, though, I will admit to having prayed a number of extra rosaries, that whole sunny week down the coast.

Meanwhile, among the several romantic developments which transpired on this trip (all of which were to prove to have the half-life of a rare radioactive element), in just three afternoons in Makarska, Miguel fell so passionately in love with a pretty and slender young Croatian (whose name escapes me) that he opted to stay in Makarska another night, and maybe longer, rather than go down the coast with the rest of us, to Dubrovnik. This young lady had connections somehow to the Croatian national basketball league, and Miguel, a starter at Holy Names, with only one year left for collegiate ball, was actively scouting possibilities for ongoing – and professional – play. I gave him Ratko's contact information, in the event that he needed to change his return ticket, and meanwhile prayed that Miguel would be in Dubrovnik by tomorrow evening, and come home with the rest of us.

Given the basketball angle, maybe I should not present Miguel's romantic attachment as being just head-over-heels. I was only the following winter to see Miguel as close to head-over-heels-in-love as I have ever seen him, and it was, in fact, a qualitatively different dynamic. Still, this young lady was very attractive, and for one more night at least, Mikey was not willing to be without her company. The other guys were quite cynical. According to Ravi, "They're selling each other a dream, Jim. She wants him to stay: that's her dream. He wants to play pro-basketball: that's his."

In any event, the rest of us let Iko drive us (in two shifts) to the bus station, and we went down the coast to Dubrovnik. Because of the desire of the guys to spend most of the day on the beach, we took the latest afternoon bus to Dubrovnik we could get. At that, the bus was a couple hours late getting into Makarska, because of a wreck somewhere up the mostly two-lane coast road. I had been vexed at this delay. But forty minutes south of Makarska the sun went down, and for the next two hours I saw the coast as I had never seen it before: its cities and resorts lit up, their lights reflected in the calm, dark sea, with the mountains rising blue-black behind them. We got into Dubrovnik late, about ten, but that was early to the guys, and after getting into our rooms, most of them took off for the Old Town, which was a twenty-minute walk above the coast, from our hotel.

We were at the Petka, a large and comfortable hotel with a good restaurant, friendly staff and unrivalled views. With the guys all off for their night in the Old Town, I went down to the patio bar and had a Heineken, enjoying the fresh and mild evening air, the scent of the oleander, and the British accents, at the next table over.

EPILOGUE

And so it is that I came to be seated at a café above the sea, in Dubrovnik, sipping peach iced teas, and watching for any sign of movement, on the part of my boys, toward taking a leap from the rocks, with the young Croatians. But my boys did not give me any cause for alarm. They were spread out over the rocks below with the girls from Italy and Sweden, and were serenely enjoying the serene afternoon: maybe at this point, none of us had anything left to prove.

We had had breakfast at the hotel, and set off for the Old Town, where we had spent most of the early part of the day. Above all, we had spent it on the walls, since several of the guys had not yet seen them. It was hot; hot in that special manner of Dubrovnik, and when, from the walls, the guys saw the palm thatch and the stone steps down to the sea, of this particular bar, they said, "Jim, we are going there, after the walls." It turned out that the boys had been at this same bar the previous night, and had loved it.

Before we came to the bar, though, we had lunch. And we had lunch with…Sanya. I was taking photos of some of the guys in the main square, when suddenly a beautiful blonde in an almost blazingly white dress crossed my field of vision. I looked up from my camera and…"Sanya?" I asked.

This time, we had time to follow her up the steps to the restaurant she was advertising. She asked where Miguel was, and Ravi assured her that he had "personal business" in Makarska. Sanya smiled – no explanations needed. Sanya told us that she studied at the university in Rijeka, up north on the coast, but worked here in Dubrovnik in the summers. She spoke several languages, as we discovered, watching her bring smiling groups of Italians, Germans and French to the restaurant's outdoor tables.

That was a fun lunch. There were some Italian ladies at the next table over who were very taken with Pancho. One of them was sure he was a movie star; the others just said he looked like one. They all wanted pictures with him. Pancho took this in stride. Sanya visited us off and on throughout the lunch, between stints in, as she put it, "my office," meaning the square. When we came back into the square, after lunch, the guys took turns posing with Sanya, who did not at all seem to mind, and who in any event, could not take a bad picture.

And so back up along the walls, and through the portal to the stone steps, leading to the bar above the sea. The guys quickly headed down to the rocks, to swim and to sun, and to mix it up with the European girls. I took the seat at the rail that would be mine the rest of the afternoon.

The young lady at the bar said to me, "You really like peach iced teas." I liked them well enough to keep drinking them. I'd have preferred raspberry or unsweetened, and after all, at three, four in the afternoon, it was too early to have real drink. Jorge dolphin-dived in the water, came up and repeated his invitation, "Come down, dude."

Ravi and Nelson, looking almost straight up from the rocks, also urged me down. "Water's great," said Ravi, and dove in. "It's our last afternoon in Croatia," Nelson called up to me, and then followed

Ravi. A few feet away, spread out with their beach towels, the other guys lolled, laughed and talked with the European girls.

I did not want to come down. I wanted to spend the rest of the afternoon there, watching my boys, praying for the young Croatian divers, and…just being…being on the last afternoon of the pilgrimage I had worked five years to bring off. The sunlight flooding Dubrovnik and its harbor that afternoon seemed to be derivative of Heaven itself. I could have stayed there indefinitely. It was, for me, truly a timeless moment.

I know that I thought of my books, there, that afternoon. I know that I flashed on the way I had felt, just a few months before, when Lisa had turned over to me the big box that contained all my novels. Somehow, I had absorbed all that. In a way I was not yet able to describe, I somehow trusted that whole situation. I had let go of my life. This radiant afternoon with my boys on the Adriatic was the result. I was going to argue with that? I don't think so. I could not at that point have described it, but somehow, light was pouring through the sorrow, the loss, I had endured, as a writer. I could not at that point have described it, but somehow, grace was at work, in circumstances I had dreaded. I knew peace, that afternoon, with all that had happened. I knew confidence and trust, in a design not my own.

Someone must have had an operational cell phone, because we received news mid-afternoon that Miguel was in Dubrovnik, at the hotel and sleeping. I was relieved to hear it. I had all eight of my boys with me, here in Dubrovnik, and tomorrow, we would all be on the flight home together. Daria was meeting us at the airport. I looked forward to telling her and Will about our adventures. They knew what this trip meant to me. For five years it had been do or die. Well, this sundrenched afternoon above the sea, we had done it.

And so much else had worked out, along the way. My thesis, my finances, my new car, my on-going preparation for the priesthood through the best job I had ever had in my life – a job I had neither looked for nor wanted. "This is not your problem," Daria had said. "This is God's problem. Let him figure it out for you." I could only smile, thinking how God had, indeed, done just that.

I was returning to the seminary. I had jumped through every hoop put up at Vocations in Sacramento the past spring and summer, knowing, as seminarians often do, that I was being "tested." I had thought the business somewhat childish, but seminarians learn to put up with such things. I had done all my applications, right and wrong, had completed all my interviews, and I had seen the letters of recommendation that had gone in, on me: one from Father Soane; the other from Daria. Among the many other reasons that I had for my deep serenity that afternoon was my happy anticipation of being back at the seminary, in less than two weeks.

I could not have guessed the bombshell that would greet me when I got home: the news that Vocations in Sacramento had refused to re-admit me to diocesan sponsorship; as far as Sacramento was concerned, I would never be a priest. This news would, for a brief but intense two weeks, have me scrambling to put things together with Oakland. It was also news which ensured the accuracy of Monsignor Church's prediction. I would be three years, after all, getting back to St. Patrick's. My first call over this business would be to a good friend of mine in the Diocese of Oakland -- Father Van Dinh. Van would fairly hoot with joy over the news, and assure me of my future with Oakland. I never saw the Sacramento decision coming: I can be really stupid, at times.

But that, all of that, was for the future. The imminent future, it is true, but the future. As I say, that afternoon above the sea was a timeless moment. I can even today visit it in memory, and recapture that deep sense of resting joy.

The guys eventually came up from the rocks. We sat around and had drinks; I continued with iced teas, though some of the guys ordered beer. We took pictures. Lots of pictures. The guys discussed their plans for their last night in Europe. They agreed to return to Old Town for dinner; to come back after dinner to this very spot, where they had been the night before, to drink, to dance, to talk about their lives and their dreams with the girls from Italy, from Sweden, from Croatia, and to watch the moonlight spread across the sea.

That sounded good to me. I reminded the guys that we had an early wake-up in the morning: I think it was five-thirty, as we had the eight AM flight to Frankfurt. They assured me they would be on-time for the van to the airport. They might be up all night – "We can sleep on the planes, Jim" – but they would make the connection to the airport. That was fine with me; I didn't care what shape they were in, as long as they made the van.

Lilin told me he was not up for a late night, and I said that the hotel would have dinner waiting for us when we got back. He thought that sounded good. He and I had a long and leisurely time of it, that night, over a very good dinner on the hotel's patio. We compared this last evening of the trip with the first -- waiting at the border -- and laughed about it.

I was to check in on Miguel, too, that evening, and discover that he wanted "water and potato chips." I was able to obtain these on the premises. He downed them gratefully and...went back to sleep. The nights in Split and Makarska had finally caught up with him.

But meanwhile, my boys and I were gathering up our things, there at the bar above the sea; the long, sundrenched afternoon was ending. Talking quietly among themselves, the guys filed up the stone steps.

I turned and gave the city, its islands and the sea one last look. I flashed back in memory to that sunny morning on the patio in June, 1997. Mom herself had told me, years later, that until it happened, she never really thought we would get the kids to Europe. I shook my head and smiled. I praised Jesus. I thanked Mary. I turned and followed my boys up the steps to the Old Town.